MW00508849

Unidentified Narrative Objects and the New Italian Epic

LEGENDA

LEGENDA is the Modern Humanities Research Association's book imprint for new research in the Humanities. Founded in 1995 by Malcolm Bowie and others within the University of Oxford, Legenda has always been a collaborative publishing enterprise, directly governed by scholars. The Modern Humanities Research Association (MHRA) joined this collaboration in 1998, became half-owner in 2004, in partnership with Maney Publishing and then Routledge, and has since 2016 been sole owner. Titles range from medieval texts to contemporary cinema and form a widely comparative view of the modern humanities, including works on Arabic, Catalan, English, French, German, Greek, Italian, Portuguese, Russian, Spanish, and Yiddish literature. Editorial boards and committees of more than 60 leading academic specialists work in collaboration with bodies such as the Society for French Studies, the British Comparative Literature Association and the Association of Hispanists of Great Britain & Ireland.

The MHRA encourages and promotes advanced study and research in the field of the modern humanities, especially modern European languages and literature, including English, and also cinema. It aims to break down the barriers between scholars working in different disciplines and to maintain the unity of humanistic scholarship. The Association fulfils this purpose through the publication of journals, bibliographies, monographs, critical editions, and the MHRA Style Guide, and by making grants in support of research. Membership is open to all who work in the Humanities, whether independent or in a University post, and the participation of younger colleagues entering the field is especially welcomed.

ALSO PUBLISHED BY THE ASSOCIATION

Critical Texts
Tudor and Stuart Translations • *New Translations* • *European Translations*
MHRA Library of Medieval Welsh Literature

MHRA Bibliographies
Publications of the Modern Humanities Research Association

The Annual Bibliography of English Language & Literature
Austrian Studies
Modern Language Review
Portuguese Studies
The Slavonic and East European Review
Working Papers in the Humanities
The Yearbook of English Studies

www.mhra.org.uk
www.legendabooks.com

ITALIAN PERSPECTIVES

In the light of growing academic interest in Italy and the reorganization of many university courses in Italian along interdisciplinary lines, this book series, founded by Maney Publishing under the imprint of the Northern Universities Press and now continuing under the Legenda imprint, aims to bring together different scholarly perspectives on Italy and its culture. *Italian Perspectives* publishes books and collections of essays on any period of Italian literature, language, history, culture, politics, art, and media, as well as studies which take an interdisciplinary approach and are methodologically innovative.

Managing Editor
Dr Graham Nelson, 41 Wellington Square, Oxford OX1 2JF, UK
www.legendabooks.com

Unidentified Narrative Objects and the New Italian Epic

K ATE E LIZABETH W ILLMAN

LEGENDA
Italian Perspectives 42
Modern Humanities Research Association
2019

Published by Legenda
an imprint of the Modern Humanities Research Association
Salisbury House, Station Road, Cambridge CB1 2LA

ISBN 978-1-78188-819-3

First published 2019

Copy-Editor: Nigel Hope

CONTENTS

TO MY FAMILY

ACKNOWLEDGEMENTS

This book originated as a PhD thesis at the University of Warwick, and I would first like to thank my brilliant supervisors Jennifer Burns and Fabio Camilletti, as well as the other staff members and my fellow researchers, who provided a lively and friendly intellectual environment throughout my time there. Special mention goes to Martina Piperno and Giacomo Comiati. My PhD would not have been possible without the funding I received from the Arts and Humanities Research Council. The three months I spent at the British School at Rome were also hugely enriching, in part due to the conversations I had with Jacopo Benci and Andrea Cortellessa. Throughout my doctoral research, I met a number of writers who were helpful and kind; thank you Roberto Bui, Giovanni Cattabriga, Giancarlo De Cataldo, Letizia Muratori and Giorgio Vasta. I would also like to thank my generous examiners, Ann Caesar and Florian Mussgnug, and everyone involved in this project at Legenda for enabling me to turn my thesis into this book, as well as Manuela Salvi for her invaluable help in answering my translation questions.

I would not have come this far without the excellent teaching and support from staff members during my previous studies at school and university. My introduction to Italian began during my BA at Bristol, where I was lucky enough to return after my PhD to teach, and I would particularly like to thank Ruth Glynn for her support over the years, as well as James Hawkey and Damien Mooney. During my MA in Comparative Literature at King's College London, I was inspired by both my fellow students — Christine Fouirnaies, Tom Livingstone and Niall Sreenan — and my teachers — Alicia Kent, Rosa Mucignat and, in particular, Federico Bonaddio. Dr Bonaddio's course on 'Conflicts of the Mind' and our discussions gave me the original idea for this project, which I would not have embarked on without his help in drafting proposals. He reminded me of how strange and compelling Roberto Saviano's *Gomorrah* is, a book I had originally read after my time in Naples as an Erasmus student, which was perhaps the very first spark for this book.

I would like to dedicate this book to my family and particularly to Sean Jackson, for giving me the support to finish this project, especially after Niamh arrived.

K.W., December 2018

INTRODUCTION

Unidentified Narrative Objects, Wu Ming and the New Italian Epic

In the twenty-first century, there has been a surge of popularity in texts that cross the borders between styles, genres and media, between real-life events and imagined ones, so that these texts are difficult to categorise or sometimes to distinguish as fiction or nonfiction. The historical novel, literary journalism, autofiction, biofiction: none of these are new forms, but they have been extensively employed in recent years, sometimes more than one in the same text, as writers have disrupted conventional generic categories to produce texts that might be called 'unidentified narrative objects' (UNOs). The term UNO was coined by the Italian writer Wu Ming 1, alias Roberto Bui, when discussing Italian literature after 2000 (2009a: 11). In a document called the Memorandum, which first appeared online in April 2008, he described how UNOs were increasingly prevalent in twenty-first-century Italian literature, and saw them as part of a phenomenon that he called the New Italian Epic (NIE), a label used to refer to a large and heterogeneous corpus whose writers had a common belief in the power of literature to effect change in society by depicting and reassessing the past and present. Some of the writers Wu Ming 1 mentioned in the Memorandum as being part of the NIE 'nebula' (2009a: 14) were already well known and widely read both within and outside Italy, such as Roberto Saviano, whilst others were perhaps more marginal voices in contemporary literature, such as Letizia Muratori. Wu Ming 1 explained that the label was used not for the entire body of work of the writers in question, but for specific texts that they had written with these particular characteristics, which may not be present in other texts by the same author. These writers are part of the same 'generazione letteraria' [literary generation],[1] as Wu Ming 1 (2009a: 11) put it, and they were (in theory) conditioned by a similar set of events, ranging from the political shake-up in Italy in the early 1990s, developments in the publishing market, the political disillusionment and media control of Silvio Berlusconi's governments, and the advent of the Digital Age.

The NIE's characteristics can be seen most clearly in the texts written by the Wu Ming collective, of which Wu Ming 1 is part. Wu Ming has two alternative meanings depending on how it is pronounced in Mandarin: 'five names', although since 2016 only three of the original five members remain, or 'no name', used by Chinese dissidents desiring freedom of expression.[2] Wu Ming initially started out under the auspices of the Luther Blissett Project,[3] under which the future members of Wu Ming wrote the novel Q in 1999, marking the beginning of their literary career. Subsequent novels were signed Wu Ming, and solo projects or collaborations with other authors saw the individual members using numbers rather than their proper names. This, combined with their refusal to appear on television or have their photographs taken, is part of Wu Ming's aim to undermine the figure of the author, both as a celebrated personality and as an isolated genius working alone. Their jointly written texts display the key features that Wu Ming 1 outlined in his Memorandum on the NIE, including literary experimentation and a commitment to encouraging their readers to reconsider the historical moments they address, whether sixteenth-century Europe in Q and *Altai*, the French Revolution in *L'Armata dei Sonnambuli* [*The Army of Sleepwalkers*], the years leading up to the American Revolution in *Manituana*, the First World War in *L'invisibile ovunque* [*The Invisible Everywhere*], the years following the Russian Revolution in *Proletkult*, or the aftermath of the Second World War in 54 and *Asce di guerra* [*Hatchets of War*].

The purpose of this study is to demonstrate that UNO is a useful term to describe increasingly hybrid recent texts in Italy, which might be seen as part of an unidentified genre that, contrary to what others (particularly Wu Ming) have argued, contains crossovers between anti-realist postmodernist experimentation and neo/realist/ic engagement. Wu Ming 1's label of NIE is more problematic, as I will demonstrate, because it tends to exclude female, postcolonial and migrant perspectives, and because it is more indicative of concerns about the late postmodern novel, although the Memorandum on the NIE raised some fascinating points about the direction of Italian literature in the new millennium that this study will develop. The UNOs I examine warrant attention, as they are fascinating negotiations of history and tradition through experimentalism, both building on what came before and taking literature in new directions. I would also suggest that the term UNO may usefully be taken beyond Italy's borders to other national literatures, where we can see comparable examples, as I highlight throughout this study.

Despite the shortcomings of Wu Ming 1's (and others') discussion of these UNOs, the Memorandum on the NIE began a lively debate on contemporary Italian literature,[4] not only in the scholarly panorama,[5] but also online, primarily through Wu Ming's widely read blog *Giap*[6] and the online journal *Carmilla*,[7] where other writers, critics and members of the public responded to and expanded on Wu Ming 1's ideas. Some of the material related to this phenomenon, through being on the internet, is ephemeral and at risk of disappearing, if it has not already disappeared, as in the case of the hypertext and extra material for Genna's *Medium* (see chapter 2), or the blog extension of Jones's text *Sappiano le mie parole di sangue* [*My Words Be Bloody*] (see chapter 4). Perhaps some of the online material I reference here will not be available in the future, but I hope to record this work surrounding Italian literature at the beginning of the twenty-first century in a more concrete way, showing that the debate started by Wu Ming 1 signals an important moment in recent Italian culture.[8] Furthermore, although Wu Ming 1 emphasises that the Memorandum was an attempt to describe the current literary climate rather than a manifesto (as I discuss in chapter 1), we will see that the concerns and common characteristics that he identified have continued to be explored by these and other writers since 2008, demonstrating the timely nature of his observations on changing approaches to literature in the new millennium. Yet, his observations also contain limitations and blind spots that I will address in this study, extending the corpus that he outlines to suggest further avenues that warrant attention. I thus aim to paint a more complete picture of the state of Italian literature at the beginning of the twenty-first century and to go further in exploring the potential of UNOs than his Memorandum.

In *The Location of Culture*, Bhabha describes the end of the twentieth century as the beyond:

> Our existence today is marked by a tenebrous sense of survival, living on the borderlines of the 'present', for which there seems to be no proper name other than the current and controversial shiftiness of the prefix 'post': postmodernism, postcolonialism, postfeminism...
>
> The 'beyond' is neither a new horizon, nor a leaving behind of the past... [...] in the *fin de siècle* we find ourselves in the moment of transit where space and time cross to produce complex figures of difference and identity, past and present, inside and outside, inclusion and exclusion. For there is a sense of disorientation, a disturbance of direction, in the 'beyond'. (Bhabha 1994: 1–2)

In the twenty-first century, we continue to inhabit and explore this beyond, this moment of transit, these '"in-between" spaces' (Bhabha 1994: 2), and UNOs are testament to this. Bhabha sees the in-betweenness of the beyond as 'the terrain for elaborating strategies of selfhood — singular and communal — that initiate new signs of identity, and innovative sites of collaboration, and contestation, in the act of defining the idea of society itself' (1994: 2). In this study, we will see that it is precisely through the hybridity of UNOs that writers could address — and, in some cases, have addressed — the areas that Bhabha outlines: 'elaborating strategies of selfhood' through the use of autofiction or biofiction that connects to wider, societal or communal experience; acting as one of these possible 'innovative sites of collaboration, and contestation' in terms of form and content, through new forms of transmedial and transnational collaboration that address notions of collective political action and of cultural conflict; and 'defining the idea of society itself' through this social action fuelled by interactive technologies and the forums they create, as well as through revised envisionings of the past and present that include or privilege perspectives that have been conventionally marginalized, in order to shape the future.

Postmodern *Impegno*

As Bhabha states, the prefix 'post-' has been controversial in its shiftiness. This is no less true of Italy, where postmodernism has generally been regarded as coinciding with the disappearance of political and ethical engagement in literature and of the figure of the public intellectual. The NIE can be seen as an attempt to work against this, although we will see throughout this study that UNOs have continued to incorporate postmodernist experimentation.

Aside from limited attempts to curb Silvio Berlusconi's power within politics,[9] intellectuals had been seen as offering limited constructive reflection on, or solutions to, Italy's recent problems. Some, such as Amato (2009) and Pardi (2008), argue that intellectuals had failed to engage with the majority of Italians or criticise the social situation in a meaningful way, only ridiculing the masses dumbed down by television without proposing alternative models.[10] Recent years have seen a sense of nostalgia about a time when figures like Pasolini played a key role on the cultural scene, as Antonello has discussed in his 2012 text, *Dimenticare Pasolini* [*Forgetting Pasolini*]. Yet, at the same time, the Memorandum was greeted with widespread controversy, with some questioning Wu Ming 1's right to comment on literature as a critic, given that he was also a writer,[11] a criticism that seems surprising in the light of the praise given to Calvino's *Lezioni americane* [*Six Memos for the Next Millennium*], or Eco's numerous critical works. These debates were taking place alongside the much-repeated adage that Italy had more writers than readers, and fears that literature had been debased by overlaps between the book market and the mass media, becoming another source of meaningless entertainment rather than a serious pursuit, as espoused by Ferroni in *Scritture a perdere* [*Throwaway Writing*] (2010). This climate was reflected in another criticism that Wu Ming 1 received about the Memorandum, that is that some of the texts he was discussing were so-called genre fiction and therefore not 'serious' literature.[12] This criticism can be associated with a perennial debate about the quality of contemporary literature and the *romanzo medio* [middlebrow novel] in Italy that goes at least as far back as Calvino, and what Benedetti described in *Pasolini contro Calvino* [*Pasolini versus Calvino*] as a sense that literature had become colourless and 'depotenziata' [disempowered], simply obeying the demands of the culture industry (1998: 21). Such controversies resurfacing around the NIE provide a fascinating insight into the Italian cultural and literary scene from the twentieth into the twenty-first century.

These controversies can also be connected to the idea of a 'postmoderno nazionale' (Benedetti 1998: 21), that is, the specificity of the way in which postmodernism has been received in Italy. In the twenty-first century, critics such as Luperini (2005) have argued that postmodernism has been taken to its logical extreme of self-referentiality and ironic playfulness, and that there is a need to go beyond it. Boscolo called one of her articles about the NIE: 'Scardinare il postmoderno' [Unhinge the Postmodern] (2008). Wu Ming 1 also voices this view in the Memorandum, as we shall see. However, throughout this study, I underline elements of continuity with twentieth-century literary production, arguing that these texts do not represent a break with postmodernism, even if at times they digest it in a distinct way from their Italian predecessors. They also show that postmodernist features and political and ethical commitment are not mutually exclusive. A key reference point in this regard is Burns's *Fragments of* Impegno (2001), which calls into question a mono-lithic understanding of political and ethical commitment in Italian literature, and highlights changes in approach to this in the 1980s and 1990s, which many of these texts continue into the twenty-first century. Burns's observation of a shift in those years 'from an author-oriented towards a reader-oriented perspective' (2001: 6) has also continued to hold true, as we shall see in terms of the participatory aspects and the various interpretations invited by the authors of these UNOs, who may write under pseudonyms or as collectives.[13] Following on from this, Antonello and Mussgnug's argument that twenty-first-century Italian literary, filmic and theatrical production can be seen as part of a *Postmodern* Impegno in their 2009 book of the same name is another cornerstone of my understanding of these recent literary developments. I employ the term *impegno* in this study in the post-hegemonic sense as outlined by Antonello and Mussgnug (2009: 9–11), referring to political and ethical engagement that is not connected to a particular agenda. *Impegno* in the corpus I examine can work in different ways across media platforms — from text to images to television/film to digital content — and it can take quite different forms depending on the writer, as we will see in the primary texts analysed here — from Saviano's political crusade to expose the Neapolitan mafia by any means possible, to Giancarlo De Cataldo's and Antonio Scurati's embellishments on history to attempt to find answers to current problems, to Laura Pugno's use of a future dystopia to comment indirectly on the present, to the personal stories of collective significance related by Giuseppe Genna, Helena Janeczek, Babsi Jones, Igiaba Scego, and Antar Mohamed with Wu Ming 2 — although these writers are all united by a common belief in the power of storytelling to interrogate the contemporary world.

The insistence on postmodernism's demise can be connected to the recurring theme of the death of the father that Wu Ming 1 identifies in the NIE, which I address in my second chapter, where I employ recent work by the Italian psychoanalyst Recalcati, as well as Brooks's earlier work on a Freudian interpretation of narrative in *Reading for the Plot*, although I also question the emphasis on fatherhood, as overlooking motherhood and female experience precludes important avenues of reflection. Psychoanalytical ideas are also not out of place when considering, as I do in chapter 4, the so-called 'return to reality' that some have observed in Italian culture in recent years, as there seems to be a desire for return to some kind of authenticity associated with neo/realist/ic literature in contrast to what Wu Ming 1 has labelled 'Postmodernismi da quattro soldi' [Two-a-penny postmodernisms] (2009a: 63), which could also be read as symptomatic of other, deeper concerns about inheritance and responsibility. The corpus I analyse represents neither a rupture with postmodernism nor a return to an idea of *impegno* that we can associate with post-war neorealism, but rather a mixture of the two combined with new elements.

History and Memory

Neumann states: 'literary fictions disseminate influential models of both individual and cultural memories as well as of the nature and functions of memory' (2010: 333). Certainly, the texts I examine give some indication of culturally prevalent concepts of history and memory. In recent years, the binary opposition between the two has broken down, as cultural memory studies have grown as an area of scholarly interest, and elements such as oral history have begun to be incorporated into historical research, making it a more all-encompassing discipline. Erll has suggested 'dissolving the useless opposition of history vs. memory in favour of a notion of different *modes of remembering* in culture [...] the past is not given, but must continually be re-constructed and re-presented' (2010: 7). These modes of remembering are precisely what we shall see in chapter 3 in the historical novels I analyse. The reflections that these texts bring to the fore about different versions of the past is also part of a more specifically Italian tradition of blurring the lines between history and fiction, raising doubts and possibilities about the past. This can be dated back to the microhistorical approach to historical research set out by Carlo Ginzburg, as well as to Alesssandro Manzoni's work in the nineteenth century, both his seminal historical novel *I promessi sposi* [*The Betrothed*] and his essay on combining historical fact and fiction, entitled 'Del romanzo storico' [On the Historical Novel], which Ginzburg (2006) would later draw on. We will see these various elements reflected in the approach of these twenty-first century writers to telling personal, individual accounts of the past against a wider backdrop of collective memory, whilst also interacting with archival documents to foreground the workings of history.

Not only have the lines between memory and history been increasingly blurred, but also those between original experience and the construction of memory. Memories are not necessarily attached to the person who experienced them, but can be transmitted to others as part of what Hirsch (2012) terms 'postmemory', which is a particular feature of Janeczek's work, analysed in chapter 3. Different memories can also be joined together across time and space, what Rothberg (2009) has called multidirectional memory in his analysis of the ways in which Holocaust remembrance has interacted with the legacies of colonialism and slavery. The texts I address likewise draw together different memories of historical events across the years and across national lines, often reappropriating experiences that their writers did not witness first-hand, and suggesting connections with the present. Rothberg sees memory as 'subject to ongoing negotiation, cross-referencing, and borrowing; as productive and not privative' (2009: 3). The various possibilities for interpretation in many of the UNOs I analyse and the echoes contained within them suggest that Rothberg is justified in seeing the productive potential of such multidirectional remembering.

Van Dijck states: 'Memory is no longer what we remember it to be' (2007: 182); she speaks in terms of the changes wrought by the Digital Age on memory and how it is mediated, changes that can also be detected in the contemporary literature I address here. New technologies mean that the ways in which we engage with our own history and with a wider understanding of History with a capital 'H' have changed, as access to archival documentation has led to more personal interaction with the past. As Derrida pointed out in 'Archive Fever': 'The archivization produces as much as it records the event' (1995: 17). Harris has described the changes in the archive with the advent of new technologies as follows:

> With digital archives, we move beyond the physical repository or final resting place of a particular material object. In the digital archive, an object continues to acquire meaning based on users' organization of the material (beyond editorial control of the primary architect), based on the continued re-mixing, re-using, and re-presentation of the object. (Harris 2014: 17)

We can investigate our own family history on sites such as ancestry.com, or research events that are further removed from us, or we can communicate with one another about memories of a shared collective experience, as Hajek (2014) has explored in relation to commemoration of the Movimento del '77 on Facebook. However, Hoskins argues that the 'unprecedented accessibility' of digital data also makes it 'more vulnerable to manipulation' (2009: 102). Wu Ming have been involved in various online discussions about the manipulation of historical data, as seen in their campaign surrounding the falsified photographs of the *foibe* killings that repeatedly resurface and are shared on social media on the Giorno del ricordo,[14] or the collective known as Nicoletta Bourbaki, a group who investigate historical manipulations online, particularly on Wikipedia, formed after a discussion on Wu Ming's blog *Giap* (Bourbaki 2014). Other risks posed by digital archives are the ephemerality and also the proliferation of the information held there, both of which could also mean that 'its potential to be rediscovered in future times is very much reduced in comparison with the materiality of its hard-copy predecessors' (Hoskins 2009: 102). Conversely, digital technologies can also disallow forgetting, resisting amnesia and preserving information and opinion in a way that may even subsequently prove problematic, as seen in the 2014 'Right to be Forgotten' ruling by the European Union's Court of Justice, which means that individuals can now request that search engines remove 'inaccurate, inadequate, irrelevant or excessive' information about them.[15] How memory operates in the twenty-first century is thus still being negotiated, and cannot be seen as purely positive or negative.

A recent e-book on transmediality edited by Brook and Patti (2014) shows the online environment to be a particularly interesting testing ground for ideas about history, politics and memory. The editors describe

> un nuovo modello ibrido della Storia in cui — attraverso video, documenti, scritti vari, suoni — si mescolano storie private e personali con la Storia ufficiale e collettiva, storie visive e storie udite [...] E così le gerarchie vengono smentite. Quello che emerge dall'era digitale è una Storia parcellizzata e frammentata, versioni del passato che possono essere in conflitto, che emergono come da un libro dei ritagli. Nonostante ciò, dietro tutti questi cambiamenti, rimane sempre una nostalgia per la Storia — una Storia olistica e totale in cui tutto va ricordano, archiviato e raccontato. È ancora da stabilire con precisione cosa questa nuova Storia ci può insegnare. (Brook and Patti 2014: Kindle locations 343–49)

> [a new hybrid model of History that — through videos, documents, different types of writing, sounds — mixes the private and personal with the collective and official History, stories seen and stories heard [...] Thus hierarchies are refuted. What emerges from the digital era is a fragmented History, versions of the past that can be conflicting, that emerge as from a scrapbook. Despite this, behind all these changes, there always remains a nostalgia for History — a holistic and total History in which everything is remembered, archived and told. It is still to be established precisely what this new History can teach us.]

Certainly, it is difficult to confirm what concrete changes have taken place in relation to these relatively new technologies, but we will see textural reconfigurations of history and History, remembering and forgetting, moving between the personal and collective, and piecing together fragments of the past in what often literally resemble scrapbooks due to the inclusion of real or fabricated archival documentation.

Representing Reality in the Digital Age

New technologies have played a role in twenty-first-century Italian literature not only from the point of view of changing ways of accessing the past. In Italy, ideas about the possibilities offered by the internet have taken on a particularly political hue, partly due to Berlusconi's monopoly over other media through his company Fininvest, as the internet has been seen as a place where alternative counter-narratives can circulate, as well as where political movements like the Movimento 5 Stelle (M5S) grew up and were able to reach a wider public (as pointed out by Brook and Patti 2014: Kindle locations 302–14). On a global level, reporting the news has also been influenced by the democratisation of technology, as it seems anyone can relay and comment on what is happening minute by minute on blogs and social media, which have been seen as a way round the corporate control of telecommunications companies, run by figures such as Berlusconi or Rupert Murdoch. The highly personal approaches to journalism that are the subject of chapter 4 would seem to reflect this more individual interaction with news stories.

However, we must not be too utopian when considering the possibilities offered by the internet. Some still have limited access to it, and it is still at the mercy of larger forces, as well as being a place where so-called 'fake news' circulates. When discussing social network sites (SNSs), such as Twitter and Facebook, Goriunova and Bernardi point out: 'While SNSs clearly provide exciting new possibilities for the articulation of political concern and organization of political movements, as corporate and proprietary environments, they also become gray zones of distrust of the free and grassroots character of their products' (2014: 457). This can be seen in recent controversies over the role of Facebook in controlling what news (whether true or not) reaches its users (see Buckley 2018).

Moreover, since the advent of both digital technologies and television, there have been concerns raised in Italy and elsewhere about the difficulties of experiencing and narrating reality in a highly mediated, hyperreal world, most notably by the French theorist Baudrillard (1994), and these concerns have also been explored by recent Italian writers, as we shall see. There is an awareness among these writers of a need to help people process the huge amount of information they are bombarded with on a daily basis, and they put themselves forward as being able to 'read the world' — as Amici (2010: 10) said of the NIE writers — for the general public through more literary approaches to this information overload. They express a common belief that their stories will help us reach a deeper understanding of their subject matter than the more superficial approach of the mass media. This is comparable to the phenomenon of New Journalism that began in the 1960s and that continues to be drawn on today by various writers, as well as being part of a long Italian tradition of *inchiesta* [investigation] novels, as I explore in chapter 4.[16]

In line with this tradition, these texts that address real-life events employ the tools of fiction and even at times incorporate invented elements, the implications of which I explore throughout this study. Siti's *Troppi paradisi* [*Too Many Paradises*], like other recent UNOs — De Cataldo's *Nelle mani giuste* [*In the Right Hands*] (see chapter 2), Jones's *Sappiano le mie parole* (see chapter 4) — includes a warning at the beginning to underline the fictionality of this seemingly true account, calling the text 'una autobiografia di fatti non accaduti' [an autobiography of events that didn't happen] (Siti 2006: 2). At the beginning of Scurati's *Il bambino che sognava la fine del mondo* [*The Child Who Dreamed the End of the World*], which is about actual news stories, but also has a picture of the author as a child on the front cover and contains autobiographical elements, we are warned:

> Questo romanzo appartiene al genere dei componimenti misti di cronaca e d'invenzione. Poiché ritiene che la vocazione della letteratura sia oggi, in un tempo dominato dalla cronaca, non già quella di confondere ulteriormente i confini tra realtà e finzione, bensì quella di superarli, l'autore invita il lettore a considerare ogni singola parola di questo libro come frutto della sua immaginazione, anche e soprattutto quando si narri di fatti riferiti a personaggi e a contesti che portano il nome di persone o di istituzioni realmente esistenti (Scurati 2010)

> [This novel belongs to the genre of mixed works of news and invention. Since he believes that the vocation of literature today, in a time dominated by news, is not to further confuse the boundaries between reality and fiction, but rather to overcome them, the author invites the reader to consider every single word of this book the fruit of his imagination, even and above all when narrating events referring to characters and contexts with the names of people and institutions that actually exist.]

Yet, whilst Bajani assures us in the 'Warning' of *Ogni promessa* [*Every Promise*] that this is 'quella particolare forma di falsificazione della realtà che chiamiamo romanzo' [that particular form of the falsification of reality that we call a novel] (Bajani 2010), Genna gives his highly fantastical 2007 text, *Medium*, which I analyse in chapter 2, the subtitle 'una storia vera' [a true story] on its first page, and labels it 'romanzo' [novel] on the text's website.[17] Clearly, there are unusual configurations of fiction and nonfiction in these recent 'mixed works', as their extra-diegetic apparatus often indicate. This is encapsulated by the epigraph to Mohamed and Wu Ming 2's *Timira* (analysed in chapter 3), which says: 'Questa è una storia vera... comprese le parti che non lo sono' [This is a true story... including the parts that are not] (Mohamed and Wu Ming 2 2012). Such approaches can be traced back to Sciascia, who asserted: 'lo scrittore non è né un filosofo né uno storico, ma solo qualcuno che coglie *intuitivamente* la verità' [the writer is neither a philosopher nor a historian, but only someone who *intuitively* understands the truth] (Sciascia 1979: 81), or to Pasolini, who famously stated: 'Io so. Ma non ho le prove. Non ho nemmeno indizi. | Io so perché sono un intellettuale, uno scrittore' [I know. But I don't have the proof. I don't even have the clues. | I know because I am an intellectual, a writer] (Pasolini 1974). While we will see Saviano claim a firmer kind of truth in *Gomorra* by repeatedly turning around Pasolini's words — 'Io so e ho le prove' [I know and I have the proof] (Saviano 2006: 233–40) — he embellishes real-life experience, as do many of the other primary texts in this study, although more openly. From De Cataldo's character of 'il Vecchio' [the Old Man] filling a gap in our knowledge about recent history (chapter 2), to Janeczek's mosaic of real and imagined stories (chapter 3), to Jones's underlining of the mythological quality of her reportage (chapter 4), we will see that these texts offer a more literary and less empirically verifiable truth, moving away from more referential forms of writing to offer what Gready (2009) would call 'novel truths' (see chapter 1), or, as Wu Ming 2 put it in the title of a talk on *Timira*, these writers are 'in search of narrative truth'.[18]

Unusual combinations of fiction and nonfiction are also present in recent Italian texts that contain autobiographical elements, which can be seen as part of a recent increased interest in experiments with life-writing from authors from a variety of countries: Rachel Cusk, Marie Darrieussecq, Geoff Dyer, Sheila Heti, Karl Ove Knausgaard, Ben Lerner and Amélie Nothomb are just a few of a huge number of possible examples. Their texts tend to be hybrid combinations of the author's real-life experiences with more or less open fictionalising, and the popularity of this autofictional mode could be partly explained by wider cultural changes in the Digital Age related to identity and subjectivity. From anonymous identities in chat rooms and on comments threads to 'managed' identities in social media profiles, we can now conceive of identity 'not only as a disembodied, fragmented and fluid phenomenon, untethered from the constraints of the human body, but also a constructed one, brought into being through people's representation of themselves online' (Doran 2014: 267). Alongside these developments, writers are called on more and more to use social media to construct a public profile that their readers can 'follow' and 'like' and interact with as if they were friends, making literature more personalised than ever before. More and more writers are openly drawing on their personal experiences for their literary output, although in the texts I examine this often takes on a particularly political dimension. Wu Ming 1 says of Beppe Sebaste in *H. P. L'ultimo autista di Lady Diana* [*H. P. Lady Diana's Last Driver*] (2007): 'usa introspezione e autofiction per narrare un fatto pubblico e "storico"' [he uses introspection and autofiction to narrate a public and 'historic' event] (Wu Ming 1 2009a: 15n). We will see this in many of the texts analysed in this study, as portrayals of the self have a wider community role in what could be seen as a rehabilitation of the personal as political.

However, the widespread use of autofiction should not necessarily be seen as part of what Shields described as *Reality Hunger* in his 2010 book, or what some Italian critics termed a 'return to reality' (see chapter 4). Rather, these are experimentations with the porous boundaries between reality and fiction, between the fragmented and the constructed self in twenty-first century liquid modernity (Bauman 2000). Doubrovsky, who first coined the term 'autofiction' in the 1970s, stated in the blurb of his autofictional *Laissé pour conte*:

> À l'inverse de l'autobiographie, explicative et unifiante, qui veut ressaisir et dérouler les fils d'un destin, l'autofiction ne perçoit pas la vie comme un tout. Elle n'a affaire qu'à des fragments disjoints, des morceaux d'existence brisés, un sujet morcelé qui ne coïncide pas avec lui-même. (Doubrovsky 1999: inside cover)

> [As opposed to autobiography, which explains and unifies, which wants to get hold of and unravel the threads of a destiny, autofiction does not perceive life as a whole. It is only concerned with separate fragments, shattered pieces of existence, a divided subject that does not coincide with him- or herself.]

Nonetheless, the fact that this term has existed since the 1970s also suggests that, whilst the Internet Age may have crystallised some of the issues surrounding identity and brought them in new directions, this divided self is again connected to an existing postmodernist cultural climate.

Genre/Gender

As I will discuss in chapter 1, Wu Ming 1's choice to call the UNOs he discusses 'epic' is problematic: despite recent reimaginings of the epic from new perspectives, it is a genre that has been traditionally associated with heroic, male adventures and western ideology, which might partly account for the white, male bias of the NIE that I highlight throughout this study. Mecchia has rightly pointed out in relation to Wu Ming's work:

> historical novel, epic tradition, adventure novel, mystery and spy stories, comic book popular culture and, in the case of the *Manituana* website, interactive videogaming [...] what Wu Ming has not been able or willing to recognize, so far, is the gender exclusivity often implicit in such modes of expression [...] It is impossible, when reading the narrative objects produced by Wu Ming, not to raise the issue of the relationship between genre and gender. (Mecchia 2009: 207–08)

This troubling relationship between gender and genre can also be extended beyond Wu Ming's texts to others of the nebula, given that most of them are written by men, feature primarily male characters and tend to focus on male experience, as seen in chapter 2 in the greater attention given to fatherhood rather than motherhood. In the cases of female writers like Pugno (see chapter 2) or Janeczek (see chapter 3), whose work — as my analysis will demonstrate — is clearly relevant to, and expands on, the fascinating points Wu Ming 1 raises, but which he places outside the nebula, this may be because they had not been as commercially succesful at the time of the Memorandum as the more mainstream male writers he includes,[19] such as Saviano or Camilleri, suggesting that market forces also play a role in the exclusion of some writers from the NIE corpus. Issues related to gender intersect with those of race and belonging, and previous discussions of the NIE, particularly by Wu Ming 1, have tended to focus on work not only by male writers, but also by writers who are white and ethnically Italian, which I problematise at various points in this study, and seek to remedy by including work by writers who have been ignored or undervalued in relation to the NIE.

When the film-maker Alina Marazzi, whose collage films explore political issues through personal, individual stories, and blur reality and fiction like UNOs,[20] visited the University of Warwick in January 2014,[21] I asked her if she saw parallels between her work and the NIE, and she answered that she could call her work 'New Italian Anti-Epic'. Perhaps the missing or inchoate attention to female experience in the nebula could be seen in terms of such portrayals sometimes being anti-epic, or anti-heroism, the expression of the experience and of the imaginary of those who are not, and do not necessarily seek to be, protagonists in history or in a (new) national story, but whose views nevertheless matter and promise to increase understanding. We will see this contrast in chapter 4 in an analysis of Saviano as the global superhero versus Jones's 'failed' project, which she explicitly distances from ideas of epic.

Moreover, a recent edited volume has rightly pointed out the 'male, heteronormative bias' of most critical work in Italian Studies on notions of *impegno*, calling attention to the dismissal of female *impegno*, sometimes due to a tendency to overlook the political potential of addressing private concerns (Standen 2015: 4). This may account for a similar bias in understandings of the NIE, which is still haunted by the figure of the male public intellectual (as we will see in chapter 2 in particular), and which Jones again distances herself from (see chapter 4). Elena Ferrante's exclusion from discussions of the NIE, despite her texts exploring political and historical issues and her anonymity as an author being more complete than that of Wu Ming, might be explained by her personal stories of women's lives not fitting into a traditional model of politically engaged literature, as well as by her refusal to be a public figure in a traditional way.

Although Wu Ming 1 (2009a: 10–14) argues that the corpus he discusses is not a genre, but a collection of texts that display comparable approaches to literature, history and contemporary reality, I find it useful to understand the texts I discuss as a new hybrid unidentified genre by drawing on Derrida's (1980) understanding of genre as resisting rigid classification (which, interestingly, is referenced by Dimock (2006) in her discussion of new reimaginings of epic, as I explore in chapter 1). Derrida points out that the law of genre 'is precisely a principle of contamination, a law of impurity, a parasitical economy [...] a sort of participation without belonging' (1980: 59); these ideas seem to be encapsulated in the concept of the UNO, which is based on contamination, hybridity and oscillating between forms and styles. This looser understanding of genre allows for the frequent stylistic and thematic differences between the texts in my corpus. Rather than taking them to be based on the epic genre and associated with male adventure stories, I see affinities between these texts in terms of disrupting conventional modes of writing and privileging unexpected or alternative perspectives, combining anti-realist postmodernist experimentation with neo/realist/ic *impegno* and slipping between forms, styles and sometimes media to provoke reflection. This can encompass work by writers who find the epic label problematic, or whose work might not be seen as displaying a traditional sense of *impegno*. By looking beyond the NIE, my corpus also incorporates more transnational concerns than the Italian label allows, and the term UNO might be applied to texts in other languages that display the kind of generic waywardness that we will see throughout this study.

Organisation and Structure

There have been a large number of texts published in Italian in the twenty-first century that might be called UNOs, so I use Wu Ming 1's nebula as a starting point for exploring the highly relevant concerns he raised, although I also remedy some of the limitations of his corpus by introducing additional texts that explore fruitful lines of inquiry that his discussion overlooks. In each of the three thematic chapters, after a theoretical discussion of the theme identified that bases it within a (transnational) cultural climate and literary tradition, I perform a close reading of three or four primary texts that, I believe, best represent the key issues surrounding the theme in question from diverse perspectives: the first two or three from Wu Ming 1's nebula, and the final one a text that has been ignored or undervalued in whatever way, but that brings other dimensions to the theme in question. My primary texts are some of the most interesting UNOs of recent Italian literature, and they were also chosen because they demonstrate connections with preceding and contemporary literary experiences and with a series of recent debates on the cultural scene. I deliberately chose not to analyse texts written by Wu Ming as a collective, as they tend to more completely encompass all of the elements mentioned in the Memorandum, and I wanted to test Wu Ming 1's ideas against the work of other writers, whilst also attempting to fill the gaps in his understanding of recent Italian literature. Some of the writers and texts Wu Ming 1 discussed receive little or no attention in this study, due to space constraints, or because they only make brief incursions into the main areas of interest that I identify. This does not intend to be an exhaustive study of Italian literature at the beginning of the new millennium, but rather a survey picking out texts that address the questions Wu Ming 1 raised in the most interesting and revealing manner, to show a set of common concerns for writers in Italy and beyond in the twenty-first century. This gives more concrete and broader illustration to a discussion that, as I have already mentioned, has been limited in some ways. A close reading of these texts may bring to light some interesting gaps between what Wu Ming or others have stated and how the texts work in practice, as well as suggesting further elements for consideration in how Wu Ming 1's ideas might develop more productively.

Other texts are briefly brought into each chapter too, and, where possible, I indicate examples of these themes being addressed in other national literatures, tending towards European and American literature due to my own familiarity with them, in order to underline my argument that these UNOs might be seen as part of a wider evolution of the novel form that is linked to changing conditions in the twenty-first century. Yet, I also highlight the Italian literary tradition and political and social context that undoubtedly account for some of the peculiarities of these texts. By illustrating the transnational elements of these writers' approach to literature and their subject matter whilst also not ignoring the specificities of Italian culture, I seek to create links between the local, the national and the global, engaging in local inquiry but, equally, showing that the conditions for these UNOs did not happen in a vacuum.

The first chapter is an analysis of the Italian literary scene at the beginning of the twenty-first century with a particular focus on Wu Ming 1's Memorandum, to outline the key themes that will be the subject of the rest of this study, creating a framework for further discussion. I treat the Memorandum as a primary text in itself, engaging, where possible, in a close reading of the document. This raises the key issues surrounding recent Italian UNOs and highlights the tensions and gaps in what could be seen as a crypto-manifesto. Although some of the Memorandum is problematic, it also helps paint a picture of what was happening in Italian culture at the turn of the millennium.

A prime example of an interesting but flawed point raised by Wu Ming 1 is that of the recurring theme of the death of the father in recent Italian literature, which shows anxieties surrounding the end of the First Republic, postmodernism and modern-day society. I analyse this in chapter 2, before engaging in a close reading of Genna's autofictional representations of the death of his real-life father from two contrasting perspectives in *Medium* and *Italia De Profundis*. In both cases, his mourning is bound up with the state of Italy today, firstly through a fantastical reimagining of his father's communist past, then through his own experiences drawing on the work of literary 'fathers' such as Pasolini and David Foster Wallace. I then turn to a very different manifestation of this theme in the figure of 'il Vecchio' who has haunted various recent Italian texts, most memorably De Cataldo's *Romanzo criminale* and *Nelle mani giuste*. The latter forms the basis of my analysis, as it portrays the problems surrounding the political turmoil in the early 1990s, the ascent to power of Berlusconi and the need to take responsibility for the new Italy of the Second Republic with which many Italian writers have been preoccupied. Finally, I move away from Wu Ming 1's corpus to analyse Pugno's dystopian novel *Sirene* [*Sirens*], arguing that a move away from a purely fatherhood and male experience opens up some fascinating reflections on the pressing issues that face us today, taking in environmental considerations and the posthuman condition.

Questions of inheritance and responsibility are also bound up with the use of the historical novel form, the subject of chapter 3, as these texts are also ways of coming to terms with the past. The two main strands of historical novels in recent Italian literature are represented in this chapter by Scurati's *Una storia romantica* [*A Romantic Story*] about the Risorgimento, which, like others in this strand, attempts to rethink the collective memory of a mythologised moment in national history, and Mohamed and Wu Ming 2's *Timira*, which, conversely, works towards uncovering a largely forgotten or disavowed element of national history, that is, Italian colonialism. I then analyse Janeczek's *Le rondini di Montecassino* [*The Swallows of Monte Cassino*], which incorporates elements of both strands by looking at a famous event — the Battle of Monte Cassino during the Second World War — through various perspectives, many of which have been forgotten by mainstream historiography. I argue that Janeczek's work makes a valuable contribution to rethinking Italy's past through its multiperspectival and transnational approach. I also link these historical novels to Ginzburg's microhistorical approach, as well as situating them within the historical novel tradition that dates back to Manzoni's *The Betrothed* and his problematising of historical knowledge in his essay on the historical novel. In many ways, these contemporary writers are seeking to answer similar questions to those of their nineteenth-century precursor: how can we approach and combine history and fiction?

The interplay between fiction and nonfiction is also the concern of those contemporary writers who have experimented with combining a journalistic mode with the tools of fiction and transmediality, which I analyse in chapter 4, centring on the work of Saviano, Jones and Scego. Whilst Saviano's *Gomorra* [*Gomorrah*] about the Neapolitan mafia known as the Camorra purports to be truthful, the use of real events is as blurred and problematic as in Jones's *Sappiano le mie parole di sangue* about the Balkans conflict, although Jones is more overt about the role of fictionalising in her narrative. I then go beyond Wu Ming 1's corpus by analysing Scego and Bianchi's *Roma negata* [*Denied Rome*] within a network of transmedial activism that seeks to remedy the silencing of migrant perspectives and the overlooking of Italian colonial history in mainstream discourse. In this chapter, I call into question the supposed 'return to reality' that some critics have observed in twenty-first-century Italian literary production by bringing out the ambiguities surrounding the approach to reality in these texts.

I chose these three themes — parental legacies, history and the so-called 'new realism' — partly because they frequently resurface in recent Italian literature, but also because they are bound together by a similar desire for an imagined, impossible authenticity or truth, and contain combinations of tradition and innovation that typify Italian UNOs in the twenty-first century. My contention is that NIE is not the most effective label to describe the UNOs I address. They are not wholly new: despite incorporating novel elements, they are the product of a literary tradition going back to the postmodern predecessors these writers may have attempted to shrug off, as well as to earlier *impegnati* writers, and can even be traced back into the nineteenth century. Moreover, the 'Italian' label is problematic, given the unstable nature of Italian-ness itself, and the presence of similar themes and approaches in contemporary literature from other countries. Finally, I point out that Wu Ming 1 and others' discussion of twenty-first-century literature has tended to focus on the contribution of white, male writers, despite the NIE purporting to look at the past and present from unexpected and subaltern perspectives. In contrast to existing work on the subject, I discuss writers who have been omitted from their corpus, but who would go further in questioning dominant narratives than many of those included, even if some of these writers might define their work as anti-epic.

That is not to say that the nebula is an artificial grouping together of contemporary texts. On the contrary, the family resemblances that Wu Ming 1 brought to the fore in his Memorandum are present, but they simply take different forms depending on the writers in question, and are present in texts that he does not mention, which often explore female or postcolonial perspectives. Whilst the Memorandum is flawed, it is a fascinating starting point for discussing twenty-first-century Italian literature and offers the concept of the UNO, which is not only valuable for analysing the primary texts here, but could be potentially applied to literature (and other artistic products) from beyond Italy's borders. In this study, we will see a constellation of comparable ideas that, despite incorporating previous experiences, express a moment in time and a new stage of development of the novel form, both within Italy and elsewhere.

Notes to the Introduction

1. Unless otherwise indicated, all translations in this study are my own.
2. For more on the Wu Ming collective, see Wu Ming 1 2010d and 2016, Baird 2006 and Willman 2016.
3. See <http://www.lutherblissett.net/>.
4. The Memorandum was downloaded approximately 30,000 times within the first few months of appearing online (Wu Ming 2009c: x).
5. Although there have been no book-length explorations of the NIE, there was a special issue of the *Journal of Romance Studies* in the spring of 2010, as well as isolated articles on the subject peppered throughout various edited volumes (in particular Serkowska 2011, Somigli 2013, Jansen and Khamal 2014).
6. Patti points out that it is one of the most visited blogs in Italy (Patti 2014: Kindle location 616). See also <http://it.labs.teads.tv/top-blogs>.
7. *Carmilla* (<http://www.carmillaonline.com/>) is a webzine that was founded by Evangelisti, who has edited it alongside Genna, De Michele and Wu Ming 1, all of whom are key NIE figures. Not only do they publish articles about contemporary literature and cinema, but they have also engaged with political issues, for example in a campaign of solidarity with Cesare Battisti (see Evangelisti and others 2004).
8. Where possible, I have saved the webpages I cite in the Wayback Machine Internet Archive: <http://archive.org/web/>.
9. Not only did Berlusconi manage to come back into power in 2001, but, as Ginsborg points out, the centre-left government of 1996–2001 failed 'to pass any law on the conflict of interests, or any law regulating the telecommunications sector' (Ginsborg 2005: 190).
10. For Amato (2009), the events at the G8 in Genoa in 2001, which I discuss in chapter 1, particularly brought this to the fore.
11. Wu Ming 1 (2009c) refers to several examples of this criticism in a blogpost on the subject, including Giacomo Manfredi, who said in an interview: 'Io penso che non tocchi agli scrittori definirsi. Gli scrittori raccontano' [I think that writers should not define themselves. Writers narrate] (Andreetto 2008).
12. This is clearly shown by the title of Rondolino's (2009) article about the Memorandum in *La Stampa*: 'Wu Ming se questa è letteratura' [Wu Ming If This Is Literature].
13. Such as Tommaso Pincio, whose pseudonym is an homage to Thomas Pynchon. Aside from Wu Ming, twenty-first-century Italian literature has been fertile ground for collaborative writing, as seen in collectives such as Kai Zen and Scrittura industriale collettiva, as well as individual writers working with others on occasion (for example Carlotto and Mama Sabot 2008, Evangelisti and Moresco 2008, Duka and Philopat 2008).
14. The *foibe* killings took place during and after the Second World War, and were mainly perpetrated by Yugoslav partisans against Italians in the regions close to the border with Yugoslavia. They are commemorated on the controversial Giorno del ricordo, established in 2004. For a summary of Wu Ming's campaign against the circulation of falsified photographs online about the *foibe*, see Purini 2014.
15. See the European Commission's 'Factsheet on the "Right to be Forgotten" Ruling', <http://ec.europa.eu/justice/data-protection/files/factsheets/factsheet_data_protection_en.pdf>.
16. I return again to Manzoni and this time to his 'Storia della colonna infame' [History of the Column of Infamy], showing how his approach can later be detected in Sciascia, Pasolini and the NIE nebula.
17. As I discuss in chapter 2, this website is unfortunately no longer available.
18. I am referring to a talk Wu Ming 2 gave at the University of Warwick on 5 March 2013, entitled 'The Historical Novel as a Means of Investigation: In Search of Narrative Truth' (event poster here: <http://www2.warwick.ac.uk/fac/cross_fac/ias/current/earlycareer/events/migration/wu_ming.pdf>).
19. As shown by the fact that both Pugno's *Sirene* [*Sirens*] and Janeczek's *Cibo* [*Food*] are out of print. However, Janeczek would go on to win the Strega Prize in 2018.

20. Wu Ming 1 (2010b: 8) has also drawn parallels between the NIE and Marazzi's work, and Recalcati (2015: 174–77), whose work I employ in chapter 2, analyses Marazzi's work in his book on inheritance and motherhood.
21. She was a University of Warwick Institute of Advanced Study Visiting Fellow, and took part in an event I organised entitled 'The Past before Us: Uses of History in 21st Century Italy', which also included the writer Giorgio Vasta; see <http://www2.warwick.ac.uk/fac/cross_fac/ias/current/visitingfellows/2013–14dateorder/marazzi/marazzi_events.pdf>.

CHAPTER 1

'Something is Happening in Italian Literature': The Memorandum on the New Italian Epic and Twenty-First-Century Italian Literature

The term 'unidentified narrative object' (UNO) was coined by Wu Ming 1 and explained in detail in his Memorandum on the New Italian Epic (NIE), which first appeared online in April 2008. In this document, he stated that certain hybrid texts published in Italy, mainly since 2000, were part of a recent phenomenon in Italian literature that experimented with new and unusual elements to explore social and political issues: 'Nelle lettere italiane sta accadendo qualcosa' [Something is happening in Italian literature] (Wu Ming 1 2009a: 10). The Memorandum begins with Wu Ming 1's explanation of how he coined the name NIE, giving numerous examples of texts that can be included in its corpus. He says he is creating links that have either been ignored or taken for granted between texts in dialogue with one another, which he refers to as a nebula to give a sense that they are loosely gathered together like particles in a cloud, rather than a school of authors who have actively grouped together to form a movement: 'Eccoli, dal centro della nebulosa già ripartono, volano in ordine sparso, le traiettorie divergono, s'incrociono, divergono...' [There they are, already leaving the centre of the nebula, flying randomly, the trajectories diverge, cross over, diverge...] (2009a: 14). He then lists the seven main characteristics of these texts — ranging from having an oblique gaze on their subject matter to telling alternative (his)stories — and, finally, reflects on the urgent need for such narratives in today's world: 'Oggi arte e letteratura non possono limitarsi a suonare allarmi tardivi: devono aiutarci a immaginare vie d'uscita' [Today art and literature cannot restrict themselves to sounding belated alarms: they must help us to imagine ways out] (2009a: 60). Publishing the Memorandum online to be freely downloaded meant that readers could leave comments and interact with what was being said, and the original document was edited and supplemented several times in reaction to the numerous responses it had received. The 'Memorandum Version 2.0' appeared in September 2008, complete with footnotes and an extra section to develop or clarify certain points, or to refer to further reading, often online. It also contained corrections, including a sentence that is crossed out and justified in a footnote (Wu Ming 1 2008a: 27). The following year, a third extended version was published in a book entitled *New Italian Epic. Letteratura, sguardo obliquo, ritorno al futuro* [*New Italian Epic: Literature, Oblique Gaze, Back to the Future*] (Wu Ming 2009b),[1] signed by Wu Ming as a whole, which supplemented the Memorandum with Wu Ming 2's essay 'La salvezza di Euridice' [The Salvation of Eurydice], Wu Ming 1's speech 'Noi dobbiamo essere i genitori' [We're Going to Have to Be the Parents] and his expansions on the original Memorandum gathered in a new section with the Spanish title 'Sentimiento nuevo', as well as an introduction by Wu Ming collectively.

The Memorandum was met with a substantial amount of controversy, and, although some of this was more indicative of issues related to the Italian cultural scene (as I argued in the introduction to this study),[2] it is also open to some of the criticism that has been levelled at it. Whilst Wu Ming 1 has always stressed that it was not a manifesto, stating in the first lines of his foreword to 'Version 2.0' in emphatic italics: '*Memorandum. Sintesi provvisoria. Primo tentativo*' [*Memorandum. Provisional summary. First attempt*] (2008a: 1), in many ways it could be seen as a crypto-manifesto. By outlining the shared characteristics between these texts, he creates a group, a 'generazione letteraria' [literary generation] (11), that is distinguished from what came before, aligning writers in a way that resembles a literary movement. Wu Ming 1's tone and the ideas he puts forward have a utopian ring about them that we might associate with a manifesto: literature can be used to change society; literature is still at the centre of culture in spite of technological developments. Despite the emphasis on participation and the democracy of literature that Wu Ming 1 discusses in the Memorandum and also attempts to enact by being part of a writing collective, he puts himself forward as the spokesperson for this literary phenomenon. Although these narrative objects are called unidentified, there are many attempts to identify them here. However, Wu Ming 1 does not *prescribe* but *describe* what is, and has already been, happening in Italian literature. The issues discussed in the Memorandum are both briefly developed and wide-ranging, as he intended it to be the beginning of a debate aimed at a wide audience of internet users. If we take the Memorandum to be a starting point, albeit one with contradictions and omissions, it is a valuable document for exploring the Italian literary scene at that time. The Memorandum contains interesting tensions between the words of Wu Ming 1 and the reality of the contemporary literary market and of the NIE texts, whilst also containing troubling blind spots regarding work by non-male, non-white and non-ethnically Italian writers.

In this chapter, I will give an overview of the key concepts outlined in the Memorandum, their strengths and weaknesses, and how they reflect the Italian cultural scene in the twenty-first century. I will treat the Memorandum as a primary text, as it is a type of UNO in itself. Wu Ming 1 tells us in the introduction to 'Version 2.0' in a parenthetic aside that he is writing 'un romanzo un racconto, sto narrando' [a novel a story, I am narrating] (2008a: 2). This is certainly not a straightforward piece of academic criticism, but an unusual hybrid that does not easily fit into existing definitions. Subsequent chapters will be based around the themes discussed here, developing them in more detail and examining individual texts from the nebula and beyond to show them in action and to suggest connected avenues that might have been overlooked by Wu Ming 1 and others. This chapter is thus a brief exploration of the threads that will later be followed, and it is divided into the three elements that constitute the phenomenon's name: its newness in relation to previous literary experiences and the Digital Age, its Italian-ness seen through the lens of its historical and social context but also placed within a wider transnational landscape, and, finally, the implications of describing these texts as epic. This analysis will make it clear why I prefer the term UNO to that of NIE to describe this approach to Italian literature in the twenty-first century, as the label NIE seems to lead to the exclusion of female and transnational perspectives, which I will go some way towards remedying through my focus in subsequent chapters on a wider range of texts than those identified by Wu Ming 1.

New

When discussing New Journalism, Tom Wolfe said: 'Any movement, group, party, program, philosophy or theory that goes under a name with "New" in it is just begging for trouble. The garbage bag of history is already full of them' (Wolfe 1975: 37). Certainly, there are problems surrounding Wu Ming 1's choice of this adjective for the NIE. The label of 'new Italian narrative' began to be used in the 1980s to refer to 'an eclectic and varied production where the growth of readerships has been accompanied by the numbers of new writers who have brought with them unfamiliar cultures, backgrounds and experiences' (Ania and Caesar 2007: 2). In the 1990s, it was connected with the young writers in an anthology edited by Franchini and Parazzoli (1996), and it was also used in the name of a critical text, *The New Italian Novel* (Barański and Pertile 1993), that analysed the work of writers such as Andrea De Carlo, Gianni Celati and Vincenzo Consolo, as well as later being applied to the Cannibal writers,[3] for example in *Italian Pulp Fiction: The New Narrative of the* Giovani Cannibali *Writers* (Lucamante 2001). Wu Ming 1 presents the NIE as distinct from experiences like these, although there is some overlap with these various 'new' literary experiences, as well as with other contemporary texts from which Wu Ming 1 tries to distance them.

Indeed, the Cannibal writers foreshadowed certain elements of both the style and approach of the NIE texts, despite obvious differences that may obscure their importance. The anthology of short stories that gave the Cannibal writers their name, *Gioventù cannibale* (Brolli 1996), was one of the first texts to appear as part of Einaudi's 'Stile Libero' series, which is undoubtedly linked to the fortunes of the NIE writers too. At a time of crisis at Einaudi in terms of its identity and finances, Stile Libero was created by Severino Cesari and Paolo Repetti for hybrid texts mixing languages, genres and styles, including *noir*, comics and science fiction, often accompanied by videos or DVDs (Ferretti and Ianuzzi 2014: 294).

The hybridity that we see in recent UNOs can be clearly linked to this innovative approach coming from a mainstream publisher. Stile Libero also tended towards new and transgressive writers, including those that would later become part of the NIE, such as Lucarelli, Pincio and Luther Blissett/Wu Ming. In addition, there is overlap between the Cannibal writers and the NIE in the ways they approach the contemporary world through literature. Mondello argues that what was truly original about the Cannibal writers was how they included the contemporary in literature, such as television, consumerism and youth culture, using slang and including music almost as a soundtrack to the stories (Mondello 2007: 10). Such reflections of contemporary life are also present throughout the NIE, part of their 'attitudine *popular*' [popular attitude] (32), as Wu Ming 1 calls it in the Memorandum (32), which often entails an oral element incorporating slang. The generational issues that Mondello sees as integral to the Cannibal writers are also a stalwart of the NIE, as I will discuss chapter 2, where I suggest that this is linked to the society of consumption, which their 1990s precursors were similarly reflecting on. Indeed, the effects of consumerism and the mass media that preoccupied the Cannibal writers are frequently depicted by NIE writers too, as seen in Walter Siti's *Troppi paradisi* [*Too Many Paradises*],[4] or in Genna's portrayal of the fashion industry and a modern world of empty enjoyment in *Fine impero* [*End of Empire*],[5] as well as in a culturally barren contemporary Italy in his *Italia De Profundis*, analysed in the next chapter. Although the Cannibal writers tended to favour short stories in contrast to the long form of the NIE, their rejuvenation of Italian literature in the light of the contemporary paved the way for many of the texts Wu Ming 1 mentions in the Memorandum.[6]

Another overlooked landmark of 1990s literature that undoubtedly influenced the NIE was the arrival of so-called migrant writing in Italy, which Burns describes as

> the arrival of a new *io* [I] — and a new *noi* [we] — in Italian literature: where women writers in the '60s–'70s in particular had established new voices telling stories of new experiences, or sometimes familiar experiences told from a different point of view, and so had written a new set of subjecthoods and perhaps a new consciousness into the Italian canon, now writers from different cultures were initiating an analogous process, attempting to mark out a specific cultural territory in which different voices describing a different Italy and a different notion of Italian-ness might be heard and responded to. (Burns 2007: 136–37)

The effects of Italian literature opening up to incorporate these new, transnational experiences continue to be felt in the twenty-first century. Significantly, in describing particular areas of interest for migrant writers, Burns individuates an engagement with 'the myth of Italy' (Burns 2007: 147), which cannot but resonate with the NIE and its concern with mythopoeia. The use of microhistories in the NIE as a means of rethinking the mainstream historical narrative, looking at history from subaltern perspectives, would seem to be carrying forward Burns's description of the 'new set of subjecthoods' that migrant writing heralded, although the approach of many of the NIE historical novels to Italy's colonial past has been criticised for focusing on white, male, Italian experience (see chapter 3), and, as I discuss in more detail later in this chapter, the nebula is short on texts by migrant writers.

The texts by migrant writers in the 1990s could also in some cases be called UNOs, incorporating a mix of personal experience, political and historical concerns and fiction, just as the NIE writers do. Indeed, Brioni referred to them as UNOs in an interview with Wu Ming 1, and pointed out that 1993, the date indicated in the Memorandum as the beginning of the NIE, was also the year in which the first important texts appeared in Italian narrating Italian colonialism from the point of view of the colonised, by Maria Abebù Viarengo, Ribka Sibhatu and Shirin Ramzanali Fazel (Brioni 2014: 279). Wu Ming 1 responds by mentioning African-Italian writers like Scego and Ghermandi, who were admitted into the nebula after the Memorandum first appeared, and states that such literary production clearly makes an impact in terms of rethinking colonialism (Brioni 2014: 280). He does not elaborate much more on this point, and his discussion of postcolonial literature seems to be very much concerned with other ideas, such as Italy being treated as a colony by the United States during the Cold War, Italy's internal colonialism and the north–south divide (Brioni 2014: 277–78), or Wu Ming's tendency to write about the past from the point of view of characters 'dalla parte sbagliata della Storia' [from the wrong side of History] (Brioni 2014: 287). As we shall see with other preceding literary experiences, there does not seem to be a full acknowledgement of the influence of migrant writing on the NIE nebula, even six years after the Memorandum appeared.

The putative newness of the NIE is very much tied up with generational issues and the failings of the generation before them and of Silvio Berlusconi's Italy, which have been seen as galvanising these writers into action. Wu Ming 1 claims that there has been a realisation among his peers that they need to grow up metaphorically and become the founders, or parents, of a new Italy. In the Memorandum, he links what has been happening on the Italian political, social and cultural scene with the recurring theme of the death of the father in the texts of the nebula (74), which I analyse in detail in the following chapter. This generation defines itself in relation to what came before, leaving a sense of emptiness in being always post-something, even posthumous: 'post-fascisti, post-comunisti, post-postmoderni, Seconda Repubblica, eccetera' [post-fascist, post-communist, post-postmodern, Second Republic, etc.] (74). As a result, the theme of absent or dead progenitors is both literally and metaphorically present in many NIE texts. Wu Ming 1 argues that this generation needs to stop thinking of itself as *problem children* (2010c), and writers need to start taking a stance on social issues through literature: 'Immaginando storie alternative, curano i difetti del nostro sguardo di postumi e ci preparano a immaginare un futuro' [Imagining alternative stories, they remedy the defects of our posthumous gaze and prepare us to imagine a future] (2008b).

This is very much connected to what Wu Ming 1 sees as the shortcomings of late twentieth-century postmodernist literary production, which he feels shied away from shouldering this responsibility after the death of the various 'fathers' we will encounter in the following chapter, although his approach to postmodernism suffers from being simplistic. In his talk on the NIE included in the print version of the Memorandum, Wu Ming 1 quotes the American writer David Foster Wallace, who significantly used a parent–child analogy to describe the latter stages of postmodernism. Wallace saw this period as reminiscent of being a high-school student throwing a wild party when your parents are away, then wishing they would come back and restore order:

> It's not a perfect analogy, but the sense I get of my generation of writers and intellectuals or whatever is that it's 3:00 A.M. and the couch has several burn-holes and somebody's thrown up in the umbrella stand and we're wishing the revel would end. The postmodern founders' patricidal work was great, but patricide produces orphans, and no amount of revelry can make up for the fact that writers my age have been literary orphans throughout our formative years. We're kind of wishing some parents would come back. And of course we're uneasy about the fact that we wish they'd come back — I mean, what's wrong with us? Are we total pussies? Is there something about authority and limits we actually need? And then the uneasiest feeling of all, as we start gradually to realize that parents in fact aren't ever coming back — which means we're going to have to be the parents. (McCaffery 1993: 150)

Wu Ming 1 called his talk 'We're Going to Have to Be the Parents' after Wallace, signalling the crucial position of the orphan metaphor in the NIE. He argues that the NIE is in contrast to what he calls 'Postmodernismi da quattro soldi' [Two-a-penny postmodernisms] (63), a term that he particularly applies to late postmodernist writing. Whilst he admits there are exceptions to the rule,[7] he maintains that late twentieth-century literature was frequently characterised by self-referentiality and cold irony, and the creative act stopped being seen as one of renewal and liberation (64). For him, postmodernism died on 11 September 2001 (66), and, since then, the NIE writers have been stepping up to attempt to become the new parents of Italy.

Such an attitude to postmodernism has been espoused by critics such as Donnarumma (2003) and Luperini (2005), who have tended to reduce the concept to what Re describes as 'the alleged triumph of shallowness and disengagement, an ironic, playful and sceptical attitude, loss of any faith in the possibility of an accurate or coherent representation or rendering of reality, epistemic nihilism, and apathetic surrender to the ruthless rules of consumer capitalism' (Re 2014: 101). Jansen has explored the difficult reception of postmodernism in Italy, which, in contrast to the American postmodernist attitude of 'anything goes', manifested itself instead more as a rejection of literature as a useless and self-referential game (Jansen 2002: 239). Such artistic production is often associated with Calvino's later work, and placed in artificial opposition with a Pasolinian 'realism' — most notably by Benedetti (1998) — and, indeed, realism is another term that has been subject to certain misconceptions, as shown by the recent debate started in the journal *Allegoria* on an alleged 'return to reality' in recent Italian literature (see chapter 4). Wu Ming 1 seems to fall victim to this more general tendency to misconstrue postmodernist experimentalism as being disengaged from reality and to propose that postmodernism has now ended as we enter a new historical and cultural phase. The fact that the main body of the Memorandum opens and closes with quotations from

T. S. Eliot's *The Waste Land* — and the presence of Eliot as a reference elsewhere in NIE texts[8] — suggests that the ideas of Wu Ming 1 and some other NIE writers align with those of critics like Luperini (2005: 13), who has observed a return to elements of modernism in recent years to search for answers to contemporary issues. Storini (2010: 82) also raises the pertinent point that Wu Ming 1's description of postmodernist literature recalls a Sausurrean approach to language, as seen particularly in his description in the Memorandum of 'un mondo dove il linguaggio rimanda sempre e ossessivamente a se stesso, i segni rimandano sempre e solo ad altri segni [...] fino all'apologia dell'indecidibilità, dell'ineffabilità, dell'assenza di qualunque senso' [a world where language always and obsessively refers to itself, signs always and only refer to other signs [...] until the apologia of undecidability, ineffability, of the absence of any meaning] (66). The allusion to Saussure, whose theories eventually led to poststructuralism and deconstruction, gives an indication of the tendency in Italy to reduce postmodernism to certain schools of thought, mainly based on the work of French theorists, rather than allowing for wider and more politically committed interpretations of the ontological doubt it ushered in.[9]

As Burns (2001) has demonstrated, a sense of political and ethical commitment or *impegno* was not absent in Italian literature in the latter decades of the twentieth century, it simply became more fragmentary rather than adhering to a collective monolithic project. It is also difficult to see a radical break with postmodernism stemming from 9/11, given that many of the concerns of postmodernist writing, such as a mistrust of traditional power and universal values, and a tendency towards openness leaving the reader to interpret the texts, are present in the NIE too. Antonello and Mussgnug (2009: 5) rightly point out that attempts to rebrand postmodernism do not address the underlying similarities between the concepts of postmodernism and current literary production. Whether this era is 'post-postmodernist' or, as Wu Ming 1 says, does not have a label yet (68), it is not one of complete rupture with postmodernism, which Wu Ming 1 does not fully address.

Certainly, the NIE could be seen as signalling a more overt and less fragmentary approach to engagement with national issues. Wu Ming 1 places the idea of engagement at the top of his list of characteristics of the NIE in the Memorandum, defining it employing English slang — 'Don't keep it cool-and-dry' (22) — perhaps as a nod to pop culture, or perhaps to distance it from the Italian tradition of *impegno* and underline its newness. He tells us that these recent writers wish to re-engage with the masses by combining narrative complexity with what he calls 'attitudine *popular*' [popular attitude] (32). The NIE writers recognise that 'il pubblico è più intelligente di quanto siamo disposti a riconoscere' [the public is more intelligent than we are inclined to recognise] (32), and that popular culture is not simply something to be demonised, but elements of it, including new technologies and the tools of genre fiction,[10] can contribute to the overall effect of these texts and help them to connect meaningfully with the reading public (32–33). It is this that Wu Ming 1 seeks to do in the Memorandum too, acting as the writer as social commentator and ethically committed intellectual reaching out to a wide audience of internet users, with complex ideas expressed in an accessible way, as part of new approach to literature.

This co-presence of 'high' and 'low' cultural elements can be seen in the Memorandum itself, which, despite addressing serious, often academic, points and including technical language, has a conversational tone, at times becoming extremely informal. This orality is present immediately from its opening as a sort of reminiscence: 'Nel pomeriggio dell'11 settembre 2001 lavoravamo a casa di Wu Ming 2' [On the afternoon of 11 September 2001, we were working at Wu Ming 2's house] (5). Later, Wu Ming 2's voice intervenes in the main section in a conversational and immediate way: 'Wu Ming 2 è qui, accanto a me, e chiede la parola' [Wu Ming 2 is here, next to me, and wants to say something] (36). At times, it displays a humorous theatricality in order to explain the points being made that is certainly not typical of literary criticism: '"Ehi, cos'è quello? È un uccello? No, è un aereo! No, un momento... È Superman!" Assolutamente no. È un oggetto narrativo non-identificato' ['Hey, what's that? Is it a bird? No, it's a plane! No, wait a minute... It's Superman!' Absolutely not. It's an unidentified narrative object] (41). This allusion to Superman is just one example of a reference to pop culture in the Memorandum — *Scary Movie* (65), Tom Cruise (66), *L.A. Confidential* (86) and *Buffy the Vampire Slayer* (137) are also mentioned, to name a few — but these are combined with 'highbrow' allusions to literature and theorists, such as Walter Benjamin (51) or Gilles Deleuze (77), who are referenced but not analysed with in-depth academic rigour, which undoubtedly provoked at least some of the opposition that the Memorandum received, with, for example, Ceserani calling it a 'dilettantesco manifesto' [dilettante-esque manifesto] (2012: 212). The print volume does not have an index, making it difficult to navigate for readers who want to do more than read it on a superficial level. Wu Ming 1 irreverently states that they are not interested in being accepted into 'qualche parnaso di stronzi' [some Parnassus of arseholes] (96), a particularly informal use of language to make his point that this discussion is not to be seen purely as the territory of intellectuals, but as relevant to the whole of society. Like other UNOs, the Memorandum tends to combine diverse registers, although some of these elements cloud the message that Wu Ming 1 is trying to communicate. This combination of high and low culture would also seem further to call into question the NIE's rejection of postmodernism, which Jameson described as a 'cultural mutation, in which what used to be stigmatized as mass or commercial culture is now received into the precincts of a new and enlarged cultural realm' (1991: 64).

This could alternatively be seen as part of another novelty that Wu Ming 1 claims for these texts in the Memorandum, when he says that their narrative voice is characterised by 'sovversione "nascosta" di linguaggio e stile' ['hidden' subversion of language and style] (37). This is listed as one of the seven main features of the NIE. The subversion is described as hidden because a superficial reading may not bring to the surface their experimentalism, as can be seen in the case of De Michele's *La visione del cieco* [*The Blind Man's Vision*], which was written without using the verb 'to be', giving the narrative an unusual feel, although the reader may not immediately identify the cause, as De Michele never states it in the text.[11] However, some of the texts of the nebula do not seem to be particularly stylistically experimental, either on the surface or underneath. The most striking and common element that we can detect in the style of the texts in the nebula is their orality. An article by Fulginiti (2009) helpfully conceives of orality in the NIE in a more articulated way than simply rendering speech mimetically, although we do see this in the NIE too. For Fulginiti (2009: 2), orality can include chorality, the fragmentation of viewpoints and the rhythm of the narrative, as well reflecting how people communicate today in Italy. Many of the techniques she identifies in these texts draw attention to language and how it is mediated; it tends to be portrayed as something that can be recycled or translated or manipulated in different ways, as we will see throughout this study in texts from within and beyond the nebula, suggesting that it is a key element of the UNO. This can be viewed as another example of a postmodernist tendency to question sources of knowledge, and it could also be linked to a need to combat misinformation from the mass media, particularly in Berlusconi's Italy, which underlies many of these writers' texts, particularly those that are journalistic.

Some of these texts use digital storytelling to communicate and spread their message, which is another way of working against Berlusconi's media control. In the Memorandum, Wu Ming 1 sees the use of new technologies in the NIE as part of what Jenkins (2006a) has called convergence culture in his book of the same name.[12] Some texts of the nebula (and the Memorandum itself) are transmedial, as Wu Ming 1 points out (45), employing different platforms to examine their subject matter. This is what Jenkins calls 'content streaming', a shift 'from media-specific content toward content that flows across multiple media channels' (2006a: 243). It can mean that the texts are not simply the paper copies of the books, but are supplemented by online material, such as pictures, photographs, secondary reading, film and/or music, either on websites or through social networks. Exploiting new technologies is connected to these writers' aim to give literature a social role. As Jenkins says, looking at the way in which culture has changed in the Information Age shows us 'new ways of thinking about citizenship and collaboration' (2006a: 246). In the Memorandum, Wu Ming 1 cites the pertinent comment made by Magini and Santoni (2008) that literature needs to adapt to the constant mutations and complexities of today's reality (71). Many of these writers use technology as a medium for reinvigorating literary tradition and engaging with national issues in a way that is relevant to the world we live in and includes the wider public.

A prime example of a text that exploits different media is Wu Ming's *Manituana* (2007b). Not only did Wu Ming release a trailer on YouTube and create a website with supplementary information about the story and period in which it was set,[13] but in the text itself readers can find a key to access a special website reserved only for those who have read the novel, called 'livello 2' [level 2], where there is further information on the characters and subject matter, as well as a bibliography, a comments thread, a section to which people can contribute spin-off stories, and a section that details Wu Ming's collaborative writing technique. This deepens the readers' experience of the narrative and also gives them a participatory role in it, as they must actively seek out this extra information and choose what to interact with. Whilst it is difficult to gauge how many readers actually access this site, there is a lively comments thread and various imaginative spin-offs, including one that connects *Manituana* to the Balkans conflict, although the pdf file with the story has now disappeared.[14] This is by far the most detailed extension of a NIE text; others tend to include extra photographs, videos and documents on blogs, Pinterest and/ or Tumblr, as in the case of Antar Mohamed and Wu Ming 2's *Timira*, and Roberto Santachiara and Wu Ming 1's *Point Lenana* (see chapter 3), or Genna's *Fine impero*[15] and his *La vita umana sul pianeta terra* [*Human Life on Planet Earth*],[16] which are also explored alongside his other texts on his blog.[17] Wu Ming's blog, *Giap*, and Genna's blog in themselves can also be seen as examples of transmedia storytelling, as they extend the messages found in their novels as places where the authors can post a wide range of materials and links. We will see this kind of transmedia storytelling again in chapter 4 in the way that Saviano's *Gomorra* and Scego and Bianchi's *Roma negata* are starting points for raising awareness on related issues through various media platforms and real-life activism.

Wu Ming 1 sees such transmediality as part of what Jenkins (2006a: 243) refers to as 'bottom-up participatory culture', in which consumers now participate actively in the media system. This often happens in the twenty-first century through blogs, fan communities, social networking and open-source principles (Jenkins 2006a: 3). We can also see this participatory culture in action in the spin-offs of some of these texts that go beyond online material, such as a stage version of Luther Blissett's *Q* and an album by the folk-rock band Yo Yo Mundi based on Wu Ming's *54* (as Wu Ming 2 tells Jenkins 2006c); the life of the texts is not limited to the original paper copies or to the control of their authors. The NIE has also been associated with various attempts to involve a wider community in writing the original texts themselves, such as Wu Ming's early project *Ti chiamerò Russell* [*I'll Call You Russell*][18] or Magini and Santoni's project Scrittura industriale collettiva [Industrial Collective Writing].[19] Italy in the new millennium has been a particularly fertile ground for new techniques of collective writing and reader participation, ideas that are at the heart of the Memorandum and of Jenkins's participatory culture.

However, in some ways, Wu Ming and Jenkins's ideas seem rather utopian,[20] and they are not always present in these texts either. The advent of new technologies supposedly leads to the democratisation of culture, but market forces still play a key role in culture in Italy and beyond, and, viewed cynically, the transmedial elements of many of these texts could be seen as effective marketing tools. Wu Ming now inhabit a mainstream position on the Italian cultural scene: their blog, *Giap*, is one of the most visited blogs in Italy,[21] and they bring out their books with Einaudi, a publishing giant that is both commercially successful and seen as the leading literary publisher in Italy, carrying notions of heritage and canonicity. Other NIE writers, such as Scurati, Genna, Evangelisti, De Cataldo and Saviano, are similarly well-known and their voices are very much heard on the Italian cultural scene (and beyond in the case of Saviano), which begs the question: to what extent can we see this phenomenon as truly including a wider public in culture? In addition, most NIE writers do not use the potential of the internet and digital technologies to involve a wider community when writing their books. Wu Ming 1 insists on the primacy of the written word in the Memorandum, despite technological developments, stating: 'L'epicentro rimane letterario, ma il sisma arriva ovunque' [The epicentre remains literary, but the earthquake happens everywhere] (89). The importance of print culture can be seen by the fact that the Memorandum eventually appeared in a definitive paper copy; for all the revolutionary aspects that Jenkins describes and Wu Ming advocate, there is an insistence on the book itself. It seems as if Wu Ming 1 wants to have it both ways in the Memorandum and, once again, there is a sense of both newness and tradition intertwined here. He may believe in the power of Jenkins's convergence culture to revolutionise literature, but literature is still centred on the book object.

Perhaps it is beneficial too to look beyond Jenkins when considering the transmedial elements of recent UNOs. It would not be out of place to liken such digital storytelling to Bakhtin's concept of heteroglossia in the novel, which incorporates extraliterary elements as part of its 'living contact with the unfinished, still-evolving contemporary reality (the openended present)' (Bakhtin 1981: 7). Piga perceptively likens Wu Ming's transmediality to Eco's conception of the 'opera aperta' [open work], seen through the lens of Deleuze and Guattari's metaphor of the book as a rhizome, as well as being placed within twenty-first-century participatory convergence culture (2014: Kindle locations 1140–44). As we shall see in chapter 3, parallels with Eco's work tend to be downplayed in the NIE, but the experimentalism of Eco can be seen as another important precedent for these writers. As Brook and Patti point out, new technologies have made it possible to realise ideas that could only be theorised by people like Eco, or Calvino in his conception of the 'iper-romanzo' [hyper-novel] (Brook and Patti 2014: Kindle locations 43–56).[22]

Wu Ming 1's aims are also not dissimilar to that of Tondelli's Under 25 project in 1985, an attempt to open up literature to young people and insert their voices into literature.[23] In common with the Under 25 Project, narrating is a political act for the NIE, and a way of getting different voices heard than those of the establishment. When presenting the project in the magazine *Linus*, Tondelli asked young writers to submit contributions in which they wrote about their reality instead of letting others speak for them:

> Perché invece non raccontate quello che fate, che sentite: i vostri tormenti, i vostri rapporti a scuola, con le ragazze, con la famiglia [...] Perché non scrivete pagine contro chi odiate? O per chi amate? C'è bisogno di sapere tutte queste cose. Siete gli unici a poterlo fare. Nessun giornalista, per quanto abile, potrà raccontarle al vostro posto. Nessuno scrittore. Sarà sempre qualcosa di diverso. Siete voi che dovete prendere la parola e dire quello che non vi va o che vi sta bene. Siete voi che dovete raccontare. (Tondelli 1998: 323)

> [Instead, why not narrate what you do, what you hear: your torments, your relationships at school, with girls, with your family [...] Why not write pages against those you hate? Or for those you love? All these things need to be known. You are the only ones who can do it. No journalist, however skilled, will be able to say them in your place. No writer. It will always be something

different. It is you who must speak and say what you do or don't like. It is you who must narrate.]

The result of this call to the pen was a collection of short stories, which found a new language that was less literary and more oral than other literature of the time (Tondelli 1998: 352), fragments that reflected the modern world's lack of unity and coherence (Tondelli 1998: 364). Wu Ming 1 does not call for stories in the Memorandum, but instead describes a similar search for new tools to speak of what is happening, a mode of expression adapted to what it is like to be alive now. The way in which this manifests itself is altered by the changing cultural landscape in the twenty-first century, but harks back once again to predecessors. The NIE draws on tradition (without acknowledging it in some cases), while simultaneously reflecting the contemporary world.

Italian

It is difficult to separate the arguments for newness from those for Italian-ness in the Memorandum. As I have already demonstrated, the debates on the genealogy of the genre have taken on an Italian hue, particularly concerning postmodernism, and, analogously, the contextual elements that I will discuss in this section are also related to the spirit of the times, new conditions that have filtered down to these UNOs. Nevertheless, I include context in the 'Italian' section of this chapter due to the peculiarly Italian light that Wu Ming 1 casts it in; he states of the changes that have taken place in recent years: 'In nessun altro contesto si sarebbe verificato lo stesso incontro di reagenti, la stessa confluenza di energie. Gli stimoli avrebbero avuto risposte diverse' [In no other context would the same meeting of reagents have occurred, the same confluence of energies. The stimuli would have had different reactions] (18). However, I seek to demonstrate here that there are both national and transnational elements to be taken into consideration when examining developments in recent Italian literature.

Before looking at the historical context, it is worth highlighting that the choice of the label Italian is striking, for two reasons. First, in an increasingly globalised world, there are notable influences in the NIE, although frequently overlooked, from writers who have come to Italy from other countries, which inevitably bring a transnational dimension to the phenomenon. Second, Italy itself is a de-centred and plural concept, with many writers operating on a regional rather than nationwide level, as we shall see. Many of the characteristics of the phenomenon are present in works originating in other national literatures, which Wu Ming 1 himself does not shy away from mentioning in the Memorandum (17),[24] and, throughout this study, I will attempt to draw parallels with recent literature in other (mainly European) countries, which have numerous comparable examples of UNOs. Rushing sees multilingualism as an unspoken characteristic of the NIE: 'as the Chinese name of the Wu Ming collective and the English title of their manifesto might suggest; this multilingualism appears unconsciously, as a natural cosmopolitanism of the internet age that requires no comment' (Rushing 2011). This is alongside the fact that many of the NIE writers look out beyond the Alps, whether it is through translation of their works into other languages (as seen in the case of Wu Ming themselves, or in that of Evangelisti), through adaptation into other media that are then exported worldwide (Saviano's *Gomorra*, for instance, which has been made into a film and hugely popular television series), or positioning their own work in terms of other national literary experiences (Genna, for example, draws on a wide range of international intertextual references in *Italia De Profundis*, as we shall see in chapter 2).

Approaches to recent literature vary from region to region, as Mondello has written about in terms of the different schools of *noir* on the peninsula,[25] and we can locate several key centres for the NIE in Italy, despite some writers being sprinkled elsewhere in the peninsula.[26] Bologna is the centre of the NIE, partly due to it being the city where writers such as Brizzi, Lucarelli, Evangelisti and Wu Ming themselves live, work and sometimes situate their texts — as seen in Wu Ming's depiction of the red city in the post-war years in *54*, or between different times frames in *Asce di guerra* [*Hatchets of War*] — and the importance of Bologna can also be attributed to its lively cultural and political scene, which undoubtedly conditioned the development of the NIE. The city was the backdrop for intellectual opposition to the establishment connected to the Movimento del '77, and it was the birth place of political initiatives such as the Indiani Metropolitani, the satirical magazine *Frigidaire*, and Radio Alice, an independent radio station which Wu Ming have in fact written about in their screenplay for Guido Chiesa's 2004 film *Lavorare con lentezza* [*Working Slowly*]. It was also an important locus for Tondelli's Under 25 Project and the Cannibal writers (as pointed out by Lucamante 2001: 19). The Memorandum and many of the NIE writers posthumously grew out of this fertile environment in Bologna. Milan and Rome constitute the other important locations for the NIE. Genna and Scurati, despite the latter originally hailing from Naples, are based in Milan, as their works analysed here indicate. Biondillo's detective stories with the protagonist Inspector Ferraro are situated in the Quarto Oggiaro district of Milan, and Philopat's *La banda Bellini* [*The Bellini Gang*] and *I viaggi di Mel* [*Mel's Travels*], which are name-checked in the Memorandum as prime examples of an epic narrative and of a UNO respectively (12 and 14), are two parts of a trilogy based on a semi-autobiographical account of the author's experiences of the Milanese underground punk movement. Philopat also moves between regions: his work written collaboratively with Duka, *Roma k.o*, looks at the Italian capital. Like the other NIE writers whose work is based in Rome — in particular De Cataldo[27] and Siti[28] — the writers of *Roma k.o.* are concerned with an alternative vision of the eternal city, with the narrative taking place on the city's peripheries and in the underworld (in another parallel with the approach of the Cannibal writers discussed earlier), rather than at the recognisable centre of the Italian state. The Roman writers very much distance their narratives from traditional visions of the capital and instead examine the modern-day reality of the city, as we will see in chapter 4 in an analysis of Scego and Bianchi's *Roma negata*. Clearly, the NIE has regional aspects that are overlooked by Wu Ming 1 in the Memorandum in an attempt to unite the work of these writers in his national project.

So how does he justify the Italian label? He outlines the events surrounding the end of the Cold War in order to paint a picture of Italian specificity, some elements of which undoubtedly do seep through into these narratives regardless of their writers' regional affiliations, although others point to an insistence on creating a common generational narrative. He argues that the comparisons to be drawn concerning the approaches to their subject matter and the forms of these unusual texts are the result of a combination of global and national events that have conditioned their writers, though different in age, and thus made them part of the same literary generation (11). Wu Ming 1 clearly situates the beginnings of the NIE in 1993, although 2001 is seen as a significant turning point for these writers. The Memorandum points to the figurative 'terremoto' [earthquake] (79) in Italy that followed the fall of the Berlin Wall as a key moment, as it ushered in an ongoing crisis as well as a liberation of energies. With the downfall of the Soviet Union came that of the Italian Communist Party and a complete shake-up of the Italian political system, accompanied by the *Tangentopoli* [Bribesville] scandals and the *Mani pulite* [Clean Hands] investigations into corruption. This 'smottamento politico' [political landslide] as Wu Ming 1 calls it (79) resulted in the 'Earthquake elections' of 1992, with higher percentage shifts and instability than had been seen since the end of the Second World War (Ginsborg 2001: 255). The political vacuum produced by this crisis was to be filled by Berlusconi, with his control of the mass media, conflicts of interest and corruption.[29] This situation seemed to be exacerbated in 2001, which saw not only the watershed moment of 9/11, but also the police violence against protestors on the occasion of the G8 Summit in Genoa and the return to power of Berlusconi. According to the Memorandum, these events contributed to the disillusionment with the supposed new world order that was to follow the collapse of the Berlin Wall and galvanised this generation of writers, as they saw that the changes the early 1990s should have heralded did not become a reality.

Wu Ming 1 (and others)[30] particularly places emphasis on the importance of the events at the G8 in Genoa in 2001 as a watershed moment for this generation of writers. It appears on the first page of the Memorandum, where it is linked to recollections of Wu Ming working on their novel *54*:

> In quei giorni curavamo ancora le ferite di Genova, 20 e 21 luglio. Ferite soltanto metaforiche, per grazia del cielo, ma a centinaia di persone era toccata peggior sorte: teste avvolte nelle bende, braccia steccate, piedi ingessati, cateteri. E un ragazzo era morto. Genova. Solo chi è stato in quelle strade può capire. (5)

> [At that time we were still nursing our wounds from Genoa, 20 and 21 July. Only metaphorical wounds, thank God, but hundreds of people had met a worse fate: heads wrapped in bandages, arms in splints, feet in plaster, catheters. And a boy had died. Genoa. Only those who were in those streets can understand.]

The last sentence is striking in its insistence on the importance of being present at this moment. It seems as if he wants to create an elite group of participants in this generation's version of resistance against the authorities, just as their parents had the protest decades of the 1960s and 1970s, perhaps as a way of addressing the feeling of being posthumous, mentioned above, which I address in more detail in chapter 2.

Yet, despite being held up as a defining generational moment, the G8 in Genoa in fact finds limited direct representation in the texts associated with the NIE.[31] This is in contrast to the glut of hard-hitting documentaries that have addressed what happened, such as Francesco Maselli's collective film *Un mondo diverso è possibile* [*Another World Is Possible*] (2001), Francesca Comencini's *Carlo Giuliani: Ragazzo* [*Carlo Giuliani: Boy*] (2002) and Daniele Vicari's *Diaz: Don't Clean Up This Blood* (2012),[32] as well as numerous responses in music and theatre (Melandri and others 2011: 147), in literature from beyond the NIE nebula,[33] and in non-fiction books.[34] In the few NIE texts that do confront Genoa directly, questions are raised about the unstable and fragmented nature of the experience of the G8 protests that undermine the solidity of Wu Ming 1's and others' portrayal of them as this generation's uniting collective experience. For example, in Duka and Philopat's *Roma k.o.* (2008), Duka recounts his life as a cultural agitator, punk and member of the underground movement; although he emphasises the importance of Genoa as a defining moment in the lives of those involved, his recollections are brief and confused, relying on the almost stock images that came out of the footage of the protests:

> A Genova mi è successo di tutto — al G8 la mia vita e quella di ogni persona presente è completamente cambiata... A Genova mi sono divertito — a Genova ho conosciuto molta gente — alcune delle persone conosciute a Genova sono diventate per me importantissime — a Genova ho pianto — ho corso molto — ho salvato delle persone [...] a Genova ho subìto la guerra — ho avuto la sensazione di stare in guerra. (Duka and Philopat 2008: 205–06)

> [In Genoa everything happened to me — at the G8 my life and that of everyone present changed completely... In Genoa I enjoyed myself — in Genoa I met lots of people — some of the people I met in Genoa have become hugely important for me — in Genoa I cried — I ran a lot — I saved people [...] in Genoa I went through war — I had the feeling of being at war.]

Similarly, Andrea's periodic, brief flashbacks to Genoa in De Michele's *La visione del cieco* [*The Blind Man's Vision*] (2008b), a *giallo* set three years later in 2004, also hinges on these stock images and sense of chaos; for example:

> *correvamo in confusione inciampando cadendo rialzando ci riprendevamo a correre ci infilavamo nei portoni per rifiatare bussavamo alle porte qualche porta si apriva qualcuno trovava riparo qualche porta restava chiusa il corridoio diventava una trappola per topi.* (De Michele 2008b: 102–03)

> [*we were running in confusion stumbling falling getting up again we started to run again we were slipping through doors to catch our breath we were knocking on doors some doors opened some people found shelter some doors stayed closed the corridor was becoming a mousetrap.*]

These texts seem to undermine the sense of ownership and collective memory that Wu Ming 1 transmits in the Memorandum, problematising Genoa as a clear-cut generational moment for these writers.

Whilst they are not mentioned in the Memorandum, the events of the so-called *anni di piombo* [years of lead] also underscore or are directly addressed in writing associated with the NIE, despite most of these writers being too young to have experienced them first-hand. As Lucarelli stressed in his book *Misteri d'Italia* [*Mysteries of Italy*], as well as in other texts and television programmes, there are still many unsolved mysteries in recent Italian history, many of which are related to the political terrorism that plagued Italy between the late 1960s and early 1980s. Traumatic events such as the Piazza Fontana and Bologna train station bombings, as well as the links between the state and organised crime, remain without clear answers. Glynn, Lombardi and O'Leary (2012) point out the persistence of the return to these years, particularly in recent Italian films, and, in the same volume, Cecchini states:

> The *anni di piombo* still represent an open wound in Italian collective memory. Unlike other countries that have emerged from bloody internal conflicts and outbreaks of war among the various groups that constitute the nation, Italy has proved to be unable to establish a Commission for Truth and Reconciliation aimed at reaching a shared consensus on re-imagining the past. (Cecchini 2012: 195)

Many recent Italian texts suggest that this generation seems to be haunted by the events of their parents' generation and the cover-ups that have still not been fully addressed by the establishment. In the nebula, Sarasso's *Trilogia sporca dell'Italia* [*Dirty Trilogy of Italy*], De Cataldo's *Romanzo criminale* [*Crime Novel*] and Genna's *Nel nome di Ishmael* [*In the Name of Ishmael*] re-examine many of the key events of those years, combining them with conspiracy theories and fictionalising in an attempt to process the years of lead.[35] The UNO might be seen as the ideal form for examining such slippery material, where fiction and nonfiction inevitably collide due to a lack of consensus on what happened in those years.

Interestingly, the need for a South African-style Truth and Reconciliation Commission (TRC) has not only been brought up in relation to the *anni di piombo*. Foot (2009: 1) alludes to it when discussing Italy's history more broadly: 'Italian memories have often been divided. Events have been interpreted in contrasting ways, and the facts themselves are often contested. [...] There has been no closure, no "truth" and little reconciliation'. Whilst there is a need for a more effective judicial processing of certain events in Italy's history, a TRC is not the only way of metabolising a difficult past. Referring to the responses of novelists to the problematic recent past in South Africa, Gready has argued that '"novel truths" have [...] unpacked the silences and "unfinished business" of apartheid and the TRC' (2009: 156). Gready points out that, unlike the truth commission report, which must identify facts and adjudicate (2009: 162), the novel 'has reflected upon ambiguity and complexity, interrogating gray areas of experience' (2009: 164), 'providing alternative grammars' that can complement more official reports (2009: 174). Literature, then, can assume an important role in negotiating difficult memories, and Italian writers have certainly looked to novel truths where official versions have been lacking, as we will see in chapter 2 with De Cataldo's use of alternative history fiction in *Nelle mani giuste*.

Wu Ming 2 significantly refers to Pasolini's famous denunciation of state-sponsored violence in reference to the unsolved mysteries of Italy in his essay included in the print version of the Memorandum (193), showing Pasolini to be an important predecessor for the NIE as an *engagé* intellectual who similarly searched for novel truths.[36] Pasolini (1974) famously declared that he knew about Italy's recent scandals despite not having proof: 'Io so perché sono un intellettuale, uno scrittore' [I know because I am an intellectual, a writer]. Writers are seen as being uniquely able to imagine what really happened and literature is the privileged domain for addressing such issues. This trope has been re-employed by writers both from within and outside the nebula — Genna, Saviano, Tabucchi and Jones have all experimented with the 'Io so' (see chapter 4) — which is indicative of how recent Italian writers have attempted to access answers through literature that may not be completely reliable or straightforward. Wu Ming 2 explains the aim of such writing:

> Se per indagare i fatti usiamo la narrativa, e non la storia o le scienze umane, è perché vogliamo permetterci di essere visionari [...] di concatenare gli eventi con simboli e analogie, di immaginare, quando ci mancano, quel che succederebbe se avessimo le prove. (190)

> [If to investigate events we use narrative, and not history or human sciences, it is because we want to allow ourselves to be visionaries [...] to link events with symbols and analogies, to imagine, when we do not have it, what would happen if we had the proof.][37]

The way in which these writers combine reality with literature has led to many texts associated with the NIE being labelled by some as 'neo-neorealismo' [neo-neorealism] (De Cataldo 2008), by others part of 'un ritorno alla realtà' [a return to reality] (Donnarumma 2008c), 'un realismo allegorico' [an allegorical realism] (Casadei 2011), 'nuovo realismo' [new realism] (Ferraris 2012) or 'realismo liquido' [liquid realism] (Magini and Santoni 2008). The latter is perhaps the most fitting of these labels, as the real-life basis of such writing is often questionable — I discuss the unusual configurations of fiction and nonfiction throughout this study — and also because, as Ceserani (2012: 212) rightly argues, Bauman's (2000) description of the current cultural climate as one of liquid modernity versus a previous solid modernity is perhaps the most fitting description of this cultural shift, as well as being an effective way of circumventing controversies surrounding the term postmodernism.

In terms of this interaction between fiction and nonfiction in recent historical novels, which I analyse in detail in chapter 3, they re-examine history not from a hegemonic perspective but rather seek to call into question accepted historiography. This is partly achieved by the choice to focus on protagonists 'dalla parte sbagliata della Storia' [from the wrong side of History], as Wu Ming put it in the blurb of *Manituana* (2007b). Such an approach is typified by the opening line of Luther Blissett's *Q*, which identifies its protagonist as literally and metaphorically not being in the foreground of history: 'Sulla prima pagina è scritto: Nell'affresco sono una delle figure di sfondo' [On the first page, it says: In the fresco I am one of the figures in the background] (Blissett 1999: 3). This is part of what Wu Ming 1 describes in the Memorandum as the 'sguardo obliquo' [oblique gaze] (26), which he sees as key to the NIE perspective, seeing events from a different, unexpected angle, although this gaze has sometimes been more effectively achieved by texts that were not included in Wu Ming 1's corpus in the Memorandum, as I will show through my analysis of Pugno's *Sirene* (chapter 2), for example. The oblique gaze is often achieved in historical novels by jumping forwards and backwards in time, or by narrating from multiple perspectives, both through having a large cast of characters and through including real or fabricated historical documentation within the narrative, which may provide different accounts of the events portrayed, as we will see in *Timira* (chapter 3).

However, for all Wu Ming's talk of looking at the past and present from unexpected, subaltern perspectives, both the NIE writers and their texts are dominated by educated,[38] white men. In the section of the Memorandum entitled 'La nebulosa' [The nebula] (10–14), in which Wu Ming 1 lists writers of UNOs, only four out of twenty-four names are women writers (approximately 17 per cent), and only one out of the twenty-four is not ethnically Italian (Janeczek). In the footnote that he added to include texts he had originally omitted due to not having read them at the time the Memorandum first appeared (13 n. 5), the percentage of women to men is even worse: only one out of sixteen names (6.25 per cent) is a woman, that is Ghermandi, who is also the only one with an ethnicity that is not completely Italian.[39] This under-representation then spills down into the novels themselves, in which the main protagonists are almost always men, with sometimes very few female characters with any agency. Mecchia makes a perceptive assessment of the female characters in Wu Ming's work:

> Women, in their novels, are witches, lovers, healers, mothers, sisters, daughters: intelligent, sensitive, beautiful and beloved [...] They are rarely given direct political agency, and since they can't plausibly take part in the physical battles that tend to represent the central part of the plot development in all of the 'narrative objects', they are confined to the domestic sphere of eroticism, motherhood and logistical support, while the heroic warriors — from the Bolognese periphery to Laos, from Venice to Istanbul — keep fighting on. (Mecchia 2009: 207–08)[40]

Other NIE texts contain worrying, gendered stereotypes, whether it is the prostitute with a heart of gold, Patrizia, in De Cataldo's *Romanzo criminale* and *Nelle mani giuste*, or the beautiful but ingenuous escort, Lara, in De Michele's trilogy. In addition, as I point out in chapter 2, it is generally fathers and sons rather than mothers and daughters who are the focus of interest in the nebula. As Mecchia rightly states in terms of Wu Ming, such limited female characterisation 'would not be a source of concern in itself, if it didn't raise suspicions of cultural conformity in an enterprise that thinks of itself as subversive' (Mecchia 2009: 208). She argues that this calls into question Wu Ming's opposition to *berlusconismo*, in that it does nothing to question the problematic female stereotypes that circulated in the public sphere under Berlusconi (Mecchia 2009: 209–10), and this could be extended to certain other writers of the nebula.

Alternative models, different voices and oblique viewpoints bring to mind not only postcolonial and feminist thinkers from beyond Italy's borders such as Gayatri

Spivak, but also point towards home-grown theorists such as Adriana Cavarero. However, whether made in Italy or abroad, concepts like these are absent from the Memorandum. By employing feminist and postcolonial readings, Burns (2001) brought to light alternative types of *impegno* in the work of women and migrant writers at the end of the twentieth century, but such experiences seem to be overlooked in the NIE's version of politically and ethically committed writing. Aside from the Italian label being more articulated than it would seem at first sight, including regional and transnational elements, we can also see it as signifying predominantly texts written by white, Italian males, an indication of the way in which the phenomenon tends to exclude writing that could truly work towards questioning dominant narratives.

Epic

The 'epic' label could be seen as another instance of this problematic slant; the epic remains tied up with heroic male adventures, in which women cannot participate or are left at home, as described by Mecchia above. Traditionally, the epic pitted western imperial ideology against what Quint has described as 'Epic's losers, the enemies of empire whom epic ideology assimilates with the East, woman, nature, irrationality, chaos' (1989: 27). The choice of the word was also a cause for controversy surrounding the Memorandum, as it was seen by some critics to be an inappropriate description of what these texts were.[41] Certainly, the texts of the nebula do not openly engage with classical tradition, despite some references to epic figures or stories (primarily in Wu Ming's work),[42] nor do they contain most of the prerequisites of the epic genre. Where are the gods in the NIE, or the heroes? Wu Ming 1 himself says in the Memorandum that if there is a hero in the texts of the nebula, s/he influences the action 'in modo sghembo' [in a crooked way] (31). In the case of Jones's *Sappiano le mie parole*, the narrator actually tells an interlocutor at one point that her approach is specifically in contrast to epic: 'Non sono venuta qui per fare della poesia né dell'epica. Sono venuta qui per capire e osservare' [I didn't come here to make poetry or epic. I came here to understand and observe] (Jones 2007: 62).

Indeed, the approach of the NIE writers differs from traditional epics in various ways. These texts tend to be on the side of history's losers, as mentioned earlier. Petrella has said of Luther Blissett's *Q* that it is an 'epica degli *ex-centris*, ovvero degli emarginati, dei reietti e degli sconfitti' [epic of the *ex-centris*, that is of the marginalised, the outcasts and the defeated] (2006: 146). Moreover, Quint states: 'telling a full story, epic claims to possess *the* full story' (1989: 14); the NIE, however, has no epic linearity moving towards a goal or sense of completion, no single-minded view of history that hinges on the rightness of western ideology. Wu Ming 1 explains in the Memorandum that the NIE tends towards alternative history fiction, or 'ucronia' (34), but this is not always employed in its strict sense. Several texts do imagine different outcomes to historical events, acting as a means of considering alternative possibilities in the past and their possible consequences, such as Brizzi's trilogy beginning with *L'inattesa piega degli eventi* [*The Unexpected Turn of Events*], in which Mussolini is not overthrown but continues to govern Italy after the Second World War. As the title of the first volume suggests, Brizzi gives a sense that events are subject to chance and to the choices we make. Wu Ming 1 explains that these texts reflect on other possibilities at these historical watershed moments, 'in cui molti sviluppi erano possibili e la storia *avrebbe potuto* imboccare altre vie. Il *what if* è potenziale, non attuale' [when many developments were possible and history *could have* taken different paths. The what if is potential, not actual] (35). This means that the past is not portrayed as immutable, but as having possibilities, just as the present contains the potential for change or new paths to follow. As we shall see in chapter 3 in an analysis of approaches to history in recent Italian literature, the NIE writers and others have asked questions about how our understanding of history was reached and what implications it has for us now, questions that were not traditionally at the centre of epic narratives.

However, recent rewritings of epic from new perspectives, such as Derek Walcott's *Omeros* (1990), a poem that reflects on history and collective memory in the Caribbean, or Margaret Atwood's feminist rewriting of the *Odyssey* through Penelope's voice in *The Penelopiad* (2005), have shown that we do not necessarily need to think of the epic within the rigid confines of tradition. It is worth remembering that the novel has been alternately described as the 'modern bourgeois epic' by Hegel (1975: 1092),[43] or 'the epic of a world that has been abandoned by God' by Lukács (1978: 88), which implies that epic and novel may not be as separate as theorists such as Bakhtin have argued. When discussing *Omeros*, Farrell (1999: 284) points out that Quint and others have recently presented 'views of the epic that are profoundly at odds with received opinion concerning the closed, monologic nature of the genre'. Dimock similarly sees *Omeros* as showing 'just how *un*moribund the epic is', and she proposes updating the Bakhtinian vision of the epic as behind us: 'I would like to see it as an archaic genre that has made a loop into the present: still evolving, still energized by foreign tongues, and reproducing itself across many scales, bearing witness to the input of many environments' (Dimock 2006: 96). She links this looser understanding of the epic genre to Derrida's 'The Law of Genre' (1980) (Dimock 2006: 85–86), mentioned in the introduction to this study as informing my understanding of UNOs as a genre. Dimock (2006: 86–87) similarly suggests that genre should be understood not in terms of strict categorisation, but as a rhizomatic spectrum of affinities, or a family resemblance, which is precisely the term that Wu Ming 1 has used for the NIE: 'Ho mappato accostamenti, parallelismi, commenti a "somiglianze di famiglia" tra il libro X e il libro Y' [I mapped comparisons, similarities, comments on 'family resemblances' between book X and book Y] (2010b). If we understand the NIE to be a genre along the lines of Dimock's conception of a kinship network, we may allow for the decidedly un-epic qualities of many of the texts in its corpus.

Yet, Wu Ming 1's words in the Memorandum on why he calls these texts epic seem to allude to a more traditional understanding of the genre. He explains his choice as follows:

Queste narrazioni sono epiche perché riguardano imprese storiche o mitiche, eroiche o comunque avventurose: guerre, anabasi, viaggi iniziatici, lotte per la sopravvivenza, sempre all'interno di conflitti più vasti che decidono le sorti di classi, popoli, nazioni o addirittura dell'intera umanità, sugli sfondi di crisi storiche, catastrofi, formazioni sociali al collasso. Spesso il racconto fonde elementi storici e leggendari, quando non sconfina nel soprannaturale.

[...] [Sono] [l]ibri che fanno i conti con la turbolenta storia d'Italia, o con l'ambivalente rapporto tra Europa e America, e a volte si spingono anche più in là.

Inoltre, queste narrazioni sono epiche perché grandi, ambiziose, 'a lunga gittata', 'di ampio respiro' e tutte le espressioni che vengono in mente. Sono epiche le dimensioni dei problemi da risolvere per scrivere questi libri, compito che di solito richiede diversi anni, e ancor più quando l'opera è destinata a trascendere misura e confini della forma-romanzo, come nel caso di narrazioni transmediali, che proseguono in diversi contesti. (14–15)

[These narratives are epic because they concern enterprises that are historical or mythical, heroic or in any case adventurous: wars, anabasis, initiatory journeys, struggles for survival, always within wider conflicts that decide the fate of classes, peoples, nations or even of the whole of humanity, against the backdrop of historical crises, catastrophes, collapsing social formations. Often the story blends historical and legendary elements, when it does not overlap with the supernatural.

[...] [They are] [b]ooks that deal with the turbulent history of Italy, or with the ambivalent relationship between Europe and America, and sometimes even go further.

Furthermore, these narratives are epic because they are large, ambitious, 'long-range', 'broad-based' and all the expressions that come to mind. The dimensions of the problems to be solved to write these books are epic, a task that usually takes several years, and even more so when the work is destined to transcend the measure and boundaries of the novel form, as in the case of transmedia narratives, which continue in different contexts.]

So, there are epic dimensions in terms of themes — the subject matter of these texts has depth and magnitude, often engaging with questions around myth-making or mythopoeia[44] — and also in terms of form — these texts are often long, taking time to read and to write, and the story may not only be limited to the book itself. Wu Ming have linked their transmediality to epic qualities outside the Memorandum too, as they have argued that, as in ancient times, storytelling has become a community activity again, with stories open to revision and different versions just as Greek myths were (Wu Ming 1 and Wu Ming 2 2007). Significantly, although parts of Wu Ming 1's description of the epic qualities of the NIE can be extended to some but certainly not all of the texts in the NIE corpus he outlines, it best fits the texts of Wu Ming themselves, which are long, historical, adventure novels that look at epic watershed moments, such as the Second World War (*54* and *Asce di guerra*), the years leading up to the American Revolution (*Manituana*), the beginning of the modern period (*Q* and *Altai*), the French Revolution (*L'Armata dei Sonnambuli*), or the First World War (*L'invisibile ovunque*). They depict what Bakhtin describes in epic as 'a world of "beginnings" and "peak times" in the national history, a world of fathers and of founders of families' (1981: 13). They focus on moments that led to a change in society and the course of history, with one way of life or power structure being pitted against another in their narratives.

In the special issue of the *Journal of Romance Studies* on the NIE, Biasini argues that we should take epic to mean an epic *mode* rather than the epic *genre*, as, unlike Derrida or Dimock, she understands genre in terms of prescribed norms.[45] Taking Wu Ming's *54* as her primary text, she outlines the following five features of an epic mode that link it to ancient, traditional epic poems: it has a collective, anonymous author; it examines the founding moment of a community; it contains the epic *topos* of the journey; it has microstories divided into separate chapters; and, finally, it borrows characters intertextually — in the case of *54*, the character Ettore came from Fenoglio's *Il partigiano Johnny* [*Johnny the Partisan*] (Biasini 2010: 72–73). Certainly, different combinations, though generally not all, of these features can be found in many NIE texts, although it is Wu Ming's work that best displays all five, and texts such as Siti's *Il contagio* [*The Contagion*] or Bajani's *Se consideri le colpe* [*If You Consider the Faults*] only have one of Biasini's five elements each: microstories in Siti and a journey in Bajani. They could also be found in a large number of historical novels from beyond the nebula. Texts that portray characters embarking on journeys, engage with how we understand the past, have a choral element or a large cast of characters: these elements are equally present in Manzoni's *I promessi sposi* or Tolstoy's *War and Peace*.

In the same special issue of the *Journal of Romance Studies*, Boscolo argues that the criticisms that the Memorandum received about the employment of the word 'epic' were related to an unwillingness to accept that Italy was in need of a type of narrative that Bakhtin defined as relating to the representation of a society: 'the return to an epic narrative mode is tantamount to admitting that Italian society urgently needs to recover the capacity for self-representation, to provide an accurate reflection of itself, in the wake of its dark history and recent political scandals' (Boscolo 2010b: 20). Wu Ming 1 seemed to be making a similar point when he argued that the last fifteen years of Italian history can be seen as mythical, requiring literature to adopt epic qualities in order to be able to describe it: 'Ogni giorno hanno luogo catastrofi, mutamenti discontinui che assimiliamo pian piano e non vediamo dalla "giusta distanza", quella che permetta di capirne la magnitudo' [Every day there are catastrophes, discontinuous changes that we slowly assimilate and we do not see from the 'right distance', one that allows us to understand their magnitude] (Wu Ming 1 2010b: 3). According to Wu Ming 1 and Boscolo, an epic approach seems to be the only way that these texts can encompass what has been happening in Italy and find a way of confronting the magnitude of recent history. This is in contrast to the theories on contemporary Italian writing put forward by Giglioli (2011) or Scurati (2006), who, as I discuss in more detail in chapter 4, have argued that the opposite is true, that this generation of writers have no great historical events that they have experienced directly to write about.

The truth, naturally, lies somewhere in between: recent history has not been more turbulent than it ever has, but neither is there a lack of important and/or traumatic events to experience and portray. Moreover, whilst there have been cataclysmic historical events — both globally and nationally — the turbulence comes not from the direct experience of them, but from the trauma of the 'open wound' created by an absence of resolution that brings back earlier national crises. This can be seen most clearly in the events at the G8 in Genoa in 2001, which was a very recent moment of crisis for Italy, but its impact was felt more through the reopening of old wounds related to previous traumatic events, with Carlo Giuliani's death recalling that of Francesco Lorusso in Bologna in 1977.[46] It can even be seen as part of a longer-standing *topos* of the failed revolution, which has run through Italian national history from the Risorgimento through the Resistance through the crisis of the early 1990s to today, which I address in chapter 3 when discussing Scurati's *Una storia romantica*.

The arguments for these texts having an epic approach to their subject matter as opposed to a novelistic one often seem to stem from a desire to reinvigorate the novel genre, which has been seen by some, particularly in Italy, as being exhausted, indulging in the aimless intellectual play of postmodernism rather than engaging with community and national issues. Biasini (2010: 72), Boscolo (2008) and Vito (2009) all quote the following words of Petrella, who said of contemporary epics like Q: 'È con questa nuova forma narrativa che il romanzo riesce a riacquistare il vigore delle grandi narrazioni. È con l'epica della "moltitudine" che probabilmente la letteratura dovrà fare i conti per uscire definitivamente fuori dall'*impasse* della postmodernità' [It is with this new narrative form that the novel manages to regain the vigour of great narratives. It is the epic of the 'multitude' that literature will probably have to deal with to definitively get out of the impasse of postmodernity] (Petrella 2006: 148). Once again, we come up against assertions that postmodernism has been exhausted, and there is a need for new forms, but this new form is found in something old, ancient even. Later in the Memorandum, Wu Ming 1 states that he does not think the epic elements eliminate a sense of realism in these texts: 'Realismo ed epica non si escludono a vicenda' [Realism and epic do not exclude one another] (68). According to him, the NIE is both rooted in contemporary reality but also opens out to epic proportions. He goes on to explain that, because realism is associated with denotation, whereas the epic is associated with connotation, an epic approach can transform the nature of this representation of the present situation, helping us to see '*tutti* i significati del racconto' [all the meanings of the story] (69). For him, it is the epic quality of these texts that makes us truly understand their political and ethical implications. In a subsequent article, Wu Ming 1 explained that these texts have a double gaze, zooming in on individual microstories but also zooming out to see Italy on a macro level, seeing their subject matter 'da lontano | da dentro' [from afar | from within] (Wu Ming 1 2010b). He seems to be combining the dichotomies between epic and novel, or approaching the aforementioned Hegelian or Lukácsian vision of the novel as a new rendering of the epic that is appropriate to the present time.

Wu Ming 1 said two years after the Memorandum first appeared: 'Il NIE è già diventato qualcos'altro. La nebulosa ha cambiato densità e profilo. Siamo oltre'

[The NIE has already become something else. The nebula has changed density and profile. We are beyond] (2010a). Later, in a 2014 interview, he went as far as saying that it no longer existed:

> Dubito fortemente che si possa parlare del NIE coniugando i verbi al presente, a meno che non sia presente storico. Se dovessi fotografare la scena letteraria italiana oggi, sei anni dopo il memorandum, ne risulterebbe un'immagine molto diversa. Già allora la mia era una 'istantanea del passato', del periodo 1993–2008. Fotografavo una scena che si stava già allontanando nel tempo. Oggi la 'vena' di molti autori i cui libri NIE avevo incluso nel memorandum si è inaridita (alcuni sono addirittura morti!), e pochi hanno lavorato per prolungare in avanti le linee di tendenza che cercavo di individuare. La lunga crisi ha accelerato il tracollo dell'editoria, un tracollo non solo economico ma culturale e di idee, e mi sembra che in Italia stia uscendo poco di davvero interessante. O almeno, esce poco che interessi a me. Delle 'tendenze' individuate nel 2008, l'unica che procede a grande velocità è quella degli 'oggetti narrativi non-identificati', ma non è certo una prerogativa italiana, l'ibridazione delle tipologie testuali è una cosa che sta avvenendo in tutto il mondo. Questo è il motivo per cui non posso parlare 'a nome del NIE' [...] in Italia non c'è più nessun NIE. (Brioni 2014: 287)

> [I strongly doubt that we can talk about the NIE conjugating the verbs in the present, unless it is the historic present. If you had to photograph the Italian literary scene today, six years after the Memorandum, you would see a very different image. Already back then, mine was a 'snapshot of the past', of the period 1993–2008. I was photographing a scene that was already moving away in time. Today, the 'spring' of many authors whose NIE books I included in the Memorandum has dried up (some have even died!), and few have worked to prolong the trends that I was trying to identify. The long crisis accelerated the collapse of publishing, a collapse that was not only economic but cultural and of ideas, and it seems to me that in Italy little is coming out of any real interest. Or at least, little is coming out that interests me. Of the 'trends' identified in 2008, the only one that is proceeding with great speed is that of 'unidentified narrative objects', but it is certainly not an Italian prerogative; the hybridisation of textual types is something that is happening all over the world. This is why I cannot speak 'in the name of the NIE' [...] in Italy there is no longer any NIE.]

I would have to agree that the concept of the UNO is the most useful, transnational and indeed increasingly widespread one to have come out of the Memorandum, whether looking back at the turn of the millennium or into the second decade of the twenty-first century. Yet, the lines of inquiry that Wu Ming 1 identified have certainly not dried up.

Since 2008, other comparable literary movements have developed, which suggests that the cultural scene has not yet moved beyond the issues the Memorandum raised. Another related phenomenon that positioned itself in opposition to the dominant culture with a strong sense of *impegno* was the TQ generation, made up of writers alongside people from other professions, whose manifesto in 2011 protested against the way in which the generation of Italians in their thirties and forties — *trentenni e quarantenni* — had been excluded from the country's 'vita politica e produttiva' [political and productive life].[47] Cortellessa (2011b) pointed out that their originality lay in their determination to work against the individualism that characterised the Berlusconi era and 'elaborare nuove pratiche comuni fondate — se possibile — su una concettualizzazione che si traduca in un'assunzione di responsabilità collettiva, comune. Dunque politica' [find new common practices based — if possible — on a conceptualisation that is translated into an assumption of collective, common responsibility]. This is also what Wu Ming and others attempted with the NIE. Although the TQ generation's blog closed in 2013,[48] and it is difficult to gauge how much they actually achieved, it is clear that the points raised by Wu Ming 1's Memorandum were relevant to others beyond 2008.

An important parallel can also be seen in the phenomenon of *narrazioni della precarietà* [narratives of precariousness], which includes books, anthologies of short stories and blogs that reflect on the precariousness of today's world, and particularly of the working world, as seen in Nove's *Mi chiamo Roberta, ho 40 anni, guadagno 250 euro al mese* [*My Name is Roberta, I'm 40 Years Old, I Earn 250 Euros a Month*] (2006). Like the NIE texts, these narratives have employed transmediality, with their writers often working across platforms, for example Nove's book was later made into a theatre production (Nove 2011), and Michela Murgia's 2006 text *Il mondo deve sapere. Romanzo tragicomico di una telefonista precaria* [*The World Must Know: Tragicomic Novel of a Precarious Telephonist*] (Murgia 2017) was an autobiographical blog, then a novel, a theatre production and a film. Some of the NIE writers, such as Santoni and Bajani, have written *narrazioni della precarietà*,[49] and the use of testimony and real-world experience in these narrations has also been seen in terms of the so-called 'return to reality' (see chapter 4), although, as with the NIE, this is a weak connection. Jansen (2014: 80) rightly points out that these are more late-postmodern than mimetic, realist texts, which is similar to my argument in chapter 4. Significantly, many of the Precarious writers do not choose as their form of expression epic, long-form books. Jansen states: '[il] racconto breve sembra essere una delle forme privilegiate per narrare esperienze di lavoro frammentarie, a tempo determinato, con una sostanza "liquida" adatta a trasformarsi nella transmedialità della rete' [[the] short story seems to be one of the privileged forms for narrating fragmentary, fixed-term experiences of work, with a 'liquid' essence suitable for transforming into transmediality online] (2014: 74). Their mix of fictional and nonfictional modes means they can be seen as UNOs (a comparison that Contarini (2010: 11) also makes), which further suggests the limitations of Wu Ming 1's insistence on the term 'epic' to describe how Italian writers in the twenty-first century have been approaching literature.

Overall, it could be argued that the Memorandum is something of an interesting failure, just as Wu Ming 1 describes Jones's *Sappiano le mie parole di sangue*, saying: 'Anche un fallimento insegna, anche un fallimento può essere interessante' [Even a failure teaches, even a failure can be interesting] (43). Like Jones's text, it brings up many interesting issues, but, in Wu Ming 1's text, they are never fully developed and appear often in random order, sometimes reappearing later and maybe elaborated on. At times, the abrupt jumps from one subject to another give a sense of arbitrariness and almost irrelevance. For example, in the section entitled 'Presto o tardi' [Sooner or Later] (55–61), he moves from discussing the allegorical opening to *54* that gives a sense that the Second World War never finished, to discussing the apocalyptic future of our planet, drawing strongly on Alan Weisman's *The World Without Us*, before returning to the idea of *impegno* in what seems a desultory ramble. He has a tendency towards incompleteness and unexpected jumps at times. This may be designed to destabilise the traditional style of academic criticism to find new forms for discussing Italian literature in the twenty-first century, but it also goes some way towards accounting for the controversial reception of the Memorandum. Nevertheless, the Memorandum is replete with ideas that can inform an analysis of recent Italian literature, even if Wu Ming 1's ideas often express something different from what he intended, as can be seen in the insistence on the epic as symptomatic of anxieties about the shortcomings of the novel in the alleged aftermath of postmodernism. The tensions that arise from Wu Ming 1's discussion seem to be inscribed into the name of the phenomenon itself, which embodies the combination of continuity and rupture I have brought to the fore: it contains the seemingly oxymoronic combination of new and epic, whilst also calling itself Italian but in English.

Yet, the Memorandum brings out the key themes that can be seen again and again in the nebula and more broadly in Italian literature from the beginning of the twenty-first century. These include: disillusionment with, and a need to take responsibility for, the contemporary situation; a need to process Italy's problematic history; and a tendency to experiment with the blurred line between fact and fiction. However, there is also a tendency to overlook important previous and contemporary literary experiences and an absence of marginal and subversive voices (especially female, postcolonial and migrant), which are important shortcomings that I will address in this study. Nevertheless, an analysis of the Memorandum demonstrates that something was indeed happening in Italian literature, that ideas were coming together in various texts that contained similar concerns and styles but, as the name of the phenomenon hints, these ideas were not necessarily completely new, only Italian, or purely epic.

Notes to Chapter 1

1. Unless otherwise stated, references to Wu Ming 1's Memorandum in this chapter will come from this text, as it is the most complete.

2. See the introduction to this study for these controversies; see also Wu Ming 1 2009c. Ceserani, in his article 'La maledizione degli "ismi"' [The Curse of 'Isms'], points to the tendency towards conservatism in Italian culture (Ceserani 2012: 204).

3. These writers were introduced by the anthology *Gioventù cannibal* [*Cannibal Youth*], which appeared in 1996 and was highly successful in terms of sales, if not in terms of critical reception (see Cesari 2003). The stories were tied together by a mutual focus on young, disaffected protagonists, who found themselves in extreme situations, described using colloquial language and at times black humour. Their combination of gratuitous violence and pop culture references meant that this type of writing was also referred to as 'pulp', a nod to the influence of Quentin Tarantino's cult film *Pulp Fiction*.

4. *Troppi paradisi* portrays a society dominated by reality TV and an obsession with body image. Siti may put more of himself into his text than the Cannibal writers did, but his concerns are very much aligned with theirs. Alongside his eloquent descriptions of today's world, Siti's text also includes oral, everyday, regionally specific language.

5. The protagonist is a failed writer working as a fashion journalist. He finds himself at endless drug-fuelled parties reminiscent of Sorrentino's film *La grande bellezza* [*The Great Beauty*]. At one party, in true Cannibal style, one of the models seemingly dies of an overdose, and the other guests only wish to distance themselves from this event, showing little sympathy, although she is later revived. Death and consumerism/enjoyment constantly overlap, as the cube-like building where the protagonist attends a fashion show reminds him of where he buried his father (73), and he sees the endless parties as 'una maschera, della morte' [a mask, of death] (186).

6. De Vivo (2015: 130) also links the Cannibal writers to the work of Scego, whom I discuss in chapter 4.

7. Wu Ming 1 concedes that DeLillo, Pynchon and Doctorow escape this definition of postmodernism, but also states: 'Nemmeno *due* o *tre* rondini [...] fanno primavera' [Not even *two* or *three* swallows [...] make a summer] (66).

8. Eliot is listed as one of Genna's literary role models in *Italia De Profundis* (see chapter 2), and a quotation from his *Four Quartets* appears at the beginning of Magini and Santoni's article 'Verso il realismo liquido' [Towards Liquid Realism] (2008), which I discuss later in this chapter. He is also referenced by Jones (see chapter 4).

9. See for example Donnarumma's 2008 text *Da lontano. Calvino, la semiologia, lo strutturalismo* [*From Afar: Calvino, Semiology and Structuralism*], which Re (2014: 101 n.) sums up as 'seeking to demonstrate that in his prose Calvino essentially did nothing but passively follow the dictates of Propp's and Roland Barthes's narratology'.

10. A frequent form used by the NIE writers is the detective novel or *giallo*, or at least an investigatory mode staged around a search for some kind of truth. They also sometimes employ the characteristics of *noir* in the depiction of their subject matter, drawing on recognisable traditions of genre fiction but resulting in something that defies categorisation. This relates to the Italian tradition of the 'inchiesta' [investigation] novel, as practised by Sciascia, another enduring influence on these writers, who addressed Italian political issues through his *gialli*.

11. He only uses the verb 'to be' in one fragment, when Andrea describes his confusion over piecing together the various bits of the mystery: 'Come una frase senza verbo essere [...] Le parole rimbalzano qua e là come palle di gomma cercando un senso a cui aggrapparsi' [Like a sentence without the verb to be [...] The words bounce around here and there like rubber balls looking for a meaning to grab on to] (De Michele 2008b: 239).

12. Wu Ming have interacted with Jenkins online in an interview on Jenkins' blog (Jenkins 2006b and 2006c) and also wrote the introduction to the Italian translation of *Convergence Culture* (Wu Ming 2007a).

13. See <http://www.manituana.com/documenti/0/0/it>.

14. See <http://inside.manituana.com/documenti/90/8329>.

15. See <http://fineimpero.tumblr.com/> and <https://uk.pinterest.com/giugenna/fine-impero/>.

16. See <https://uk.pinterest.com/giugenna/la-vita-umana-sul-pianeta-terra/> and <http://lavitaumana.tumblr.com/>.

17. See <http://www.giugenna.com/>.

18. Wu Ming wrote the first chapter of a sci-fi novel, then anyone could write and send subsequent chapters, which were selected by a jury online. It led to the creation of another Italian writing collective, Kai Zen (<http://www.kaizenlab.it>).

19. They wrote the historical novel *In territorio nemico* [*In Enemy Territory*] with 115 authors. See their website for details of how their collaborative writing technique works: <http://www.scritturacollettiva.org/>.

20. Indeed, there was a special issue of *Cultural Studies* in 2011, entitled 'Rethinking Convergence/Culture', which was dedicated to the need to scrutinise and problematise elements of Jenkins's work (see Hay and Couldry 2011). Patti (2016) has also perceptively pointed out the limitations in the collaborative work of Wu Ming.

21. As pointed out by Patti (2014: Kindle location 616). See also <http://it.labs.teads.tv/top-blogs>.

22. This idea appears in Calvino's story 'Il conte di Montecristo' [The Count of Montecristo] in the collection *Ti con zero* [*t zero*] (1967).

23. I also discuss Tondelli as a literary influence, although once again unacknowledged, for Genna in *Italia De Profundis* (chapter 3, note 2).

24. After referring to Italian literary tradition and its effects on the NIE, he states: 'Tuttavia, in un mondo di flussi, mercati e comunicazioni transnazionali è non soltanto possibile, ma addirittura inevitabile essere eredi di più tradizioni e avere influenze oltre a quelle nazionali' [Nevertheless, in a world of transnational flows, markets and communications, it is not only possible, but even inevitable to inherit more traditions and to have influences beyond the national ones] (17). He mentions the American writer James Ellroy, but particularly points to Latin American writers, such as Paco Ignacio Taibo II, Daniel Chavvarría, Rolo Diez and Miguel Bonasso (17), a list to which we could also add Roberto Bolaño.

25. Mondello (2010: 18) outlines the different regional groups: the Gruppo 13 from Bologna, the Scuola dei Duri in Milan, and the Neonoir group in Rome.

26. Saviano's *Gomorra* is firmly based in Naples, Carlotto's *gialli* centre on a private detective known as the Alligatore who lives and works in Padua, and Camilleri is grounded in the Sicilian context.

27. De Cataldo's *Romanzo criminale* and *Nelle mani giuste*, as well as *Suburra* which he wrote with Carlo Bonini, look particularly at the mafia phenomenon and political corruption in Rome.

28. Siti's 2008 text *Il contagio* [*The Contagion*] is situated in a Pasolinian Roman *borgata* or working-class suburb and mixes fiction and reality to make wider points about society: 'ho usato nomi fittizi, calcato le tinte, inventati episodi per garantire alla trama più appeal. Ma la casa esiste, in un angolo di borgata che potrebbe essere tutte le borgate' [I used fictional names, exaggerated the colours, invented episodes to guarantee the plot more appeal. But the house exists, in a corner of the *borgata* that could be every *borgata*] (Siti 2008: 26).

29. Despite managing to shake off various corruption charges, he was convicted of tax fraud in 2013.

30. Amato (2009) states: 'L'impressione suscitata dal G8 fu immediata, e, in Italia, più profonda e significativa degli attacchi terroristici dell'11 settembre. L'onda sismica scatenata a Genova coinvolse la coscienza di molti intellettuali, e si è propagata in latitudine fino ai giorni nostri' [The impression created by the G8 was immediate and, in Italy, deeper and more significant than the terrorist attacks of 11 September. The seismic wave caused by Genoa swept up the conscience of many intellectuals and spread outwards until today].

31. However, the numerous historical novels that address failed revolutions, which I discuss in chapter 3, could be seen as allegorically reflecting on Genoa, although they generally do not directly state this.

32. Niwot states: 'So far, over thirty documentaries and one feature-length film dedicated to Genoa have emerged in an attempt to inform what will be remembered of these events' (2011: 67).

33. Melandri and others (2011: 148) provide a list, and point out that these are often *noirs*.

34. These range from testimony from protestors, such as Lorenzo Guadagnucci's *Noi della Diaz* [*We of Diaz*] (2002), to revisionist accounts defending police and government actions, such as Fabrizio Cicchitto's *Il G8 di Genova: mistificazione e realtà* [*The G8 in Genoa: Falsification and Reality*] (2002).

35. This processing has also been carried out by various writers from beyond the nebula, such as Giorgio Vasta in his 2008 text *Il tempo materiale* [*Time On My Hands*], whose experimentalism and concerns very much align with the NIE, although he has been excluded from the nebula.

36. Wu Ming 1 (2009d: 19–20) has also referred to Pasolini's *Petrolio* as an example of a UNO, and it is an important reference point for Genna in *Italia De Profundis*, as I explore in the following chapter.

37. Pasolini's presence can be felt throughout the nebula in various ways: a quotation from *Petrolio* appears at the beginning of the second section of the Memorandum (63) and also at the beginning of Genna's *Italia De Profundis* (see chapter 2), and Genna refers to Pasolini again in

Fine impero (2013: 158); there is a character called Pasolini in Lucarelli's *L'ottava vibrazione* [*The Eighth Vibration*] (2008); Pasolini's death is mentioned in De Michele's *Tre uomini paradossali* [*Three Paradoxical Men*] (2004: 122) and in his *La visione del cieco* (2008b: 196); Scurati quotes Pasolini (although unattributed) at the end of *Una storia romantica*, calling himself 'una forza del passato' [a force of the past] (2007: 547); and Siti references Pasolini in his depiction of the seedy underside of Rome and modern consumerism in *Il contagio* [*The Contagion*] (Siti 2008: 309). Pasolini certainly has not been 'forgotten' by this generation, to use Antonello's (2012) term.

38. Not only did the NIE develop in and around the University of Bologna, but some of its writers, such as Siti and Scurati, are academics as well as writers.

39. Ghermandi was born in Ethiopia of an Italian father and Ethiopian mother and lives in Bologna. It is worth pointing out that, when Wu Ming 1 talks about the Italian literary tradition, he does acknowledge some female writers: he mentions Anna Banti in the main body of the Memorandum (16), and in 'We're Going to Have to Be the Parents' he discusses Goliarda Sapienza (125). However, Elsa Morante's *La Storia* [*History*] is a glaring omission from discussions of the historical novel form, and, as I have already discussed in this chapter, migrant writing is very much overlooked too.

40. Wu Ming have acknowledged their shortcomings in this area: 'It is difficult for male writers to depict convincing female characters, that was the problem with Q, the way we described women was... lame. We're very self-critical about that' (Celluloid Liberation Front 2013). However, I am not convinced that their subsequent work has remedied this. As Mecchia (2009: 207) argues (quoted in the introduction to this book), and as I discuss in the following section of this chapter, this is partly a problem of genre.

41. See, for example, Di Stefano 2008, or Ferroni, who made the damning indictment: 'Col proposito di chiamare a raccolta una vasta generazione di narratori, qualcuno ha coniato un'apposita etichetta, piuttosto balzana in verità, quella di *New Italian Epic*; distorcendo completamente ogni possibile accezione di 'epica', con un proposito di valorizzazione e monumentalizzazione di testi che sono perfettamente agli antipodi di ogni epica possibile, giocati su di una scrittura neutra e priva di respiro o su artifici esteriori e ripetitivi.' [With the purpose of summoning up a vast generation of storytellers, someone has coined a special label, rather boldly in fact, that of New Italian Epic; completely distorting every possible meaning of 'epic', in order to valorise and monumentalise texts that are completely poles apart from every possible epic, employing neutral and stifling writing or external and repetitive artifice] (Ferroni 2010: 39–40). However, he goes on to analyse what he sees as the positive qualities of NIE works such as Siti's *Il contagio* and Saviano's *Gomorra*.

42. Wu Ming's *Altai* (2009a), for example, apart from centring on a dramatic odyssey and the clash of East and West, contains references to Heracles (20), Ulysses (183), and the battles of Thermopylae (158) and Salamis (170). In Wu Ming's *54*, when Pierre goes to find his father, we are told: 'Telemaco andava incontro a Ulisse' [Telemachus was going to meet Ulysses] (Wu Ming 2002: 252); this is also interesting in terms of the discussion of Recalcati's Telemachus Complex in chapter 2. Wu Ming 4's *Stella del mattino* [*Star of the Morning*] depicts J. R. R. Tolkien and Robert Graves, whose work explored myths and epics, and near the beginning there is a lecture from Professor Murray who discusses Aristotle's *Poetics* and how to translate into English the concept of mythopoeia (Wu Ming 4 2008: 22–24), a key NIE theme.

43. Translation modified: I have changed Knox's translation of 'romance' to 'novel' and 'popular' to 'bourgeois', in line with others who refer to Hegel's conception of the novel as a 'modern bourgeois epic', such as Rancière (2004: 71).

44. For a discussion of mythopoeia in the work of Wu Ming, see Piga 2010.

45. 'Most important, then, is the distinction between "epic" as a genre and "epic" as a mode; the former indicates a precise, highly codified and historical literary genre; the latter, formally theorised by Northrop Frye (1957), refers to a wider category, a recognisable characteristic found even in modern novels and in other literary and artistic works.' (Biasini 2010: 71)

46. Hajek has charted the way in which the memory of the events of 1977 in Bologna was taken up later by the No Global movement, as they were 'in search of a political, collective identity' (Hajek 2013: 139), with Giuliani's death compared to, and often conflated with, that of Lorusso

by various groups (Hajek 2013: 143–45). There were also other parallels drawn between the G8 in Genoa and the *anni di piombo*. Lucarelli states: 'erano anni che non si vedevano scontri come quelli di Genova, di tipo militare come quelli degli anni Settanta' [it had been years since we had seen clashes like those in Genoa, of a military type like those of the 1970s] (2009: 57), and Nando Dalla Chiesa (2011: xii–xiii) saw the event as this generation's Piazza Fontana.

47. *Manifesto TQ*, <http://download.repubblica.it/pdf/2011/Manifesto-TQ.pdf>.

48. See Prudenzano 2013. They last tweeted in April 2013: <https://twitter.com/GenerazioneTQ>.

49. See Santoni's 2007 text *Personaggi precari* [*Precarious Characters*] (Santoni 2017) and Bajani's *Mi spezzo ma non m'impiego. Guida di viaggio per lavoratori flessibili* [*Sooner Break Than Be Employed: A Travel Guide for Flexible Workers*] (2006).

CHAPTER 2

We're Going to Have to Be the Parents: Exploring Parental Legacies and Taking Responsibility

Concerns about parental legacies and taking responsibility resurface time and time again in twenty-first-century Italian literature. These preoccupations are signalled in the title of Wu Ming 1's talk on the New Italian Epic (NIE), 'We're Going to Have to Be the Parents', although he particularly focuses on the way writers have repeatedly staged and explored the death of the father to address Italy's current social and political situation and to metabolise a difficult past, overlooking explorations of motherhood in recent literature and more oblique perspectives on how to come to terms with what has been inherited from previous generations. Wu Ming 1's and other recent Italian writers' insistence on fatherhood can be read through a psychoanalytical lens: whilst I will reference the work of the Italian psychoanalyst Massimo Recalcati when examining this focus on the death of the father, I also refer to Peter Brooks, who drew on Freud to show the role of plot in expressing conscious and unconscious desires in *Reading for the Plot*. The nineteenth-century novels he analysed were specifically preoccupied with fatherhood and legitimacy, and the conditions that Brooks describes as characteristic of these texts and at the root of their structural force — 'the conflict of movement and resistance, revolution and restoration, and [...] the issues of authority and paternity' (Brooks 1984: 65) — have parallels in the conditions that I will put forward as creating the repetition compulsion, to use Freud, of recent Italian literature continually revisiting 'la morte del Vecchio' [the death of the Old Man] (Wu Ming 1 2009a: 74). A similar social and political climate of dealing with the aftermath of failed ideals and negotiating between tradition and innovation is present in the conditions surrounding these twenty-first-century Italian writers, and thus similar parallels can be drawn between their narratives' subject matter and their writers' (and readers') anxieties and desires.

Yet, the clearly gendered slant of Wu Ming 1's and others' discussion has meant that pressing issues that face us in today's world have been neglected by only concentrating on 'la morte del Vecchio'. In his exploration of the problems that face us in today's world through the lens of psychoanalysis, Recalcati (2011: 15) emphasises that when he refers to fathers, gender is not important, and that he does not necessarily mean a family member; yet, his discussion, like the portrayals that Wu Ming 1 holds up as exemplary of the theme of 'la morte del Vecchio',[1] tends to hinge on either one or both of these elements. In the case of the NIE, this is partly due to the fact that its corpus is heavily dominated by male writers and portrayals of male experience, as I discussed in chapter 1. Recalcati's recent text, *Le mani della madre* [*The Mother's Hands*], has instead moved his discussion of inheritance to considerations about the mother figure. He argues that, while fathers pass on the Law through testimony (as I will discuss in the first section of this chapter), maternal inheritance 'concerna la dimensione della vita come tale, il diritto di esistere, il diritto di essere nel mondo' [concerns the dimension of life as such, the right to exist, the right to be in the world] (Recalcati 2015: 154), seeming to cast maternity in ethical terms, related to the endowment of meaning in life. Likewise, there is an ethical impetus behind a need to look beyond only the paternal. Motherhood in Italy has been given greater attention in recent years: it is a common theme chosen by writers for their novels,[2] which have in turn been examined in academic texts,[3] and feminist thinkers, such as Adriana Cavarero and Luisa Muraro, have been exploring the importance of motherhood and female relationships since long before Recalcati, although he only briefly mentions Muraro in a footnote in *Le mani della madre* (2015: 62 n. 31), and Cavarero is completely absent from the text. As Hirsch (1989) and Giorgio (2002) have argued, the mother–daughter relationship has been effaced from western culture for years, and its marginalisation in the NIE suggests that there is still work to be done in this regard. I will argue that the NIE's myopia when it comes to considerations of the maternal excludes some important avenues of exploration when considering inheritance and responsibility in today's world.

This chapter begins with examining why the theme of parental legacies is so present in recent Italian literature and how it connects to broader issues. The analysis then moves to two NIE writers whose portrayals of absent father figures in their narratives are distinctly contrasting.[4] In *Medium* and *Italia De Profundis*, Genna takes an autofictional approach in two very different directions, whilst in both texts linking the death of the author's own father with national issues. In contrast, De Cataldo's *Nelle mani giuste* [*In the Right Hands*] portrays a shadowy father figure known as 'il Vecchio', an imaginary secret puppet master controlling the Italian state until the early 1990s, involved in various conspiracies and unsolved mysteries in Italy's recent past. De Cataldo traces the period after his death in order to chart the rise of Berlusconi and how we arrived at today's situation. My analysis will show that both authors use the death of a patriarch to represent the end of an era and a lens through which to examine the past, present and future of Italy, connecting ideas about paternity, responsibility and engagement in their unidentified narrative objects (UNOs). However, as my subsequent analysis of Pugno's *Sirene* [*Sirens*] demonstrates, these issues are limited by the focus on paternity. Although Wu Ming 1 excludes Pugno's text from the nebula, we will see that her dystopian imaginings show the potential of the NIE's oblique gaze to consider wider problems of our time.

'Our Posthumous Condition'

When reflecting on fatherhood and responsibility, Recalcati (2011: 13) has described the implications of an age characterised by what he calls, after Lacan, the evaporation of the Father, drawing on Freudian and Lacanian theories about the father as representative of the social order and also as a regulator of desire, connected to the symbolic order. He has looked at narratives from both within[5] and outside[6] Italy to show the ways in which they express our unease in the modern world and explore ways of receiving guidance through testimony from our 'parents' (biological or otherwise), whilst also finding independence and assuming responsibility. Following Lacan, Recalcati portrays the 1960s and 1970s in terms of getting rid of paternal authority, but he argues that those protest years only ushered in new forms of repression, and paradoxically led to the strengthening of capitalism and the wish for unlimited enjoyment at the root of many societal problems today. We now have the hypermodern fantasy of being the liberated 'I', free of responsibility and with no sense of the consequences to our acts (Recalcati 2013: 46–48). There is a danger in the contemporary world of adults disappearing; instead of positive father figures, the prevalent model has become that of 'la figura del *genitore-figlio*' [the figure of the *parent-child*] who has abdicated responsibility (Recalcati 2013: 59). Berlusconi is a prime example of such a figure. Recalcati (2013: 78) states that, although the problems he describes in terms of fatherhood are present in other countries too, they have been given particular accent in contemporary Italy due to the lack of responsibility on the political scene making it resemble 'un party adolescenziale forsennato' [a frenzied teenage party]. It is Recalcati's belief that we no longer live under the sign of the symbolic Oedipal father characterised by Freud and later Lacan, nor the anti-Oedipus ushered in by the 1968 protests,[7] but he instead puts forward today's model of the son as Telemachus, searching the horizon for his father, who represents liberty through the proper transmission of the Law (Recalcati 2013: 12). This Law is not related to authoritarianism or punishment, but rather is understood as the passing on of testimony to show that '*la vita può avere un senso*' [*life can have a meaning*] (Recalcati 2013: 14). Such ideas also come into play in the narratives analysed in this chapter, as well as elsewhere in this study. Recalcati's emphasis on the importance of passing on testimony to give meaning is a concept that resounds throughout the texts I analyse, whether they explore testimony about the past through historical novels (chapter 3) or about the present through hybrid journalistic texts (chapter 4).

Wu Ming 1's arguments about fatherhood express similar anxieties to those of Recalcati concerning the aftermath of the protest generations and the problems of Berlusconi's Italy. He explains in the Memorandum that the recurring theme of the death of the father is connected with what he calls 'la nostra condizione di postumi' [our posthumous condition], as this generation feels it is always post-something: 'postfascisti, postcomunisti, post-postmoderni, Seconda Repubblica, eccetera' [post-fascist, post-communist, post-postmodern, Second Republic, etc.] (Wu Ming 1 2009a: 74). As we saw in the previous chapter, he has expressed a sense of disappointment about the Second Republic and the ascent of Berlusconi after the crumbling of the Italian Communist Party, perceiving recent writers and intellectuals as lacking engagement in addressing current problems, in contrast to the *impegno* or commitment of previous generations. He states in 'We're Going to Have to Be the Parents':

> I tempi in cui viviamo sono condizionati dalla morte dei fondatori, dei 'capostipiti', dei genitori che se ne sono andati lasciandoci con problemi enormi. Noi siamo gli eredi delle loro allucinazioni, ormai ci rendiamo conto che la crescita, lo sviluppo, il consumismo, il prodotto interno lordo, tutto questo ci fa correre su un binario morto, e ci chiediamo se lungo la corsa vedremo uno scambio, e chi scenderà ad azionare la leva. (Wu Ming 1 2009b: 118)

> [The times we're living in are affected by the death of the founders, the 'progenitors', the parents who went away and left us with enormous problems. We're the heirs of their delusions; now we're becoming aware that growth, development, consumerism, the gross domestic product all keep us running on a dead track, and we ask ourselves if there's any railroad switch and who's going to pull the lever.]

In a blog post on *Giap* that references Recalcati,[8] Wu Ming 1 argues that, rather than being able to fill the void left empty by the deaths of various 'fathers' before him, Berlusconi was only 'un vuoto circondato di vuoto, un buco nel grande buco lasciato dalla scomparsa dei genitori' [an emptiness surrounded by emptiness, a hole in the big hole left by the disappearance of the parents] (Wu Ming 1 2010a). Both Recalcati and Wu Ming 1 thus draw a line from the illusions of their parents' generation to the current problems of late capitalist society. The after-effects of their parents' actions have left this generation searching for some kind of order and a desire for progenitors who can hand on responsibility to them, rather than leaving them waiting and watching the sea for a return in Recalcati's terms, or for someone who can help steer a different course in Wu Ming 1's terms. Wu Ming 1 implies that it is precisely the NIE engaged writers who can initiate this change. Although Umberto Saba famously pointed out that Italian history was characterised by fratricide rather than patricide,[9] the insistence of Wu Ming 1 and other recent authors on the theme of 'la morte del Vecchio' could be read as a desire to push forward change and break with the past, at a point in time that has been seen as one of political, economic and cultural crisis in Italy; as Saba states: 'è solo col parricidio [...] che si inizia una rivoluzione' [it is only with patricide [...] that a revolution starts] (1993: 16).

Italian writers have been seen as having similar failures to their politicians, shying away from ethical responsibility to engage seriously with this reality. Significantly, late twentieth-century literature was diagnosed as being in a posthumous condition by Ferroni in his 1996 text *Dopo la fine. Sulla condizione postuma della letteratura* [*After the End: On the Posthumous Condition of Literature*], and late postmodernism has been seen as symptomatic of this condition due to its irony and alleged disengagement, in contrast to the overtly politically committed writing that came before it. As discussed in chapter 1, Wu Ming 1's title 'We're Going to Have to Be the Parents' comes from a quotation from David Foster Wallace, who was describing the way in which postmodernist writing had descended into a lack of any rules and a feeling that there was a need for some kind of authority that would have to come from this generation. Wallace states: 'The postmodern founders' patricidal work was great, but patricide produces orphans, and no amount of revelry can make up for the fact that writers my age have been literary orphans throughout our formative years' (McCaffery 1993: 150). Wu Ming 1 made his speech 'We're Going to Have to Be the Parents' in the wake of Wallace's suicide, the death of a literary father figure that we will see Genna address in *Italia De Profundis*. The theme of the death of the father can therefore be related to a need to overcome an idea of writing as ironic, tongue-in-cheek and self-referential play, 'Postmodernismi da quattro soldi' [Two-a-penny postmodernisms] in Wu Ming 1's (2009a: 63) words, although, as I have already argued, and as we will see once again here, the putative lack of engagement of postmodernism and rupture between twenty-first-century Italian literature and what came before are based on a series of misconceptions.

It would not be inappropriate to see recent Italian writers' rejection of post-modernism in terms of an attempt at separation from their fathers, or a mis-understanding of their literary inheritance. In *Senza padri* [*Without Fathers*], Godani argues that recent proclamations of the end of postmodernism and the beginning of a new realism are artificially pitting 'l'era dell'autenticità contro lo sperimentalismo e la sovversione dei codici' [the era of authenticity against experimentalism and subverting the rules] (Godani 2014: 34), with the latter associated with the fatherless state that Recalcati and others have described. Godani suggests that not only is this a misunderstanding of postmodernism, but also that such experimentation should be seen in a positive light, just as he argues that the return of fathers should not be wished for, but rather their absence can be seen as liberating, bringing with it new possibilities: 'quella dissoluzione figura semmai come la condizione di una "comunità" di eguali, senza legami fissi' [that dissolution appears, if anything, as the condition of a 'community' of equals, without fixed ties] (Godani 2014: 20). Godani's analysis of recent texts and films shows that: 'non solo contribuiscano attivamente, con le loro sperimentazioni, alla moderna dissoluzione dei limiti e dei legami, ma di questa dissoluzione si trovino a esaltare la portata liberatoria' [not only do they contribute actively, with their experimentation, to the modern dissolution of limits and ties, but they are also exhilarated by the liberating scope of this dissolution] (2014: 13). In the course of this chapter, we will see that the NIE texts that deal with the death of the father similarly incorporate postmodernist experimentation, even if it is not acknowledged as such, and there is a sense of freedom, or at least of openness, in this, as well as in the future of their protagonists and of Italy and the world.

As the reference to Wallace suggests, such ideas surrounding postmodernism/experimentation versus realism/responsibility are not only part of the conversation in Italy. For example, the British writer Edward Docx (2011) has proclaimed postmodernism dead, welcoming in an 'Age of Authenticism',[10] and interestingly in terms of echoes of the NIE, Docx sees long-form novels like Jonathan Franzen's *The Corrections* as part of this supposed authenticism. Yet, it is striking that in Italy and further afield, writers have often chosen experimental modes of writing to address questions surrounding parental legacies that certainly do not insist on being 'authentic'. This can be seen in this chapter in the range of different imaginative genres that are incorporated into these primary texts: science fiction (Genna and Pugno), alternative history fiction (De Cataldo), noir (De Cataldo), autofiction (Genna).

Indeed, autofiction has frequently been used in recent years to address the kind of issues surrounding parenthood that I have outlined above. For example, in Italian literature, Siti's *Troppi paradisi* [*Too Many Paradises*] portrays the death of the autofictional protagonist's father while considering questions about contemporary consumer society; in addition, Giovanni Maria Bellu's *L'uomo che volle essere Perón* [*The Man Who Wanted to Be Perón*] (2008), an investigation of claims that Juan Domingo Perón was actually Sardinian, the autofictional narrator significantly refers to his father as 'il Vecchio' and describes the conflict with his father coming from a fascist background in contrast to the son's '77 generation. Beyond Italy's borders, perhaps the most well-known example of autofiction that addresses parenthood is Karl Ove Knausgaard's exploration of the death of his father and of becoming a father himself in *Min Kamp* [*My Struggle*], while elsewhere writers such as Rachel Cusk or Marie Darrieussecq have addressed motherhood in recent autofictional texts, and Chloé Delaume's body of work has approached the legacy of her troubled family history from various creative angles. Another example that stands out is Bret Easton Ellis's *Lunar Park* (2005), which imagines the American author's father coming back to haunt him and his family from beyond the grave; there is a clear parallel with Genna's supernatural approach in *Medium*, as we shall see, and Genna (2005) reviewed Ellis's book for *Carmilla*, showing a line of influence. Recent texts that have dealt with deceased parents, as we will see in this chapter too, are often staged around an investigation into the past, which may reflect on both personal and national history. These are problematic pasts, tied up with parents that their children never truly knew or understood, although they seek to now. Recalcati says in relation to Philip Roth's 1991 text *Patrimony: A True Story*, which depicts the decline and death of the American author's father: 'La morte del padre pone [...] il problema delle nostre radici, della nostra provenienza e dell'impossibilità che queste radici e questa stessa provenienza giungano a costituire un terreno solido, sicuro, al riparo dall'aleatorietà della vita' [The death of the father poses [...] the problem of our roots, of our origin and of the impossibility of these roots and this origin becoming solid ground, protected from the randomness of life] (Recalcati 2011: 124). The gaps between fiction and reality that are foregrounded in autofiction mean that it has been a frequent choice of genre to depict this unstable relationship with our parents and our roots. Yet, this is not only limited to fatherhood, but also applies to the lives of mothers and our relationship with them, as Janeczek does in *Lezioni di tenebra* [*Lessons of Darkness*], for example, an autofictional text that is saturated with uncertainty or darkness about her mother's experiences during the Second World War, as the title foregrounds.

We cannot underestimate the importance of motherhood in exploring testimony about problematic and unstable pasts and their effects in the present, and in how we relate to the world and one another. In *Tu che mi guardi, tu che mi racconti* [*Relating Narratives: Storytelling and Selfhood*], Cavarero (1997) underlines the importance of women passing on self-narration to one another to show the particularity of identity. Similarly, but without acknowledging Cavarero's work, Recalcati (2015: 17) emphasises the power of the particularity of a mother's testimony, which he sees in terms of combatting the discourse of capitalism. The problems of our late-capitalist world are what Wu Ming 1 was concerned about this generation addressing in his statement quoted earlier, when describing the emptiness of a world of 'growth, development, consumerism, the gross domestic product', but his NIE nebula fails to include maternal testimony, aside from Andrea Bajani's *Se consideri le colpe*, which addresses the death of the (male) narrator's mother (Wu Ming 1 2009a: 74). The NIE largely excludes female writers, most notably Elena Ferrante, who has examined motherhood throughout her innovative texts, as well as excluding Pugno, whose approach to questions of inheritance certainly reflects on the possible damage of capitalism taken to its extreme in a male-dominated world ravaged by environmental disaster, as we shall see later in this chapter, which I will connect to the work of the feminist theorist Rosi Braidotti and her recent text *The Posthuman* (2013). Motherhood and female concerns might be seen as closely connected to the kind of environmental issues that Pugno's text raises; as Fulginiti (2014: 163) points out, concerns about an apocalyptic 'earthicide' can be linked to ideas about matricide, in that they address the death of mother nature, and this link is made by Pugno's text too, as we shall see.

Significantly, Wu Ming 1 is particularly insistent in the Memorandum about the importance of addressing the environmental crisis that we are facing in the twenty-first century. He discusses the inevitability of humans being wiped out in the future, as a result of the environmental damage we have done, in order to emphasise the importance of writers imagining the post-human future that awaits us:

> Ci rifiutiamo di ammettere che andiamo incontro all'estinzione come specie. Certamente non nei prossimi giorni, e nemmeno nei prossimi anni, ma avverrà, avverrà in un futuro che è intollerabile immaginare, perché sarà *senza di noi*.
>
> [...] Eppure l'antropocentrismo è vivo e vegeto, e lotta contro di noi. Scoperte scientifiche, prove oggettive, crisi del Soggetto, crolli di vecchie ideologie... Nulla pare aver distolto il genere umano dall'assurda idea di essere al centro dell'universo [...].
>
> Perciò è tanto importante la questione del punto di vista obliquo, e diverrà sempre più importante — come aveva intuito Calvino — la 'resa' letteraria di sguardi extra-umani, non-umani, non identificabili. (Wu Ming 1 2009a: 56–58)

> [We refuse to admit that we are going extinct as a species. Certainly not in the coming days, nor in the next few years, but it will happen, it will happen in a future that is unbearable to imagine, because it will be *without us*.
>
> [...] Yet, anthropocentrism is alive and well, and fights against us. Scientific discoveries, objective evidence, the crisis of the Subject, the collapses of old ideologies ... Nothing seems to have diverted mankind from the absurd idea of being at the centre of the universe [...].

Thus, the question of the oblique viewpoint is so important, and — as Calvino guessed — the literary 'rendering' of extra-human, non-human, unidentifiable gazes will become increasingly important.]

Literature's ethical role in Wu Ming 1's terms is not only to reimagine the past and comment on the present, but to move away from anthropocentrism to imagine this posthuman future through the NIE's oblique gaze, exploring what he goes on to describe as 'un pensiero *ecocentrico*' [*eco-centric* thought] (Wu Ming 1 2009a: 59). Yet, as well as the oblique gaze being limited by the male-dominated nature of the nebula, this *pensiero ecocentrico* is largely absent from the texts that focus on fatherhood, which tend to look back into Italy's past rather than looking forward to the world's future. We will see that Wu Ming 1's eco-centric thought is enacted by Pugno's investigation of the possible legacy that awaits us in her imaginings about environmental apocalypse in *Sirene* through considerations about matrilinearity, matricide and the possibilities of a post-anthropocentric reality.

Brooks (1984: 62) states that there is a fundamental question at the root of the obsession with paternity in Stendhal's work: 'To whom does France belong?'. A closer analysis of Genna's and De Cataldo's portrayals of patricide and generational conflict in this chapter will raise the question: to whom does Italy belong? Genna and De Cataldo explore how we can relate to a personal and collective past through addressing both real and symbolic father figures, and they ask what literature can do, in attempts to find a way forward in the current political and cultural climate. However, we will also see that these writers are examining these questions from a clear position of male, Italian-national centrality, which we will move beyond in the final section of this chapter in an exploration of the wider issues raised by Pugno's *Sirene*. In the NIE texts that deal with the theme of orphanhood, a direct paternal inheritance seems to be investigated but not fundamentally challenged. The oblique gaze should ideally provide an alternative to the dominant, male viewpoint that is still found in many NIE texts.

Medium and *Italia De Profundis* by Giuseppe Genna

Genna is an important figure in twenty-first-century Italian experimental literature, and his work is also highly relevant to Wu Ming 1's ideas about the NIE, which he has engaged with critically through articles on *Carmilla*, writing about texts that form part of Wu Ming 1's corpus (see, for example, Genna 2007a, 2007b, 2007c), and positioning himself as part of the phenomenon. His innovative texts are among some of the most interesting examples of UNOs in the nebula, given their incorporation of transmediality and of a range of genres, including autofiction, biofiction and *giallo*, often to address real-life events. Several of his texts explore issues relating to fatherhood. The texts I analyse here — *Medium* (2007d) and *Italia De Profundis* (2008b) — do so through the death of his real-life father. Fatherhood is then examined from a different perspective in his later text *Fine impero* (2013), which opens with the funeral of the main protagonist's baby daughter and explores not the loss of a father but the condition of a mourning father, although he has overlaps with the autofictional Genna we will see in this chapter.[11] Genna's work tends to work in this way, with texts picking up the themes of previous ones and re-examining them from different perspectives.

Here, we will examine *Medium*, published online in 2007, and *Italia De Profundis*, published in print a year later, which both open with the death of his father, Vito Genna, before going on to ask questions about history and literature in today's world. Vito Genna's death was a real-life event that Wu Ming 1 refers to at the beginning of 'We're Going to Have to Be the Parents', but in the two UNOs it is explored through the lens of the character Giuseppe Genna in two different ways. Whilst in *Medium* it leads to an investigation into his father's and Italy's past that culminates in supernatural revelations, *Italia De Profundis* goes on to relate a series of fragmentary experiences that followed in what is a critique of modern-day Italy, 'un luogo che ho disimparato ad amare' [a place that I have unlearned to love] (11). Although Vito Genna's death was something that Giuseppe Genna actually lived through, it was also, as Wu Ming 1 points out, 'un'esperienza allegorica soverchiante' [an overwhelmingly allegorical experience] (Wu Ming 1 2009b: 103), and this can be seen by the ways in which it is woven into these narratives, reflecting on the concerns that Wu Ming 1 and Recalcati have outlined in relation to 'la nostra condizione di postumi' [our posthumous condition] (Wu Ming 1 2009a: 74).

In *Medium*, the death of Vito Genna suggests the end of an era and Wu Ming 1's idea of being 'post-communist'. Vito was a staunch communist and travelled to East Germany during the 1980s; the text centres on that period as Giuseppe tries to understand his father's involvement with communism. Before his death, Vito was living in a now very right-wing Milan, a sick old man and an alcoholic, as if unable to cope with the modern-day Italy in which his ideals have been set aside. Wu Ming 1 explains:

> Il padre di Giuseppe Genna aveva dedicato buona parte della vita a un partito che non esisteva più, nella speranza di una rivoluzione che non c'era stata, nel quadro di una sinistra politica che moriva in metafora mentre lui moriva *alla lettera*, moriva di cancro in un appartamento desolato di una città desolata e conquistata dalla destra tanto tempo prima. Un infarto improvviso gli aveva risparmiato mesi di strazio, e il figlio aveva sentimenti contrastanti: aveva il cuore a pezzi, ma provava sollievo.
>
> Il figlio sapeva che la morte del padre stava per la morte di un'epoca, la morte di un mondo. Il lutto per il padre era anche il lutto per l'epoca. (Wu Ming 1 2009b: 104)

> [Genna's father had devoted most of his life to a party that didn't exist anymore, hoping for a revolution that never came, in the context of a political left that was metaphorically dying as his father was *literally* dying; he was dying of cancer in a lonely apartment in a lonely city that had been taken over by the right wing long before. A sudden heart attack saved him from months of pain, and his son had mixed feelings: he was heartbroken, but he also felt relieved.
>
> The son knew that the death of the father symbolised the death of an era, the death of a world. Mourning the father was also mourning that era.]

Giuseppe goes through his father's books on communism, relics of a now distant past, where he finds a clue to unlocking what his father did in Germany, a letter written by the mysterious 'G' that can help answer his question: '"*Chi era* mio padre?"'['*Who was* my father?'].[12] He first goes to the communist archives in Rome in order to begin truly to understand his personal and political past, and, whilst there, communist imagery merges in his mind with memories of his father in 'un passato che nell'infanzia avevo mitizzato' [a past that I had mythologised in childhood] ('Discesa nella città eterna'). The reconsideration of these paternal myths becomes part of his coming to terms with the loss of his father. Understanding the politics of the past is inextricably linked to understanding and mourning his father.

It is no coincidence that Wu Ming 1 refers to Genna as playing the role of Telemachus when he later follows his father's trail to Berlin (Wu Ming 1 2009b: 106). Recalcati refers to Telemachus' journey to gain knowledge of his father in the myth as an important part of his inheritance, as he actively chooses to seek him out: 'Cerca le tracce del padre, cerca notizie della sua vita' [He searches for the father's traces, he searches for news of his life] (2013: 134). This is precisely what Genna does, embarking on a search that puts him at risk, but, ultimately, following these traces results in proper recognition of his father. As in the Homeric tale, proper acceptance and inheritance of his father's legacy can only be done after Telemachus' journey. Genna is staging through fiction what Recalcati and Wu Ming 1 have spoken about this generation needing to do, that is go in search of their inheritance.

There is both a personal and community function to Genna's investigation of history. *Medium* was first published online complete with hypertext references, available for free download with recordings of the author reading sections, and a no-profit print version was also made available.[13] As a result of sharing his story and making his mourning public, Genna received messages from readers who wanted to share similar experiences with him (as Wu Ming 1 (2009a: 105) points out). This is in keeping with the tendency in the NIE, discussed in the introduction to this study, to use autofiction as part of a sense of *impegno* or commitment: 'introspezione e autofiction per narrare un fatto pubblico e "storico"' [introspection and autofiction to narrate a public and 'historic' event] (Wu Ming 1 2009a: 15n9). Genna states in the text: 'Mio padre è *il* padre' [My father is *the* father] ('Magia rossa'), implying a desire for universality. Although this is a deeply subjective account, he seeks to connect with a wider public through it.

Yet, despite the subtitle of *Medium* being 'una storia vera' [a true story], Genna chooses a highly fictional mode in order to do so. The first line states: 'Questo libro non è sincero' [This book is not sincere], and the first few pages repeatedly tell the readers: 'Immaginate' [Imagine] (Ritrovamento'). Indeed, as the text goes on, it descends into supernatural events and moves away from the more realist feel of its opening section. It transpires that the letter he found does not indicate that his father had a love affair in Germany, but alludes to visualisation experiments he undertook there with the Theosophical Society, involving a woman called Frau Hinze, who wrote the letter, and the real-life figure of the writer Peter Kolosimo.[14] We learn that these visualisation experiments were undertaken to look into the future, in order to ensure the survival of communism. In doing so, Genna's father foresaw not only his own death as it would actually happen, but also the end of the world in 2080 due to an asteroid hitting the Earth.[15] Wu Ming 1 has said of Genna's imaginings in *Medium*:

> Descrivendo il padre come un veggente, Genna [...] lo omaggia per aver almeno immaginato un futuro, impresa che le ultime generazioni trovano molto difficile. In questo modo, Genna elabora il lutto e rende l'elaborazione importante per tutti noi.
> [...] Una questione personale si è trasformata in meditazione sui destini della nostra specie, del nostro pianeta, del nostro cosmo. (Wu Ming 1 2009b: 108)

> [By depicting his father as a psychic, Genna [...] pays tribute to him for having at least imagined a future, a task that the latest generations find very difficult to accomplish. In this way, Genna elaborates the mourning, and makes the elaboration important for all of us.
> [...] An individual matter has become a meditation on the destiny of our species, our planet, our cosmos.]

The community role of the text is certainly more complex than a simple sharing of the experience of grief after losing a parent, but rather provokes reflection through a psychic game of mirrors: this real, present event leads Giuseppe on an imaginary investigation into the past in which Vito saw both the past and future. The death of his father also coincides in the text with Giuseppe Genna expecting his own child with his girlfriend Federica, again combining past and future as legacies are explored and to be handed on. This is complicated by the fact that Giuseppe witnesses himself communicating with his father from the future in one of the visualisation experiments. He then has the presentiment that his baby, which was probably conceived in a deeply Freudian moment of lovemaking on the spot where his father's body was found, and which Federica eventually miscarries, was 'una nuova manifestazione di mio padre' [a new manifestation of my father] ('Io'). Genna acts as the medium between these entangled times, inviting reflections through his narrative that channels reality and fiction.

However, it is unfortunate that, despite the interesting ideas that Genna puts forward in *Medium*, it is limited in engaging with a wider audience because its transmedial elements have now disappeared on Genna's new website, which is testament to the ephemerality of online material, as we will see in chapter 4 too with Jones's digital extensions to her text *Sappiano le mie parole di sangue*. Readers can no longer access the hypertext references or the recordings of Genna reading the text, both of which deepened the unusual autofiction that Genna was engaging in through combining his imaginings with real-life elements. In the case of the recordings, this was done through the fantastical narrative being read in Genna's voice, embodying the story in the author himself. The hypertext references similarly anchored the fictional elements in reality through sending readers of this fantastical narrative to fact-based websites such as Wikipedia (for example, on the pentacle in the chapter 'L'occulto assalto', among many other examples), a tourism site about the Berlin Wall ('Il canale nero'), or the website of the real-life hospice Vidas mentioned by Genna's father's oncologist ('Ritrovamento'). The links at times also provided maps or photographs, giving visual representation to elements of the story in order to create again a reality effect in a narrative that decisively and explicitly moves away from reality. Transmediality through online material seems to be particularly suited to autofiction, as it recalls the kind of autofiction that many of us engage in in an age of social media, carefully curating information about ourselves through a combination of text, links and visual material to create a public profile that may coincide more or less closely with our lived experience. Like many contemporary writers, Genna maintains an active online presence through Facebook, Twitter (@giuseppegenna) and his blog, with which the wider public can interact. As I suggested in the introduction to this study, the increasingly widespread use of social media may go some way towards explaining the recent popularity of autofiction, as authors feel increasingly compelled to experiment with their private and public selves. It is no coincidence that another contemporary Italian writer who has employed transmediality extensively through supplementing her text with online material is Jones, whose text can also be described as autofiction (see chapter 4). However, the transmedial expansions of both Jones's *Sappiano le mie parole di sangue* and Genna's *Medium* have disappeared, meaning that later readers/users are unable to access the extra material and engage fully with the autofiction these authors are experimenting with, leaving these texts rooted in a moment in time that has now passed.

Genna took quite a different approach in his other autofictional text about the death of his father: *Italia De Profundis*. Whilst *Medium* is an investigation into the past, *Italia De Profundis* is firmly situated in the present, as mourning his father leads Genna's textual avatar to reflect on the problems in both his own life and modern-day Italy. It moves from his hometown of Milan to Venice during the film festival, then to a tourist resort in Sicily. Genna tells us in the acknowledgements at the end of the text that it could equally have been entitled ' "*Giuseppe Genna*" *De Profundis*' (347), giving a sense of his autofictional, constructed self as both separate from him in its inverted commas and bound up with Italy, which his name could replace. In Santoro's words, Genna superimposes himself onto an Italy that is 'malata, divorata da un male, un cancro in avanzata metastasi, come quello che divora il corpo vivo del padre e l'anima dello stesso autore' [sick, devoured by an illness, a cancer in advanced metastasis, like the one that devours the living body of the father and the soul of the author] (Santoro 2010: 36).

The text is also less supernatural than *Medium* in approach, and this difference in tone is established from the description of the discovery of his father's body, which corresponds in many details with the description of the same event in *Medium*, but without strange phone calls and mysterious visitors. It instead focuses on practicalities, made up of brief fragments outlining the arrangements he made and the thoughts he had; as he states: 'Non c'è nulla di sovrannaturale' [There is nothing supernatural] (27). However, that is not to say that this book is firmly rooted in reality or indeed realism. Whilst it avoids experiments with time travel, we do encounter a psychic shaman and some distinctly Lynchian undertones, and indeed overtones when he thinks that he is living through one of Lynch's films

(191). Indeed, he then narrates his experience of seeing *Inland Empire* at the Venice Film Festival, where he also meets Lynch, whom he sees as 'uno dei genii della nostra epoca' [one of the geniuses of our era] (227). The American director says of his work that, despite examining various subjects, his gaze is inward, observing himself (222). Genna deeply admires *Inland Empire*, a strange web of stories loosely based around the theme of adultery, saying that its allegorical drive means that there is no plot (211), and his own text seems to mirror this approach: rather than a straightforward, easily decipherable story, there are variations on a theme, open to psychoanalytical interpretation.

Indeed, although Genna is offering his personal story, what is in front of us is another UNO that is stylistically unusual, searching for forms to represent reality in a world in which, as Genna tells us repeatedly: 'La parola sta cadendo. | L'immagine sta cadendo' [The word is falling. | The image is falling] (55, and then in various forms on pages 78–79, 139, 153–54, 208). The loss of a father is linked to a loss of stability in understanding and representing the world. *Italia De Profundis* even comments on itself in postmodernist metafictional moments. One that particularly stands out is his warning to the reader:

> ATTENZIONE
> Da questo punto, fino a pagina 91, tutto diventa noiosissimo. Al fine di evitare tale noia, si consigli vivamente di saltare a pagina 92, dove non è neppure detto che non ci si annoi. Comunque, ciò che segue è più noioso di quanto sia umano immaginare e inoltre si tratta di una parte che abbassa le vendite del libro. Si raccomanda di saltarla a piè pari, davvero. (73)

> [ATTENTION
> From this point, until page 91, everything becomes very boring. In order to avoid this boredom, it is strongly recommended you jump to page 92, where you will not necessarily not get bored. However, what follows is more tedious than humanly imaginable and, moreover, it is a part that reduces the sales of the book. Skipping it completely is recommended, really.]

Santoro (2010:38) points out that we are faced with a *mis-en-abyme* of the self, as Genna the textual protagonist's story is interrupted by an extra-diegetic Genna telling us what to do, but arguably also encouraging us not to do it. Do we read the more straightforward, linear and banal 'descrizione della "scena italiana"' [description of the 'Italian scene'] (70), then skip ahead to the next step of the narrative, or do we embark on the stream of consciousness filled with abstract images that are open to the reader to interpret? As with his changing statements about the truth status of *Medium*, Genna seems to be asking what literature can do, highlighting its artificiality whilst considering political and ethical issues. His technique at this point is reminiscent of Julio Cortázar's experimental 1963 novel *Rayuela* [*Hopscotch*], in which the readers are encouraged in the author's note at the beginning to find their own paths through the novel, possibly jumping over the 'Expendable Chapters' (Cortázar 1966: 351). This makes readers share the work of constructing the text, as the author tries to shake them out of passivity. The encouragement to participate in Genna's work is reinforced by its transmedial dimension, which, in contrast to *Medium*, focuses less on anchoring the text in authorial embodiment and real-world places and facts: as well as four book trailers, there is a 'ipertesto della "scena italiana come inferno"' [hypertext of the 'Italian scene as hell'] on Genna's blog, where the reader can seek out further explanation and references that help to unravel the obscurity of the section from page 73 to page 91 that Genna seemingly advises his readers to skip.[16]

Such elements suggest that, once again, Genna does not want to invite easy identification with his subject matter, but rather aims to encourage readerly work. This is also true of his earlier, highly unusual text *Dies irae* (2014), in which he interwove an autofictional investigation of the story of Alfredino Rampi with a science fiction narrative and various other microstories. In *Italia De Profundis*, Genna meets a man who tells him he loved *Dies irae*: 'Alfredino, gli anni Ottanta, Moana Pozzi: io ricordo tutto. È andata veramente così' [Alfredino, the eighties, Moana Pozzi: I remember everything. It really went like that] (310). On hearing this, Genna now thinks the novel was 'un mezzo fallimento' [a half failure] (310), as the reader was not meant to identify with it and nostalgically share the memory of the 1980s. Rather than the reader being simply a 'spettatore' [spectator] (310), Genna's work is supposed to shake up expectations, and this is precisely what we can see him trying to do in *Italia De Profundis* too. Each reader must construct his or her own interpretation when confronted with these strange stories, loosely following the clues or hypertext to reach a possible understanding of what is being said, which will never be spelled out by the author.

From the opening extract taken from *Petrolio* onwards, Genna also draws on Pasolini's work in order to experiment with form in *Italia De Profundis*. Pasolini has been an important reference point for recent Italian writers, as I discuss in chapter 4 in the resurfacing of his 'Io so' [I know] in the twenty-first century, and he could also be seen as the deceased father of intellectual *impegno*, even if he never styled himself as a paternal figure. In *Dimenticare Pasolini* [*Forgetting Pasolini*], a text that seeks to evaluate more critically this now mythologised figure, and investigate how nostalgia about him illustrates the current Italian cultural climate, Antonello repeatedly refers to Pasolini's influence today in terms of inheritance: he describes 'un continuo e sempre rinnovato dibattito sulla sua eredità, sul suo lascito testimoniale' [a continuous and always renewed debate on his inheritance, on his testimonial legacy] (2012: 97), and asks in terms that strongly recall Recalcati: 'Cosa ci resta della sua eredità? Cosa dobbiamo farcene della sua lezione? Come recuperarla, se recuperarla è possibile?' [What is left of his legacy? What should we do with his lesson? How to recover it, if it is possible to recover it?] (2012: 100). Pasolini, whilst being an inspiration to recent writers, also overshadows their work due to the tendency of critics and the media to evoke him in exemplary and hagiographical terms, something that Antonello rightly calls into question. There is a sense that the past, that of the parents of these recent writers, looms over their attempts at finding new ways of engaging with national issues.[17] However, in Genna's text, Pasolini is relevant more in terms of narrative practice, rather than being a model he looks to emulate in his act of *impegno* as Saviano has, for example (see chapter 4). Patti rightly says of the epigraph: 'the quotation from *Petrolio* would seem to aim at developing a metaliterary discourse on writing and the problematic representation of reality' (2010: 87). In answer to Antonello's question about Pasolini's legacy, Genna's way of recovering this inheritance here is by looking beyond the classical novel form and style as Pasolini did. This is an attempt to 'seize reality' as Pasolini put it in the quotation Genna includes (Pasolini 1992: 419), although, like the texts analysed in chapter 4, this does not imply a mimetic, realist approach. Rather, as Patti states, Genna draws on the Pasolinian concept of writing 'in an experimental, unpredictable and undetermined way' (Patti 2010: 88). Through the fragmentary quality of his narrative, the gaps, the metaliterary discourse and the extra material online, Genna experiments with form and leaves the text, as Pasolini did *Petrolio*, as 'an open puzzle yet to be completed' (Patti 2010: 93).[18]

Italia De Profundis is rich with intertextual connections beyond Pasolini and Lynch, which further develop Genna's desire for a type of narrative that is innovative and requires his readers' participation. By directly invoking his literary precursors to address today's world, Genna looks back in order to look forward, and also explicitly places his work within a transnational framework, further demonstrating the way in which the NIE is not confined to Italy's borders. Genna points out that his description of the tourist resort also owes a textual debt to Michel Houellebecq's *Plateforme* [*Platform*] (340), although he also says of the French writer: 'mi sento distante dalla sua perenne inclinazione depressiva' [I feel distant from his perennial depressive inclination] (321). Despite this dismissal, *Plateforme*, opening with the death of the character Michel's father and going on to explore modern issues, and in particular those related to sexual relationships and desire, against the backdrop of modern tourism, is an important reference point for Genna's text. Houellebecq's resort in Pattaya is destroyed by a terrorist bomb at the end of *Plateforme*, whilst Genna makes his Sicilian resort go up in flames, as both texts seem to be sending out warnings about the dangers of the mindless enjoyment they explore. Genna also refers to William S. Burroughs several times, and his influence is evident in the fragmentary nature of the text resembling a cut-up, as well as in one of the vividly depicted 'Quattro storie di merda che non ricordo più' [Four shitty stories that I don't remember any more] (113) in which Genna takes heroin. T. S. Eliot's *The Waste Land* is mentioned alongside Burroughs in a list of literary precursors (72), and the text comes to a close with a quotation from that poem, the same extract that concludes the main body of Wu Ming 1's Memorandum; thus Genna makes a clear connection between his work and the NIE phenomenon.[19] It is worth pointing out that this extremely diverse list of literary precursors/progenitors provided by Genna — which also includes Leopardi and Celan alongside Pasolini, Burroughs and Eliot — is completely male, again leaning towards 'fathers' rather than 'mothers'. Genna tells us that all of them were chosen because they make the reader work; they are characterised by self-awareness (72). We must reflect on what is being put in front of us, which, like *Medium*, may initially appear to be autobiographical, but is something more experimental and thought provoking in the vein of his range of literary references.

Genna seems to be discouraging us from being like the shallow 'neoitaliani' [neo-Italians] that he encounters in the tourist resort in Sicily. These people are the epitome of Recalcati's vision of the more problematic parts of today's capitalist world, endlessly consuming and searching for pleasure, but unable to access true desire. The narrator tells us: 'Parlano solo di cose, di soldi. E di sesso, di prestazioni sessuali, di storie tra amanti — e invece cercano l'amore' [They only speak about things, about money. And about sex, about sexual performance, about affairs between lovers — and yet they are looking for love] (304). He is among this crowd and admits that he is one of them too, as we all are (323). We see him dealing with his own feelings about relationships and desire, as shown by the 'four shitty stories', in which he seems to be experimenting with his more transgressive compulsions, which are connected to his malaise in this modern world. In a country portrayed as dominated by television and mobile phones, with declining literary and cinematic culture, the narrator's existential angst plays itself out through these extreme experiences related to desire, whether sexual desire, the desire for drugs, or the desire to die in the euthanasia sequence. They are part of his self-discovery and of his exploration of national issues; as he narrates his country he also asks himself: 'Cosa vuoi autenticamente? | Cosa desideri autenticamente?' [What do you authentically want? | What do you authentically desire?] (250).

It is his stay in the tourist resort that brings to the fore perhaps the most important element in the dense intertextuality of *Italia De Profundis*, that is Wallace, who is also important in the NIE conception of the death of the father, as we have seen. However, I would argue that there is a certain misunderstanding of Wallace's work in *Italia De Profundis* that is representative of a wider misunderstanding of postmodernism and irony. In the tourist resort, Genna likens himself to Wallace in the American writer's essay about his experience of a cruise holiday, 'A supposedly fun thing I'll never do again', which similarly examines western consumerism (321). However, he also argues that Wallace was wrong to observe the cruise ship passengers with irony and amusement, from a distance that Genna is unable to achieve (322–23). He claims that Wallace can engage in sterile theorising about 'il superamento del postmoderno' [overcoming the postmodern] (322), but Genna instead waits for the tragic culmination of the barrenness he observes. In a lengthy footnote worthy of Wallace's style, Genna describes the American writer's death, calling it 'un gesto fondativo — probabilmente il più fondativo della mia generazione letteraria' [a foundational gesture — probably the most foundational of my literary generation] (324), although he is unable to explain why it happened. Genna's digression on Wallace's death is followed in the narrative by the discovery of the unknown man who died in his room in the tourist village. Significantly, he is found by Genna in the same position as his father's corpse (330); this indicates that, like Wallace's body or his father's, the discovery will lead to some kind of deeper knowledge or interrogation of beliefs. Nobody had noticed this single man, alone, and, after his death, they simply want to continue enjoying their holiday. It is as if his death is an intimation of something they want to ignore; it is described as the ghost of Banquo (334). A possible interpretation of this is that we need to connect with others, that detachment through intellectual endeavour or social invisibility will ultimately lead to tragedy. Boscolo argues that Genna is implicitly suggesting that the pain that led to Wallace's suicide 'derived from the awareness that he was no longer able to distinguish between himself and the masses he described with irony and detachment' (Boscolo 2010b: 23). She goes on to say that, in the light of today's global conflicts and environmental disasters:

> Irony and detachment are [...] no longer acceptable means of representing society, in that everyone, including authors and narrators, is part of the society that is depicted. The chosen few who can look down on the behaviour of the masses no longer exist. (Boscolo 2010b: 23–24)

However, Wallace was not simply the superior writer looking down on his subjects. Whilst there are laugh-out-loud moments in Wallace's essay, poking fun at some of the cruise ship passengers he observes,[20] his irony is not synonymous with detachment. He has a deeply serious message to communicate about the nature of consumption in today's world, in which people pay vast amounts of money to return to a childlike state of being pampered, watched over by staff who 'keep reassuring everybody that everybody's having a good time' (Wallace 1998: 260), all in an attempt to 'triumph over [...] death and decay' (Wallace 1998: 264). As with Genna's holiday village, or Houellebecq's, there are strong psychoanalytical undertones about the nature of pleasure and enjoyment today in Wallace's essay. Rather than simply inhabiting a position of detached distance from the experience, Wallace finds himself depressed by it: 'There is something about a mass-market Luxury Cruise that's unbearably sad [...] on board the *Nadir* — especially at night, when all the ship's structured fun and reassurances and gaiety-noise ceased — I felt despair' (1998: 261). Even if Wallace himself said that 'Irony's gone from liberating to enslaving' (McCaffrey 1993: 147), the irony we see in 'A supposedly fun thing I'll never do again' can be seen as a form of attachment or responsibility, rather than of detachment or distancing. Moreover, I would argue that such irony, and even humour, are not absent from Genna's texts, which play with his readers' expectations and with the blurred lines between reality and fiction, between Genna the author and Genna the fictional character, to make serious points about today's world.

Di Martino rightly states that 'attempts to deny the existence of a continuity between postmodernism and contemporary literature are often due to the misconception that postmodernist irony is associated only with a poetics of relativism and self-referentiality, and does not carry a message of solidarity that promotes social commitment' (2011: 137). In arguing that there is continuity in the ethical use of irony from Pirandello to Gadda to Eco and finally to the NIE, Di Martino draws on both Hutcheon's work on postmodern irony as a 'complicitous critique' of reality (Hutcheon 1988: 3) and Burns's argument in *Fragments of Impegno*, in which the writers she analyses are described as employing both 'a superficial, sparky sort of irony', but also 'a much weightier, more cogent and even cruel irony, which exposes the "dark side" of contemporary life and asks the reader to recognise it [...] This is an irony which intends to make a point, and a very sharp point' (Burns 2001: 183).[21] Interestingly, Burns also suggests that, although such a use of irony is a tradition of European literature, it can also be seen as specifically Italian — 'running from as far back as Dante, through Ariosto, Leopardi, Verga, Svevo, to Pavese and Calvino, who forefronts the seriousness of games' (Burns 2001: 183) — and Di Martino makes a similar argument for this Italian tradition of irony. It is no coincidence, then, that we see it also being employed by many recent Italian writers, despite Wu Ming 1's belief put forward in the Memorandum that postmodernist irony is 'cool-and-dry' (Wu Ming 1 2009a: 22). There is an emotional engagement that can be detected, which I will return to in chapter 4 when discussing other recent autofictional narratives. Here we have seen that the loss of Genna's father seems to trigger a search for new affective connections in texts that, despite their use of irony, supernatural elements and heavy fictionalising, have a real sense of social responsibility.

Nelle mani giuste by Giancarlo De Cataldo

De Cataldo's *Nelle mani giuste* (2007) contains certain crossovers with Genna's work in its enquiry into the past and reflections on the present through ideas connected to paternity and responsibility through literature, but goes in a different direction. It is the sequel to his hugely successful 2002 text *Romanzo criminale*, which depicted the true story of the Magliana gang, and was subsequently made into an acclaimed film and a television series. Like Genna's *Medium*, *Romanzo criminale* and *Nelle mani giuste*, as well as De Cataldo's Risorgimento novel *I traditori* [*The Traitors*], centre on an investigation into the past, examining traces to explain how we arrived at the present situation, and in all three of De Cataldo's texts this relates to the mafia phenomenon and its links with the state. Although *Nelle mani giuste* is a work of fiction, De Cataldo, a former judge, says in the text's foreword that it is also based on research: 'Il lavoro di ricostruzione si basa prevalentemente sulla lettura di atti giudiziari [...] Quanto al "frasario" e al *modus operandi* dei mafiosi, essi sono tratti in massima parte da trascrizioni di intercettazioni' [The reconstruction work is mainly based on reading legal documents [...] The 'jargon' and the *modus operandi* of the mafia are mostly taken from transcripts of wiretapping] (2). De Cataldo has written another UNO with the journalist Carlo Bonini that explores Roman *mafiosi*, *Suburra*, which has been adapted into a television series. In a 2008 article in *La Repubblica*, De Cataldo spoke about recent books, films and theatre productions in Italy beginning to investigate national issues with a renewed sense of *impegno* that he, like so many others, connects to the Pasolinian legacy (De Cataldo 2008). Interestingly, he does not reject labels like neo-neorealism or, indeed, NIE — 'Le etichette lasciano il tempo che trovano' [The labels will be found over time] (De Cataldo 2008) — but, like me, instead opts to call this 'una letteratura "non identificata"' [an 'unidentified' literature], although he sees it as purely addressing Italian concerns rather than considering a more transnational perspective (De Cataldo 2008).

Some of the characters of *Romanzo criminale* reprise their roles in *Nelle mani giuste*, such as Scialoja, the police officer who investigated the Magliana gang before becoming disillusioned, or Patrizia, the sex worker he falls in love with, but the sequel has a distinct approach and tone compared to the original, and this is strongly tied up with ideas related to the theme of 'la morte del Vecchio'. Where *Romanzo criminale* was a sprawling history of the gang, spanning the years from 1977 to 1992, *Nelle mani giuste* maintains a tight focus on the period between autumn 1992 and December 1993, not coincidentally addressing the year that has been seen by Wu Ming 1 as the starting point of the NIE phenomenon, but also the missed opportunity for revolutionary change. This is the watershed moment of the changeover between the First and Second Republic, the Tangentopoli scandals and the rise of Berlusconi, and De Cataldo repeatedly refers to it in terms of a paradigm shift, alternatively 'il crepuscolo degli dèi' [the twilight of the gods] (186), or 'una Nuova Alba Italiana' [a New Italian Dawn] (195). Within the fictional world of the text, it also signals the death of the character 'il Vecchio' [the Old Man], who had been controlling the country from behind the scenes: mediating between state and mafia, overseeing the so-called 'strategy of tension' and creating the Catena, a secret organisation behind the real-life hidden network known as the Gladio. 'Il Vecchio' also stored a huge number of documents containing state secrets, reminiscent of Andreotti's secret archive. Scialoja, one of the many 'orfani' [orphans] of 'il Vecchio' (19), receives this extensive store of documents as his successor, and is left to negotiate a difficult legacy, as, once more, the end of an era coincides with the death of a patriarch, and a search for a new way forward.

Scialoja battles with a sense of inadequacy in the face of his inheritance, as he feels unable to fill the shoes of 'il Vecchio'. Despite having come a long way from the police officer of *Romanzo criminale* — 'Nella sua vita precedente, quand'era un semplice sbirro infarcito di ideali' [In his former life, when he was a simple cop stuffed with ideals] (38) — and learnt about the mechanisms of power, in a familiar story arc charting the loss of ideals and acceptance of corruption, he makes mistakes or fails fully to understand his new position. He questions why he was chosen as successor, telling himself: 'non sei il Vecchio! Non sei lui, e non sei nemmeno come lui' [you aren't the Old Man! You aren't him and you aren't even like him] (106). The death of this father figure is linked to a need to step up and assume new responsibilities, although there are no familial ties here, and, over the course of the book, it becomes clear that the patriarch wished to toy with Scialoja and maintain power even from beyond the grave, deliberately creating a rivalry with Stalin Rossetti, the head of the Catena, who feels he is the rightful heir. There was no neat passing-on of the inheritance of 'il Vecchio', but rather a desire to create fraternal infighting and maintain chaos as his legacy. Neither is Scialoja's inheritance something to be desired, but rather a cross to bear as he struggles with his own authority and legitimacy against the backdrop of Berlusconi coming to power and, towards the end of the narrative, the various bomb attacks around Italy at that time, connected to Cosa Nostra. This is one of the epic threshold moments discussed in chapter 1.

Generational issues are present in the text in the many different facets of society depicted, not simply in the figure of 'il Vecchio' in politics. De Cataldo introduces the already deceased character of 'il Fondatore' [the Founder], who represents the capitalist patriarch, head of a successful business, the control of which has now been passed down to the next generation. 'Il Fondatore' is remembered by his daughter Maya as controlling and authoritarian; she desired an affectionate and normal father: 'Non grande, non invidiato, non terribile come Giove in terra. Non come quel Fondatore' [Not great, not envied, not terrible like Jove on earth. Not like that Founder] (247). Outside the law, Cosa Nostra is portrayed as following a similar power structure. It is wrestling with the now absent father figure of Totò Riina, with a nostalgia for a glorious past and with its younger members pushing back against their elders. Zu' Cosimo — who bears a strong resemblance to Bernardo Provenzano, the real-life Mafia Godfather — tells the boss of the new guard: 'è cosa triste, Angelino, quando i giovani voltano le spalle ai vecchi' [it is a sad thing, Angelino, when the young turn their backs on the old] (188). Every aspect of De Cataldo's world is dealing with authority and generational problems.

Nelle mani giuste is described by Wu Ming 1 (2009a: 12) in the Memorandum as an experiment in poetic prose, and, certainly, De Cataldo's use of language when exploring this key point in time draws attention. Aside from the strongly oral quality that is present in many NIE texts, expressing the varieties of spoken Italian, such as the Sicilian background of characters like zu' Cosimo or the cadences of Rome, De Cataldo frequently employs rhetorical and poetic effects. The first time the reader comes up against this is near the beginning, when the narrator elucidates what can be seen as a sort of 'A to Z' of Italian culture and society, accumulating an alliterative list starting with 'Artigiani, assassini, architetti, antifascisti, anticommunisti, artisti' [Artisans, assassins, architects, anti-fascists, anti-communists, artists] (35). Elsewhere in the text, the use of rhetorical questions and anaphora is widespread. To give one of many of examples: 'Stalin Rossetti trafficava con la sacra corona unita. | Stalin Rossetti trafficava con i serbi. | Stalin Rossetti trafficava con gli albanesi' [Stalin Rossetti trafficked with the United Sacred Crown. | Stalin Rossetti trafficked with the Serbs. | Stalin Rossetti trafficked with the Albanians], and so it continues (92–93). This gives the text a certain vibrancy and liveliness that Wu Ming 1 would align with epic qualities, and it also foregrounds language and how it is being used. As Genna self-consciously instructs his readers how to approach his text in *Italia De Profundis*, De Cataldo seems to want to direct our focus towards his own storytelling, rather than simply drawing the reader into a verisimilar world.

Within such playing on words, the text's title resonates in various ways. The 'right hands' recall the 'Clean Hands' judicial investigations of the time. They also imply Scialoja's hands into which 'il Vecchio''s power and archive of documents have been placed: 'Che immensa fonte di potere, nelle mani giuste' [What an immense source of power, in the right hands] (332). The 'right hands' also suggest the inverse, the 'wrong hands', which is arguably the sensation given to the reader when Senator Argenti reflects towards the end of the text, on the eve of Berlusconi's election win: 'La Storia avrebbe consegnato l'Italia nelle mani giuste' [History would put Italy in the right hands] (295). Despite Argenti's assertion, there is a strong sense that in 1993 something did not change hands correctly. Yet, there is also a certain amount of ambiguity whether the situation can be corrected, as shown by the repetition of ideas about change: 'le cose cambiano' [things change] (89, 90, 91), 'Ma le cose possono mai cambiare?' [But can things ever change?] (162), 'le cose cambieranno' [things will change] (273, 274), 'Cambieranno?' [Will they change?] (273). In the epilogue, when Rossetti becomes the new successor of 'il Vecchio', he reflects: 'Le cose tornavano al loro posto' [Things were going back to their place] (331). This recalls the idea famously expressed in Giuseppe Tomasi di Lampedusa's historical novel *Il gattopardo* [*The Leopard*]: 'Se vogliamo che tutto rimanga come è, bisogna che tutto cambi' [If we want things to stay as they are, things will have to change] (1969: 41).[22] Perhaps the right hands are simply the hands that have always held the power.

Nevertheless, De Cataldo has Rossetti killed almost immediately after he gets his hands on the inheritance, and the secret archive is burnt down, like Genna's tourist resort in *Italia De Profundis*. By burning these secrets, and having Scialoja disappear without trace — 'Nessuno sa che fine abbia fatto' [Nobody knows what happened to him] (336) — De Cataldo leaves the text open as to what remains of the father figure, and of Italy's shadowy recent past. As in Genna's text, razing this fictional space to the ground arguably leaves a sense of possibility regarding both their inheritance and the future. In the final pages, just after Rossetti's death, the narrator poses the question: 'Ma esistevano mani giuste?' [But did the right hands exist?] (332). The text resists a sense of closure, leaving open questions about paternity and succession. This can be compared to Stendhal's approach in *Le Rouge et le noir*, whose narrative, after a postponed conclusion, abruptly ends with the guillotine. Brooks says of the text:

> *Le Rouge et le noir* solicits our attention and frustrates our expectation because we have some sense of the fitting biographical pattern: one in which sons inherit from fathers and pass on [...] a wisdom gained, a point of understanding attained. Stendhal's perversity may make us realize that such a patterning is both necessary and suspect, the product of an interpretation motivated by desire. (Brooks 1984: 89)

De Cataldo and Genna similarly destabilise their readers' desire for closure, or for a straightforward story about the loss of a father figure, instead posing questions about inheritance and responsibility. The ending of *Nelle mani giuste* could be seen as part of a desire to question that 'natural' order of things in Italy, as the new inheritor Rossetti is immediately killed, and the former inheritor disappears, and even what they were to inherit goes up in flames. In Recalcati's terms, De Cataldo, like Genna (or Stendhal), would seem to be calling on this generation to reconquer their inheritance through this frustration of expectation.

Giglioli, however, sees De Cataldo's work in terms of a renunciation of responsibility. He takes issue with the figure of the Grande Vecchio, the puppet master controlling events from behind the scenes that appears in De Cataldo's texts and others, such as the eponymous protagonist of Luther Blissett's *Q*. For Giglioli, the need for such a figure springs from anxieties about agency in the modern age, the result of a godless universe where texts no longer have a Manzonian idea of providence to give meaning to events.[23] In the choice of contemporary writers to fictionalise about history in this way, Giglioli detects a 'forte impulso risarcitorio' [strong compensatory impulse] (2011: 47), which supposedly demonstrates their desire to justify the failures of the present through their historical novels, and, in doing so, to underline both our impotence and lack of culpability in today's world.

However, it is arguable whether De Cataldo is offering us reassurance of any kind through his fictionalising in *Nelle mani giuste*. He has said that he specifically conceived of the character of 'il Vecchio' in order to provide a godlike figure who represented chaos as opposed to a Manzonian divine providence (Antonello and O'Leary 2009: 355). As described above, there is not a neatness to his legacy, neither is there a clear order in his approach to politics, in which he seemed simply to pursue power for power's sake. By adding the Catena behind the real-life Gladio network, De Cataldo multiplies the levels of secrecy and conspiracy of his fictional world, giving a strong sense that there may be no centre to these manifold layers, no transcendental organisational principle to the chaotic entanglements of mafia and state. Yet, this does not signal Giglioli's impulse to compensate; rather, De Cataldo is negotiating the holes in public knowledge about what happened in the early 1990s, and indeed earlier in the case of *Romanzo criminale*. By narrating conspiracies and inventing a fantastical and omnipotent patriarch, he is inserting his fiction into the gaps of history. In an interview, De Cataldo linked his approach precisely to that of Manzoni in *I promessi sposi* [*The Betrothed*] and 'Storia della colonna infame' [History of the Column of Infamy] in the ways Manzoni negotiated between 'true' and 'verisimilar' (Antonello and O'Leary 2009: 358). This is particularly interesting in reference to the discussion of the historical novels that I address in the next chapter, tracing the approach of these writers back to the 'father' of the modern Italian historical novel. Like Manzoni, De Cataldo's allegorical approach to his subject matter helps to shed light on the present. We are not supposed to take his 'solutions' to the unsolved mysteries of the recent past at face value, or see them as replacing a Manzonian providence. Like Genna's *Medium*, this is a flight of the imagination, yet one that has a bearing on reality.

Moreover, whilst Giglioli (2011: 29) may refer to writers like De Cataldo writing paranoid stories, the use of conspiracy theories is entirely appropriate in reference to Italy's recent past. The Bologna bombing and Moro's death that are addressed in *Romanzo criminale* are just two well-known examples of the many Italian mysteries that continue to unfold, as shown by the ongoing revelations of the investigation into the Moro kidnapping.[24] The 'Mafia Capitale' scandals that were uncovered in 2014 demonstrate that De Cataldo's portrayals of the links between organised crime and state officials in Rome are not very far removed from the reality. De Michele (2008a) places De Cataldo's text among others that are attempting to 'dire l'indicibile nel paese dei misteri' [say the unsayable in the country of mysteries], and Genna said of De Cataldo in a review of *Nelle mani giuste*:

> affronta il soggetto più difficile, imprendibile e scivoloso che uno scrittore
> italiano possa mettersi in testa di romanzare — cioè il passaggio post-Muro

> e la stagione delle bombe agli Uffizi, al PAC di Milano, alle chiese di Roma, oltre che l'attentato a Costanzo, nel '93 [...] un periodo circa il quale non si è confortati da nulla, da nessuna opera di riflessione e ricomposizione. (Genna 2007c)

> [he tackles the most difficult, impregnable and slippery subject that an Italian writer can decide to fictionalise about — the post-Wall transition and the time of bombs in the Uffizi, in the PAC in Milan, in the churches in Rome, as well as the attack in Costanzo, in '93 [...] a period with nothing comforting, with no work of reflection and recomposition.]

By reimagining events such as the Via dei Georgofili Massacre,[25] De Cataldo helps Italy begin to confront a traumatic recent past that had been previously overlooked by writers.

De Cataldo tells us in the 'Warning for the reader' at the beginning of the book that he does not betray history, but rather interprets it by representing 'eventi reali sotto il segno della Metafora' [real events under the sign of the Metaphor] (2). From a psychoanalytical angle, the word 'metaphor', eye-catchingly capitalised, recalls Freud's *The Interpretation of Dreams*, or Lacan's thesis that the unconscious is structured like a language. The choice of word can thus be read as another conscious or unconscious signal that we are addressing a repressed and unresolved conflict through this narrative. Like Genna's fictionalising around his father's death in *Medium*, De Cataldo seems to be playing out his (and his readers') wish to deal with something that resists being dealt with in a straightforward way, due to a lack of knowledge about, or understanding of, the past. De Cataldo uses the power of storytelling to help process a difficult and incomplete legacy even without the proof. As Genna said in a review, De Cataldo was one of the first writers to truly address the period following the end of the Cold War: 'è il primo intellettuale e narratore a compiere il gesto: gli anni Novanta entrano nella letteratura. Questo è l'inizio di un metabolismo' [he is the first intellectual and narrator to make the gesture: the nineties enter literature. This is the beginning of a metabolism] (Genna 2007c). With a continuing lack of closure, how can the gaps of the past be bridged if not through fictionalising, and how can this generation begin to digest what happened?

Sirene by Laura Pugno

Sirene (2007) fictionalises our future rather than our past in order to consider parental legacies and responsibility. It was Pugno's first novel — she also writes poetry — and, like much of her work, it includes fantastical elements, here in imagining a future dystopia in which mermaids exist. It is one of a large number of twenty-first-century Italian novels that have a dystopian setting; as Fulginiti rightly states: 'it is hard to deny that a dystopian tide is rising in Italian science fiction' (Fulginiti 2014: 161). This can be seen, for example, in Wu Ming 5's *Free Karma Food* (2006), set in 2025, when cows and pigs have been wiped out,[26] or Tommaso Pincio's *Cinacittà* (2008), which takes place in a Rome suffering a constant heatwave due to weather changes. Like *Sirene*, this could also be labelled cli-fi or climate change fiction, using literature to think through the possible consequences of the environmental damage being done now to our planet.

Whilst Wu Ming 5 and Pincio are NIE writers, there has been some controversy over whether Pugno's text can be seen as part of the nebula, although I would argue that it certainly aligns with its characteristics. Combining intermedial elements — as the author acknowledges in her 'Note' at the end, she was inspired by a range of different artistic expressions, including Japanese manga, art and architecture (147) — in a science fiction narrative that comments on some of the pressing concerns facing humanity through an oblique gaze, Pugno's text certainly seems to be a UNO, as well as adhering to Wu Ming 1's formulation of '*Complessità narrativa, attitudine* popular' [*Narrative complexity, popular attitude*] (Wu Ming 1 2009a: 32). Yet, Pugno is another female author whose work has been excluded from the nebula: as Wu Ming 1 explains in a comments thread on *Tabard* under an article by Mari reviewing *Sirene*, he had not read the text at the time of the Memorandum, and his debate with Mari seems to conclude that Pugno's text is not political enough for the NIE, particularly because it does not take a position regarding history (see Mari 2008). However, Jansen has rightly called into question this reading, pointing out that Pugno's poetics are more similar to those put forward in the Memorandum than this debate acknowledges (Jansen 2010: 105–06), and Rushing too has convincingly argued that '*Sirene* is an excellent exemplar of the NIE' (2011). We will certainly see a strong political undertone to Pugno's narrative, which, even if it does not engage with history to the extent that Mari and Wu Ming 1 feel it should, indirectly shows how the past and present might contribute to the future Pugno imagines — Rushing (2011) interestingly calls it 'a counter-factual history of the future' — as well as considering generational issues from a different perspective from other writers in the nebula. Pugno was also one of the writers interviewed as part of *Allegoria*'s special issue on the alleged 'return to reality' in recent Italian literature that I address in chapter 4; like many of the other writers interviewed, she expressed scepticism about it (Donnarumma and Policastro 2008: 21–22). She states of her own realism that it comes not from being realistic, but from her texts being 'radicati fortemente nel presente: per me il realismo è questo, essere nel nostro presente (e nel futuro)' [firmly rooted in the present: this is realism for me, being in our present (and in the future)] (Donnarumma and Policastro 2008: 22). We will see that, even within the imagined dystopia of *Sirene*, we can detect important elements of Italy's and the world's current reality, and warnings about our possible future.

In *Sirene*, parts of the Earth have been submerged under water due to climate change, and the human population has been decimated by a new contagious strain of skin cancer: 'Qualcosa era cambiato nell'atmosfera, negli strati di protezione che separavano la Terra dalla stella del suo Sistema, e ora il sole sembrava voler divorare l'umanità come un dio maligno' [Something had changed in the atmosphere, in the layers of protection that separated the Earth from the star of its System, and now the sun seemed to want to devour humanity like a malicious god] (10). This must be a near future, still in the twenty-first century, judging by the only clue we have in the text regarding the time it is set: the main protagonist, Samuel, notes that the white suits they wear to protect themselves from people suffering from the contagious disease are 'da astronauti anni Sessanta del secolo scorso' [from astronauts in the sixties of the last century] (78). The story takes place on the coast of Nuova Baja California or NuBaCa, where the privileged live in the city of Underwater protected from the sun's harmful rays; the poor must take their chances above ground, where there is a continuous state of emergency, with the authorities attempting to contain the cancer victims with Tasers (78). This is a cruel reality that continues to be dictated by capitalist structures even after the apocalypse has come. Before the epidemic of skin cancer, mermaids were discovered; Pugno thus inserts a mythological element into this world she imagines in a fantastical unsettling of the otherwise realist portrayal of her dystopia. However, as I will show later, the figure of the mermaid contains familiar elements that are indirect critiques of our world. The mermaids are 'read' in different ways by the humans in the book, from the Mermaid Liberation Front who believe that they are the world's only hope (35) to those who believe that they signal the end of humanity, 'una mutazione genetica [...] per fronteggiare un mondo da cui l'essere umano era destinato a sparire' [a genetic mutation [...] to face a world the human being was destined to disappear from] (10), to those who even think that 'I mostri sono tornati. Sirene e lebbrosi. È l'era dei mostri. Siate pronti' [Monsters have returned. Sirens and lepers. It is the era of monsters. Be ready] (77). They seem primarily to reflect human desires and anxieties, and, indeed, they are only seen through human eyes for much of the text, objects rather than subjects of the narrative, until the very end. They are immune to the sun's harmful rays; yet, scientists realised they could not reproduce this in humans, and so they are simply exploited for their meat and as sexual objects. Samuel is in charge of mermaids kept in captivity by the Yakuza, who control much of NuBaCa. In secret and to his surprise, Samuel manages to impregnate a mermaid, who gives birth to perhaps the first human–mermaid hybrid, whom he names Mia. Samuel attempts to hide Mia from the Yakuza and also impregnates her, eventually managing to free her from captivity into the ocean, pregnant with Samuel's child as he is dying from skin cancer.

At first glance, Pugno's text might be seen as quite far removed from those that explore 'la morte del Vecchio', not just thematically but also in terms of its style, which lacks Genna's postmodernist metafictional moments or De Cataldo's rhetorical flourishes, instead displaying an understated and pared back use of language. Yet, there are several parallels with the concerns that we have seen Wu Ming 1 and others voice. The world of *Sirene* is in a posthumous condition, given the fate of many humans and of the world above ground as we know it. By the end of the narrative, the Yakuza are abandoning NuBaCa for Africa, where some people are immune to skin cancer, but there is a sense that it might be too late for humanity's salvation. Not only is Samuel a survivor of this catastrophe — at least for most of the narrative, until he is struck down with the deadly disease — but he is also an orphan. His father, who was a hitman for the Yakuza, killed his mother then himself when Samuel was just a child, which doctors made Samuel forget in a process now available called 'memory cleansing' (14); in this repressive brave new world, traumatic past events must be erased rather than processed, as humanity seems to hurtle towards its demise without examining its own legacies. Questions of inheritance are also explored in the hybrids that Samuel fathers, Mia and her child, whom he realises towards the end of the narrative might be the salvation of humans, giving them resistance to skin cancer: 'Il dna di sirena era forse la cura. I corpi della nuova specie di ibridi, miscelata al giusto grado di homo sapiens, sarebbero stati immune?' [Siren DNA was perhaps the cure. Would the bodies of the new species of hybrids, mixed to the right degree with Homo sapiens, be immune?] (138). Yet, these questions of inheritance are left open as they are in Genna's and De Cataldo's texts, as Mia simply swims off into the ocean with other mermaids at the end without knowing where she is on a human map (145).

Through the mythological figure of the mermaid, Pugno raises issues related to animal cruelty, gender and race alongside her exploration of environmental issues, in a text that is more wide-ranging than Genna's and De Cataldo's focus purely on Italy through a male lens. Pugno's employment of mythological elements thus opens out to consider wider issues, just as Wu Ming 1 envisaged for the NIE, although these go beyond the limited focus of his nebula. In a resemblance to how we treat many animals today, mermaids have been overfished so that they are almost extinct in the wild, and those in captivity are given hormones and fattened up to be more fertile for breeding, leading to birth defects (28–29) and tumours (58), all to provide food for humans, despite the best efforts of the Mermaid Liberation Front to protect them. Those who can afford it enjoy types of mermaid meat that recall controversial meat products in our world, such as siren veal (59) and siren *foie gras* (76). Pugno is making an indirect comment on our eating habits now and the effects that they have on our environment and on animals, who, like mermaids, may be closer to humans than many realise.

It is interesting that Sadako, Samuel's now deceased girlfriend, was a vegan; ecological damage and unethical consumption come from men in Pugno's narrative, as environmental and gender issues seem to go hand in hand. Indeed, this nightmarish future has been created not only by natural disasters, but also by the actions of humans, specifically men. There are only two human female characters in the narrative, who have little agency and are violently exploited by men, both ultimately dying: Ivy, the Mermaid Liberation Front activist blackmailed by Samuel until she commits suicide, and Sadako, who was given to Samuel as a 'gift' by the Yakuza, and whose life before she died of skin cancer was characterised by sexual exploitation by men. She was even branded like a mermaid by the Yakuza (63), and, after her death, Samuel wanted to eat her (65–66). Clear parallels are drawn between Sadako and Mia when Samuel decides to tattoo the mermaid with the same tattoos as his girlfriend had; both Sadako and Mia are described in identical wording as being 'carta di riso' [rice paper] (95 and 96), like blank canvases that men can use as they wish. The female mermaids have become the objects of human desire and exploited sexually in brothels, and there are various rapes of mermaids in the narrative: Samuel rapes both Mia's mother and Mia, whose name indicates the sense of possession he feels he has over her. The damaging effects of male-dominated patriarchal culture are shown by Pugno through her portrayal of this violent and environmentally damaged world that treats females badly, whether mermaids or humans. Fulginiti rightly states: 'Matricide and earthicide clearly overlap in the environmental dystopia in *Sirens*, whose plot is marked by metaphors of maternal fluids (blood, milk, and water), by a succession of female generations, and by violence against bodies gendered female' (2014: 163). Science fiction is generally a male-dominated genre, but Pugno's approach brings up gender issues, which have not traditionally been at the centre of the genre. In the future depicted, female emancipation has not advanced, and if anything has been set back. Pugno's text is a warning that human progress is not always linear and forward-moving, but, as De Cataldo shows too, although overlooking sexual politics, it can stagnate or even move backwards. Pugno enacts the kind of eco-centric thought that Wu Ming 1 describes but with a feminist slant.

There are also racist, colonial undertones to the treatment of mermaids in *Sirene*. When they are first discovered by humans, they are washing up dead on the shores, obliquely suggesting the bodies of migrants who have died trying to reach Italy's shores in recent years. As a child, Samuel visits a mermaid museum but has a fever when he comes home; his father comments that he must have 'il mal di sirena' [the siren bug], saying that it is incurable like 'il mal d'Africa' [the African bug] (15), wording that suggests a parallel with an orientalising gaze on an African Other. Despite the men in Pugno's narrative lusting after these exoticised creatures that are both familiar in their human traits and seen as Other, only sterile mermaids are sent to brothels, recalling colonial fears of miscegenation. Clearly, there is an underlying historical element in Pugno's text, contrary to the debate on *Tabard*.

The ending of *Sirene* is left ambiguous by Pugno and can be interpreted in different ways, as encapsulated in the final line: 'La mente di Mia era tabula rasa' [Mia's mind was a tabula rasa] (145). Although, as Rushing points out, it seems that humans will not survive in the future — the Yakuza's slim hope of the cure to the skin cancer epidemic in the semi-extinct bushmen in Africa is ironically described as 'un future radioso' [a radiant future] (144), 'as this "radiant" future is assuredly a future that is radioactive, more filled with the sun's deadly rays than ever before' (Rushing 2011) — I would disagree with Rushing's argument that 'Pugno's grim "tabula rasa" is an image of "no future"' (2011). Mia and the child she is carrying could offer a new path for humanity through hybridity, and the future, like Mia's mind, seems to be a blank slate. Indeed, through *Sirene*'s portrayal of the damaging effects of (male) human actions and the sense of community and possibility in the group of mermaids we are left with at the end, Pugno suggests that there might be hope in a post-apocalyptic, post-anthropocentric, possibly posthuman world. She does not seem to be saying that this world will certainly be a positive one, but insists on ambiguity. We see this too earlier in the narrative, when the wildness of the coast of NuBaCa after the epidemic has forced most humans underground is described as having 'una bellezza ancora maggiore, più antica e atroce, era un mondo a sé stante, splendido e inospitale' [an even greater beauty, more ancient and atrocious; it was a world of its own, splendid and inhospitable] (87); the posthuman landscape may be more beautiful, but it is also more savage. Pugno is encouraging her readers to consider what might lie in store for us without offering straightforward answers, just as we have seen an openness in the endings of Genna's and De Cataldo's texts. It is striking that when Samuel jumps into the ocean at the end to save Mia from captivity, which will lead to his death, it is described using a birth metaphor, likening the water to a placenta (117); again, Pugno's narrative has a sense of ambiguity, here linking together death and life, endings and beginnings.

Pugno's text invites comparisons with Braidotti's work on the productive potential of thinking through non-dominant perspectives in our posthuman condition. Braidotti sees this condition 'as an opportunity to empower the pursuit of alternative schemes of thought, knowledge and self-representation. The posthuman condition urges us to think critically and creatively about who or what we are actually in the process of becoming' (Braidotti 2013: 12).[27] Pugno thinks through what Braidotti (2013: 60) describes as 'the opportunistic trans-species commodification of Life that is the logic of advanced capitalism' in imagining an extreme version of this commodification through the addition of the species of mermaids, who are ruthlessly exploited for profit and consumed in ways that recall our treatment of animals in today's world, alongside humans at the mercy of where they can afford to live in this world ravaged by skin cancer but still adhering to capitalist logic. The mermaids embody the 'blurring of the distinction between the human and other species when it comes to profiting from them' (Braidotti 2013: 63), given that the females are repeatedly shown to resemble humans so closely at times that it is unsettling to the humans, as seen when Samuel must repeatedly remind himself that Mia's mother is a mermaid — 'È una sirena, si ripeté, non un essere umano' [It is a siren, he repeated to himself, not a human being] (32) — just as he reminds himself in almost the same wording about Mia — 'Era una sirena, non un essere umano' [It was a siren, not a human being] (57). There is an additional sense of blurring the human–mermaid distinction in the linking of the exploitation of the human women with that of the mermaids, as I explored above. Pugno's text critically and creatively thinks through humans' treatment of nature and animals and the anthropocentrism that we operate under in today's world.

Interestingly, as mentioned earlier, Wu Ming 1 has underlined the importance of perspectives that might be seen as very similar to Pugno's. In the Memorandum, he argues that, in the light of imminent disasters of different kinds, the oblique gaze of the NIE can help us consider other points of view: 'è tanto importante la questione del punto di vista obliquo, e diverrà sempre più importante — come aveva intuito Calvino — la "resa" letteraria di sguardi extra-umani, non-umani, non-identificabili. Questi esperimenti ci aiutano a uscire da noi stessi' [the question of the oblique view point is so important, and — as Calvino guessed — the literary 'rendering' of extra-human, non-human, unidentifiable gazes will become increasingly important. These experiments help us to come out of ourselves] (Wu Ming 1 2009a: 58). This is a particularly interesting proposition by Wu Ming 1, but one that finds limited responses in the nebula he sets out, which could be linked to the male focus of the NIE. Moving away from patricide can help reflect on questions of responsibility for the planet's future, and Pugno's narrative very decisively calls into question a male-centric and, indeed, anthropocentric viewpoint. Wu Ming 1's reference to unidentifiable gazes suggests that the UNO is not only unidentified in its generic hybridity, but that it is fertile ground for exploring new and unexpected perspectives that might help shed light on the complexities of our world today. Narratives such as Pugno's can alert us — like the alternative meaning of the sirens in the text's title — to the damaging effects of our behaviour in the present in an attempt to have an impact on the future. Wu Ming 1 states: 'Oggi arte e letteratura non possono limitarsi a suonare allarmi tardivi: devono aiutarci a immaginare vie d'uscita' [Today art and literature cannot restrict themselves to sounding belated alarms: they must help us to imagine ways out] (2009a: 60). Yet, an insistence on patricide in the NIE in order to drive forward cultural change could be seen as sounding belated alarms, or at least as a limited way of addressing the current situation.

It is significant that all of the texts I have analysed in this chapter that address parental legacies and responsibility include apocalyptic elements, as seen in *Medium* when Genna's father foresees the end of the world, in the fires that close both Genna's *Italia De Profundis* and De Cataldo's *Nelle mani giuste*, and in Pugno's imaginings about environmental apocalypse. Apocalypse and inheritance are certainly not completely divorced from one another as narrative concerns: they both intertwine questions of endings and beginnings, as seen, for example, in what Mussgnug has described as 'last man fictions' (2012: 333), in which the protagonist has responsibility for the continuation of the species. Kermode has argued that the ways in which narratives construct endings illustrate anxieties about their authors' own times and world-view: 'The apocalyptic types — empire, decadence and renovation, progress and catastrophe — are fed by history and underlie our ways of making sense of the world from where we stand, in the middest' (Kermode 2000: 29). Kermode's wording here very much recalls the quotation from Brooks in the introduction to this chapter about 'the conflict of movement and resistance, revolution and restoration' (Kermode 1984: 65). The focus of these texts on questions of apocalypse gives a sense, once again, that these writers feel that they are at a watershed moment; they are attempting to make sense of the world in the midst of what has been perceived as a crisis in terms of the political, economic, cultural and environmental situation.

Contrary to what Giglioli has implied, imagining alternative realities, as Genna, De Cataldo and Pugno do, does not signal a desire to escape reality by finding easy answers to difficult questions. Rather than being an abdication of responsibility, it can be seen as part of a need to take responsibility, one that is done through storytelling. However, this responsibility needs to be considered beyond the questions of paternity that have been the primary focus of the NIE. Despite the interesting and experimental approaches to narrative that we have seen in the male writers analysed in this chapter, whose focus on the theme of 'la morte del Vecchio' begins to metabolise the difficult recent past, Pugno's text indicates that moving away from questions of paternity and from male — or indeed anthropocentric —

viewpoints can help to address some of the more urgent questions in the present through new perspectives, as part of an enlarged community. As Godani states: 'non è più tempo di re, *non è più tempo di padri*' [the time of kings is over, *the time of fathers is over*] (2014: 20).

Notes to Chapter 2

1. The only exception indicated in Wu Ming 1's list that explores the death of a female progenitor is Bajani's *Se consideri le colpe* [*If You Consider the Faults*] (Wu Ming 1 2009a: 74), in which the protagonist goes to Romania after his mother's death to learn about her life there, working through 'le macerie del passato' [the rubble of the past] (Bajani 2007: 51). Recalcati also examines this text in *Le mani della madre* (Recalcati 2015: 128–30).

2. Sambuco points to the growth of interest in examining the mother–daughter relationship since the 1980s, as seen, for example, in the work of Francesca Sanvitale, Fabrizia Ramondino and Elena Stancanelli (Sambuco 2012: 5). Lucamante has shown how Italian women's writing since the 1960s has interestingly and experimentally examined both the mother–daughter and the father–daughter relationship (Lucamante 2008).

3. See, for example, Giorgio 2002 and Sambuco 2012. See also the AHRC-funded network 'La Mamma Italiana: Interrogating a National Stereotype' (https://lamammaitaliana.wordpress.com/).

4. I have chosen to focus on texts by Genna and De Cataldo as they make explicit connections between their stories and Italy's current situation. However, the subject matter of 'la morte del Vecchio' does resurface in other early twenty-first-century Italian texts, albeit in slightly different forms, as Wu Ming 1 points out in the Memorandum (2009a: 74).

5. For example, Nanni Moretti's film *Habemus papam* (Recalcati 2013: 20–21) or Tornatore's film *Nuovo Cinema Paradiso* (Recalcati 2013: 142).

6. For example, Cormac McCarthy's novel *The Road* (Recalcati 2011: 155–70) or Clint Eastwood's films *Million Dollar Baby* and *Gran Torino* (Recalcati 2011: 171–89).

7. Deleuze and Guattari's *L'anti-Oedipe* (1972) ushered in a new, decentred and rhizomatic paradigm. Recalcati (2013: 103) has said of *L'anti-Oedipe* that it mobilised his generation, that linked to the 1977 political protests. Indeed, Deleuze's influence can be detected in Radio Alice, the Bolognese independent radio station linked to the protests of 1977, an important reference point for recent Italian writers (as we saw in chapter 1).

8. As well as referencing Lacan, Deleuze and Guattari, and employing psychoanalytic terminology, Wu Ming 1 draws strongly on the theories of Recalcati, and refers to him directly in the notes at the end of the post, directing readers towards a video of the psychoanalyst (Wu Ming 1 2010a).

9. 'Vi siete mai chiesti perché l'Italia non ha avuta, in tutta la sua storia — da Roma ad oggi — una sola vera rivoluzione? La risposta — chiave che apre molte porte — è forse la storia d'Italia in poche righe. Gli italiani non sono parricidi; sono fratricidi. Romolo e Remo, Ferrucio e Maramaldo, Mussolini e i socialisti, Badoglio e Graziani [...] Gli italiani sono l'unico popolo (credo) che abbiano, alla base della loro storia (o della loro leggenda) un fratricidio.' (Saba 1993: 16). [Have you ever asked yourselves why Italy has not had, in all of its history — from Rome to today — a single true revolution? The answer — a key that opens many doors — is perhaps the history of Italy in a few lines. Italians are not patricidal; they are fratricidal. Romulus and Remus, Ferrucio and Maramaldo, Mussolini and the socialists, Badoglio and Graziani [...] Italians are the only people (I believe) who have at the basis of their history (or of their legend) a fratricide.]

10. This is also referenced by Godani (2014: 33–34).

11. The main protagonist of *Fine impero* also has a father who was an alcoholic and a communist, who died of cancer, and who had tried to commit suicide in the past. We also see the protagonist interviewing Houellebecq. As with *Italia De Profundis*, the ensuing story examines the emptiness

of modern-day Italy, reflecting on the difficulties of textual representation today: 'A fine impero è possibile descrivere soltanto. Non rappresentare, non troppo fingere' [At the end of empire it is only possible to describe. Not represent, not pretend too much] (Genna 2013: 128).

12. Owing to a lack of page numbers, I should specify that this quote comes from the 'Magia rossa' section. Further section references will be given in parentheses after quotations.

13. Other writers associated with the NIE have also embraced 'copyleft' principles: Luther Blissett/ Wu Ming, Kai Zen and De Michele made some or all of their texts freely available online.

14. An Italian writer most prolific in the 1960s and 1970s, Kolosimo engaged in what has been called *fantarcheologia* [archaeology fiction], or *archeologia spaziale* [space archaeology]: 'una fantascienza tesa a esplorare il remoto passato della Terra e a inventare spiegazioni legate all'esistenza di civiltà extraterrestri per le evidenze archeologiche lasciate dai popoli antichi' [a science fiction aimed at exploring the remote past of the Earth and inventing explanations related to the existence of extraterrestrial civilizations for the archaeological evidence left by ancient peoples] (Iannuzzi 2014: 107). Wu Ming have written about Kolosimo's unusual conflation of science fiction and political reality (Wu Ming 2014b), which Genna's text comes to resemble as it goes on.

15. I will return to ideas about apocalypse later in this chapter.

16. See <http://www.giugenna.com/2008/12/03/da-italia-de-profundis-ipertesto-della-scena-italiana-come-inferno>.

17. Antonello (2012: 23) points out that in Italy this nostalgia for the past is more acute given the paternalistic nature of Italian society and culture, as shown by the recent movement known as the TQ, whose 2011 manifesto protested against their generation's exclusion from the country's political and productive life (see chapter 1). As Antonello (2012: 23) states, it is striking that they framed this protest precisely in terms of age (TQ refers to people in their thirties and forties), demonstrating the clear presence of generational conflict in Italian public life that has spilled over into cultural production. Twenty-first-century Italian writers have also attempted to fight against limiting views about their generation and, as we shall see here and in chapter 4, in some ways revive Pasolini's legacy for the twenty-first century.

18. See Patti 2010 for a detailed and effective analysis of precisely how Genna draws on Pasolini and *Petrolio*.

19. He also mentions Wu Ming 1's 'We're Going to Have to Be the Parents' when discussing Wallace's death (324).

20. 'I have seen a toupee on a thirteen-year-old boy [...] I've seen fluorescent luggage and fluorescent sunglasses and fluorescent pince-nez and over twenty different makes of rubber thong. I have [...] watched a woman in silver lamé projectile-vomit inside a glass elevator' (Wallace 1998: 257).

21. Genna (and also Wallace) could arguably be seen as inhabiting the position that Burns describes in relation to Tondelli in his work, that of 'being at once present and absent, inside and outside [...] It is the condition of the observer, detaching himself from the scene to attain a perspective which allows thorough examination of that scene, so generating a cognitive or emotional participation' (Burns 2001: 117). Tondelli must be an unspoken reference for Genna, not only through this positioning, but also in his exploration of desire in order to indirectly comment on contemporary societal issues. Genna's *Italia De Profundis* particularly echoes Tondelli's *Rimini*, which similarly explored the empty enjoyment of holidaymaking and the pain of thwarted desires through a series of fragments loosely bound together, reflecting himself in the character of Bruno May.

22. This comparison seems particularly relevant in that *Il gattopardo* addresses another failed revolution and foundational moment of the Italian state, the Risorgimento, which is also represented in the historical novels that I discuss in chapter 3.

23. For Brooks, such anxieties were already present in the nineteenth-century novels he analyses: 'The enormous narrative production of the nineteenth century may suggest an anxiety at the loss of providential plots: the plotting of the individual or social or institutional life story takes on new urgency when one no longer can look to a sacred masterplot that organizes and explains the world.' (Brooks 1984: 6).

24. For example, there have been revelations surrounding the role of the American Steve Pieczenik in Moro's kidnapping and death (see Bianconi 2014).

25. In 1993, a car bomb planted by Cosa Nostra exploded on a street behind the Uffizi Gallery in Florence, killing five people.

26. It is also transmedial in its extension through a well-developed website: https://www.wumingfoundation.com/italiano/freekarmafood/index.html.

27. Fulginiti (2014: 162–63) also draws parallels with Braidotti's work, but with the productive and transgressive potential of monstrosity in *Metamorphoses* (Braidotti 2002), and Fulginiti then connects this to the Memorandum on the NIE, but with a focus on questions of consumption and animality through comparing *Sirene* to Wu Ming 5's *Free Karma Food*.

CHAPTER 3

On the Historical Novel

In 1992, the same year seen as the beginning of the New Italian Epic (NIE), Fukuyama famously claimed that we were reaching the end of history. Subsequent momentous historical events, such as the terrorist attacks of 9/11, clearly undermined the post-Cold War optimism of Fukuyama's statement. Since then, there have also been substantial developments in the study of history, related to the growth in importance of cultural memory studies, as well as to a renewed interest from novelists in history, as seen in the huge popularity of historical fiction in the new millennium. Anderson states: 'Today, the historical novel has become, at the upper ranges of fiction, more widespread than it was even at the height of its classical period in the early 19th century' (2011). Just glancing at the winners of literary prizes in several western European countries at the beginning of the twenty-first century, we can see a large number of examples. In France, the Goncourt Prize since 2000 has been dominated by historical novels, including Jonathan Littell's *Les Bienveillantes* [*The Kindly Ones*], which won in 2006, or Laurent Binet's *HHhH*, which won the Goncourt Prize for a First Novel in 2010.[1] In Britain, the Booker Prize has been won by Margaret Atwood's *The Blind Assassin* (2000), Peter Carey's *True History of the Kelly Gang* (2001), Alan Hollinghurst's *The Line of Beauty* (2004), and Hilary Mantel's *Wolf Hall* (2009) and *Bring up the Bodies* (2012). In Spain, Javier Cercas won the National Novel Prize for *Anatomía de un instante* [*The Anatomy of a Moment*] in 2010, the same year that Antonio Pennacchi won the Strega Prize in Italy for *Canale Mussolini* [*The Mussolini Canal*].

This boom in historical fiction could be seen as surprising in the light of what Jameson (1991: 22) has described as a 'crisis in historicity' that characterised late twentieth-century cultural production, and the structuralist and poststructuralist turn that saw theorists such as Roland Barthes (1986) arguing that history was a discourse that only generated a reality effect. However, Boxall has noted in the twenty-first century 'an attempt to rethink the relationship between history and narrative, and to gain a new understanding of the way that historical material asserts itself in the contemporary imagination' (2013: 41). In his analysis of recent historical fiction, such as W. G. Sebald's *Austerlitz* (a prime example of an unidentified narrative object from beyond Italy's borders) and Ian McEwan's *Atonement*, Boxall detects a 'twin pressure — the political desire for historical realism and the self-reflexive aesthetic engagement with the limits of narrative in capturing experience' (2013: 81). We will see a similar twin pressure in the texts analysed in this chapter.

That is not to say that there has not been a radical break between twentieth-century historical novels and those of the new millennium. Elias describes many texts of the latter half of the twentieth century as embodying a concept of history as something that can never be fully accessed or grasped: 'for the post-traumatic metahistorical imagination, history is desire, the desire for the unceasingly deferred, sublime space of History' (2001: 187). As Boscolo argues, this desire can also be detected in the historical novels of the NIE nebula (2010b: 25–28),[2] and, I would argue, in recent historical novels from beyond the nebula, as well as from beyond Italy's borders. It is interesting that Elias sees the desire to confront the past in the texts she analyses as linked to a sense of trauma, or '"history that hurts"' (2001: 187), in some cases related to the legacy of colonialism. Similarly, as we have already seen previously and will see once again here, these UNOs often address or 'remediate'[3] traumatic, unresolved experiences from the past.

Contemporary writers display a similar commitment to those analysed by Elias to portraying a past that, even if it cannot be fully grasped, can be aimed at and evoked. Like Binet or Cercas, these writers often bring to the fore the author's role as historical researcher or investigator, and interweave personal memories with their subject matter, implying the subjective, contingent nature of the historical knowledge their texts offer, whilst also attempting to paint a vivid picture of the past events they address. In *The Anatomy of a Moment*, Cercas describes his approach to unravelling the Spanish coup of 23 February 1981 as follows:

> I propose to [...] describe the plot of the coup, an almost seamless fabric of private conversations, confidences and understandings that I can often only try to reconstruct from indirect testimonies, stretching the limits of the possible until they touch the probable and with the pattern of the plausible trying to outline the shape of the truth. Naturally, I cannot guarantee that everything I am about to tell is true; but I can guarantee that it is concocted with truth and especially that it is the closest that I can get to the truth, or to imagining it.
> (Cercas 2011: 239)

We will see the writers discussed here similarly approaching, but not claiming to capture fully, some kind of truth about the history they depict.

Despite parallels with recent literature from outside Italy, I will begin this chapter by examining the ways in which recent Italian historical novelists engage with specifically Italian questions about history and memory, bound up with what Foot (2010) has characterised as divided memory, and a tradition that can be traced back to Manzoni's archetypal historical novel *I promessi sposi* [*The Betrothed*] and his theories about combining literature and history that would be taken up a century later by Italian microhistorians. I will then look at the two main ways in which recent Italian writers have used the historical novel form through the analysis of two primary texts. The first is that of rethinking well-known historical events in order to save them from mythologisation and to indicate the lost opportunities they represent, as seen in Scurati's *Una storia romantica* [*A Romantic Story*].[4] The second approach inserts into an accepted version of the past the story of a marginalised individual who has been traditionally forgotten or excluded from historical memory, as seen in Mohamed and Wu Ming 2's *Timira*. I then go on to analyse

Janeczek's *Le rondini di Montecassino* [*The Swallows of Monte Cassino*], which can be seen as bridging the two strands, in that it considers a highly commemorated event of the past — the Battle of Monte Cassino during the Second World War — but does so through forgotten or subaltern perspectives. We will see that all three of these texts have parallels, both in the tools they employ to dig up the past, and in the concerns that underlie their representations of history and historiography.

A mode of historical fiction that I will not examine here, but that Janeczek dips her toes into, is alternative history fiction, or 'ucronia' as Wu Ming 1 calls it in the Memorandum (Wu Ming 1 2009a: 35), as seen in De Cataldo's *Romanzo criminale* and *Nelle mani giuste* (discussed chapter 2), Brizzi's trilogy beginning with *L'inattesa piega degli eventi* [*The Unexpected Turn of Events*], in which Mussolini is not overthrown but continues to govern Italy after the Second World War, or Wu Ming 5's *Havana Glam*, which reimagines David Bowie in the 1970s as a communist sympathiser. Yet, the approaches that I have chosen to focus on are united by being moments in history that can be seen in Wu Ming 1's terms as 'ucronie potenziali' [potential uchronias] (2009a: 34), that is, moments in which there are fractures or *pieghe* or gaps, whether due to lost potentialities or because of attempts to forget, and these gaps are then filled by fiction. As Mantel put it in a short story that imagines the assassination of Margaret Thatcher: 'History could always have been otherwise' (2014: 240). The novels we will see here show that they can reflect on other possibilities in the past even when they do not employ alternative history fiction, and, by doing so, provoke reflection on identity and historiography today.

History, Memory and Historical Fiction in Italy

As described in the previous chapters, recent Italian literature has been influenced by the after-effects of the events of the early 1990s, such as the end of the Cold War and the ensuing liberation of energies, the fall of the Italian Communist Party and the Clean Hands investigations, all of which contributed to a profound shake-up of the Italian political establishment and ushered in the Second Republic and the years of Berlusconi's influence over the country. Yet, it was not simply changing historical conditions but historiography itself that experienced a shake-up at the beginning of the 1990s, which undoubtedly also affected the concerns that are at the centre of recent Italian unidentified narrative objects (UNOs).

Since the late 1980s, memory studies have grown in importance, broadening history as a discipline, as I described in the introduction to this study, and Italian national history in this period also started to be reframed in a more transnational context. Holocaust memory, which was associated in Italy with the figure of Primo Levi, opened up from the mid-1980s onwards to become part of what Gordon has described as a broader Americanisation of the Holocaust in the 1990s, with Levi 'as a central figure in testimony and world literature' (Gordon 2006: 94). In the wake of 'the post-Cold War reconfiguration of Europe and its emerging postcolonialities' (Lombardi-Diop and Romeo 2012: 2), the Italian colonial project also began to be re-examined, and it was placed within a wider understanding of postcolonial studies.

Foot (2010) has argued that Italian history since the Risorgimento can be characterised by the idea of divided memory, due to the disagreements surrounding events and their commemoration that endure today. He also points out that the term 'la memoria divisa' was first used in the 1990s, when alternative versions of the events of the Second World War began to come to light and be addressed by historians: 'the idea of divided memory relates to a specific set of events and historical research, emerging in part from a post-cold war opening out of research into the past' (Foot 2010: 10). Beginning with the publication of books such as Claudio Pavone's seminal *Una guerra civile* [*A Civil War*] in 1991, and the study of alternative, family memories and oral history, the accepted version of the Resistance and the myths surrounding it began to be substantially revised,[5] and this had a knock-on effect of reassessing other historical events. It is no coincidence that so many twenty-first-century Italian writers have chosen to look at such contested historical moments as the fascist period, the Second World War and Italian colonialism, and in doing so place emphasis on modes of understanding history, which I will discuss further in this section with reference to the legacy of Manzoni and microhistory. If Italian history is characterised by divided memory, so is its historical fiction, which has used these divisions fruitfully to explore different bifurcations of the past.

Despite writing the seminal Italian historical novel, Manzoni went on to reject literature as a means of accessing history. *I promessi sposi* and Manzoni's theoretical writings on history and fiction raise some fascinating ideas and tensions that were later picked up by Italian historians and writers, and continue to be present in more recent historical novels, which have even directly referenced Manzoni, as we will see in the case of Scurati.[6] Serkowska's statement about the twentieth-century historical novelists she analysed continues to hold true in the twenty-first century: 'Manzoni è presente nel DNA e nel subconscio dei nostri scrittori' [Manzoni is present in the DNA and subconscious of our writers] (Serkowska 2012: 412).

A function of *I promessi sposi* that later writers have drawn on is that of provoking reflection on modes of understanding history. Codebò argues that the way in which Manzoni incorporated documentation into his novel makes *I promessi sposi* the precursor to the new historical novels of the twentieth century, whose writers 'wanted to discuss the methods for apprehending history rather than luring readers into illusory worlds' (Codebò 2010: 72). Such foregrounding of the historical operation has been taken beyond new historical novels to more recent ones, which often contain detailed notes about sources at the end, or 'Titoli di coda' [Credits] as they are called in Wu Ming's work, or provide extra material online, as we will see in the case of *Timira*, which also incorporates documentation within the narrative itself through the various 'reperti' [exhibits] we will see dispersed throughout. Like Manzoni's interjection on the *bravi* in chapter one of *I promessi sposi*, for instance, this interrupts the narrative and reminds readers that this work of literature was based on historical research. In the twenty-first century, we can detect ethical charge and significance in this archival and intellectual labour, which is foregrounded heavily, and in which author/s and readers are seen as having the opportunity to participate as (notional) equals, co-investigators and co-producers of the text they are reading.

Yet, Manzoni had a dual approach like many recent writers; as well as breaking the illusion with the inclusion of historical detail, he aimed to bring his readers closer to the past. *I promessi sposi* calls into question the grand narrative of History, typified by the reference to 'L'historia' (Manzoni 2010: 5) in the manuscript reproduced in the foreword that the narrator has supposedly found. With its stuffy and archaic historical narration, it represents a past that seems far removed from us, cold and dead. After that, the text moves to the contemporary language of the narrator, and then to the personal viewpoint of Renzo, thus closing the gap between then and now (as Della Coletta (1996: 65) points out). It also shifts its focus from the traditional subject matter of History, that is great events and important people, or what the manuscript describes as 'le Imprese de Prencipi e Potentati, e qualificati Personaggi' (Manzoni 2010: 5) ['the Enterprises of Princes and Powers and such qualified Personages' (Manzoni 1972: 19)], to the story of Renzo and Lucia, choosing to focus on history with a small 'h' and the ways in which ordinary people, whose stories are often forgotten or silenced by History, are at the mercy of wider historical events.

Many recent historical novels in Italian similarly centre on a personal and individual story, or the stories of several individuals, in order to raise points about history and historiography. Despite obvious differences, Lucia and Renzo's displacement and quest to be united against a backdrop of wider historical events, which Manzoni refers to with evident irony — 'Molte cose importanti, di quelle a cui più specialmente si dà titolo di storiche, erano accadute in questo frattempo' (2010: 545) ['Many important events, of the sort which we specifically call historical, had happened in the meanwhile' (Manzoni 1972: 526)] — find echoes in the twenty-first century. Ferrante's Neapolitan quartet provides prime examples of ex-centric historical novels, showing how the lives of working-class women in southern Italy are affected by wider historical developments in the twentieth century, although, as I mentioned in the introduction to this study, Ferrante is another surprising omission from the NIE.[7] *In territorio nemico* [*In Enemy Territory*], written by 115 contributors under the project Scrittura industriale collettiva [Industrial Collective Writing], describes two of the main protagonists Adele and Matteo searching for one another but constantly delayed by the struggles in a war-torn Italy that recalls the devastation of Manzoni's description of a plague-ridden Milan. In *Una storia romantica*, we will see Aspasia and Jacopo find their love thwarted as they are separated by larger forces in a close resemblance of Manzoni's betrothed, and they could be described as Scurati describes the real-life figure of the politician Casati: 'sospinto dall'onda degli eventi' [carried on the wave of events] (Scurati 2007b: 148). This conception of a wider History as a powerful force is most clearly present in *I promessi sposi* when Manzoni characterises it as 'un turbino vasto, incalzante, vagabondo' (2010: 526) ['a great whirlwind, wandering and trampling through the countryside' (1972: 508)]. Recent Italian writers have drawn on the Manzonian model of subaltern characters that are buffeted by the whirlwind of history.

The idea of needing to reinvigorate the past and, like Manzoni, work against the coldly academic version of 'l'historia' is widespread in twenty-first-century historical novels in Italian, whose writers strive to bring the past back to life in all its detail, rather than leaving it set in stone. An example of this can be seen in Evangelisti's introduction to his text *Controinsurrezioni* [*Counter-Insurrections*], written jointly with Moresco, which, like Scurati's *Una storia romantica*, re-evaluates the Risorgimento from unusual angles. Evangelisti states that this period has become embalmed, commemorated only by official versions in school history books and cold monuments, its iconography 'fatta di statue e di cimeli' [made of statues and relics] (Evangelisti and Moresco 2008: 11). To rescue it from such oblivion, he and Moresco each contributed to the volume sharply contrasting short stories based in 1848 and 1849. In Evangelisti's introduction, he argues that writers can paint more colourful pictures than historians can and use poetic licence: 'Solo la narrativa può restituire, in parte, il sapore di ciò che accadde. Gli odori, i colori: una verità che lo storico, vincolato a criteri quantitativi e a valutazioni asettiche, non può permettersi' [Only narrative can bring back, partly, the flavour of what happened. The smells, the colours: a truth that is not afforded to the historian, who is bound by quantitative criteria and sterile evaluations] (Evangelisti and Moresco 2008: 13). It is significant that Evangelisti uses the word 'verità' to talk about what writers can do, as the idea that there is a type of more literary truth that is not empirically verifiable frequently resurfaces in the texts I examine in this study, and this is no less true of the historical novels.

In 'Del romanzo storico' [On the Historical Novel], Manzoni would reject such an approach to writing, although this essay also contains several contradictions that imply he had not fully resolved some of the tensions that are present in, and have in fact been embraced by, more recent Italian *romanzi storici*. Manzoni (1973: 1727) criticised historical novels by raising two main qualms: either they do not distinguish clearly enough between history and fiction, or, if they do separate the two, this ruins the unity of the work. Yet as Bermann (1984: 45–46), de Groot (2010: 31) and Pocci (2012: 230) have pointed out, *I promessi sposi* constitutes a good example of the ways in which history and fiction can coexist in a novel without merging into one another or misleading the reader. Moreover, the essay is not the outright condemnation of historical novels that it would seem to be. Twice Manzoni uses map similes to compare historical and literary interpretations, which on closer analysis suggest a more nuanced conception of both history and historical novels as referring to the same object, whilst neither being a substitute for the original events. His first metaphor is put in the mouth of his imaginary interlocutor, who describes the distinction between traditional historical writing and historical novels as follows:

> la stessa differenza, in certo modo, che tra una carta geografica, dove sono segnate le catene de' monti, i fiumi, le città, i borghi, le strade maestre d'una vasta regione, e una carta topografica, nella quale, e tutto questo è più particolarizzato (dico quel tanto che ne può entrare in uno spazio molto più ristretto di paese), e ci sono di più segnate anche le alture minori, e le disuguaglianze ancor meno sensibili del terreno, e i borri, le gore, i villaggi, le case isolate, le viottole. (Manzoni 1973: 1727–28)

> [In a way, there is the same difference [...] as between a geographic map that simply indicates the presence of mountain chains, rivers, cities, towns, and major roads of a vast region and a topographic map, where all of this (and whatever else might be shown in a more restricted area) is presented in greater detail and, indeed, where even minor elevations and less noteworthy particulars — ditches, channels, villages, isolated homes, paths — are clearly marked. (Manzoni 1984: 63–64)]

This is not in fact an opposition between the two representations, as both maps are describing the same territory simply on a different scale (as pointed out by D'Angelo 2013: 141). In fact, it recalls Evangelisti's statement, quoted above, about the benefits of a literary representation of history that can give more details for readers to engage with. Evangelisti's description of the writer being able to evoke smells and colours that the historian cannot is even more similar to the second reference to maps made by Manzoni, in which he describes the role of narration and conjecture in history as being 'come chi, disegnando la pianta d'una città, ci aggiunge, in diverso colore, strade, piazze, edifizi progettati; e col presentar distinte dalle parti che sono, quelle che potrebbero essere, fa che si veda la ragione di pensarle riunite' (1973: 1734) ['almost like someone who, when drawing a city map, adds in a distinctive colour the streets, plazas, and buildings planned for the future and who, while distinguishing the potential from the actual, lets us see the logic of the whole' (1984: 75)]. Here he seems to be saying that if writers simply create a distinction between what happened and what could have happened, between fact and conjecture, then there is enough unity in the fact that it is gesturing towards reality, and, indeed, this combination can give us a better, and more vivid, overall understanding of the past.

This is a view that more recent writers seem to subscribe to. Wu Ming 2 explains the aim of NIE texts in similar terms:

> Se per indagare i fatti usiamo la narrativa, e non la storia o le scienze umane, è perché vogliamo permetterci di essere visionari, [...] di concatenare gli eventi con simboli e analogie, di immaginare, quando ci mancano, quel che succederebbe se avessimo le prove. (Wu Ming 2 2009: 190)

> [If to investigate events we use narrative, and not history or human sciences, it is because we want to allow ourselves to be visionaries, [...] to link events with symbols and analogies, to imagine, when we do not have it, what would happen if we had the proof.]

He is also alluding to Pasolini's famous statement 'Io so, ma non ho le prove' [I know, but I don't have the proof] (1974), another key reference point for the combinations of reality and possibility that we see in this study, as I discussed in chapter 1. Like Pasolini's belief that he knew about the secrets he was revealing 'perché sono un intellettuale, uno scrittore, che cerca di [...] immaginare tutto ciò che non si sa o che si tace' [because I am an intellectual, a writer, who tries to [...] imagine everything that is unknown or unsaid] (1974), there is a sense in the work of these writers that Manzoni's more colourful, embellished maps of the past reveal something more profound than straightforward historical accounts based solely on proof.

It was Manzoni's map metaphors that Carlo Ginzburg would seize on a century later in defence of the role of conjecture and literary narration in historical accounts in his postscript to Natalie Zemon Davis's *The Return of Martin Guerre*. Ginzburg finds Manzoni ahead of his time in imagining a possible type of history that would describe what Manzoni's interlocutor calls the private effects of public, historic events (Manzoni 1973: 1728). Ginzburg (2006: 307–08) saw this as a highly innovative approach and a challenge that it took a century for historians to take up, which they did so with microhistory. In reducing the scale of analysis as Manzoni did in *I promessi sposi*, microhistorians could examine how the systems of power impacted on the forgotten protagonists of history, and then move from this small-scale analysis to wider implications. They tended to use a literary mode to relate these stories of individuals or small social groups, and drew less of a stark distinction between history and conjecture than their predecessors did.

This approach can be seen both in Davis's text and in Ginzburg's influential work of microhistorical analysis, *Il formaggio e i vermi* [*The Cheese and the Worms*] (1976), which, as Pocci (2012) has pointed out, has several parallels with Manzoni's *I promessi sposi*, and it is also another important precursor for the texts I address here. In a novelistic style, Ginzburg analysed the life of one man, Domenico Scandella, known as Menocchio, trying to piece together the story of this subaltern subject of history and what it showed about sixteenth-century Italy, but also equally reflecting on how we apprehend history. In keeping with a microhistorical approach, recent historical novels tend to focus on the minor protagonists within the time period depicted in order to consider how people understand and experience history, but these fragments of the past are left open to questions and doubts. This approach to history is a political choice; Szijártó states: 'Microhistory seems to be the best medicine against the "simple truths" of history' (Magnússon and Szijártó 2013: 63). Recent Italian writers emulate this by validating perspectives that disrupt the dominant 'truth' constructed by national (and international) historiography.

Despite being an advocate of reading signs, symptoms and clues to decipher reality, Ginzburg never glossed over the role of aporia and gaps in our knowledge about history. In *Il formaggio e i vermi*, he instead sought to bring these aspects to the fore, without blending them into the story, which Manzoni would have approved of: 'le ipotesi, i dubbi, le incertezze diventavano parte della narrazione; la ricerca della verità diventava parte dell'esposizione della (necessariamente incompleta) verità raggiunta' [the hypotheses, the doubts, the uncertainties became part of the narrative; the search for truth became part of the exposition of the (necessarily incomplete) truth reached] (Ginzburg 2006: 256). Indeed, Ginzburg pointed out a perceptive distinction in relation to *The Return of Martin Guerre*: 'La ricerca (e la narrazione) della Davis non s'impernia sulla contrapposizione tra "vero" e "inventato" ma sull'integrazione, sempre segnalata puntualmente, di "realtà" e "possibilità" (al plurale)' (2006: 298–99) [Davis's research (and narration) are not based on the juxtaposition between 'true' and 'invented' but on the integration, always precisely indicated, of 'reality' and 'possibility' (in the plural)]. This harks back to what Wu Ming 2 said about exploring what could have happened in the past in order to bridge the gap between what we know and what we do not. Like Ginzburg or Davis, recent Italian historical novels tend not to be misleading about this operation (as we shall see in all three texts analysed in this chapter), but rather 'come clean' about their conjectures. They frequently use introductions or postscripts or moments of metafictional reflection to disrobe the ways in which the facts were used in order to empower their readers to reach a deeper understanding of their message and of the past in a way Ginzburg, and also Manzoni before him, would advocate.

It is worth analysing how microhistory, whilst based on evidence, is also closely tied up with literature not only in the way its approach has later been detected in novels, or in its literary style of narration. It is telling that Ginzburg said that the impetus for writing *Il formaggio e i vermi* came from reading Tolstoy's *War and Peace*; he was inspired by its intersections between the public and private domains, and Tolstoy's desire to narrate the stories of all the people who participated in these past events (Ginzburg 2006: 257). In an essay about Stendhal, who saw his novels as containing more truth than history, Ginzburg suggests that fiction, and in particular the use of free indirect discourse as one of the narrative tools that can help reach an understanding of history, could benefit historians, rather than being in opposition to historical knowledge:

> i procedimenti narrativi sono come campi magnetici: provocano domande, e attraggono documenti potenziali. In questo senso un procedimento come il discorso diretto libero, nato per rispondere, sul terreno della finzione, a una serie di domande poste dalla storia, può essere considerato come una sfida indiretta lanciata agli storici. Un giorno essi potrebbero raccoglierla, in forme che oggi non riusciamo a immaginare. (Ginzburg 2006: 184)

> [narrative procedures are magnetic fields: they provoke questions and attract potential documents. In this sense, a procedure such as free direct discourse, born to answer, in fiction's territory, a series of questions posed by history, can be considered an indirect challenge to historians. One day, they could pick it up, in forms that we cannot imagine today.]

Ginzburg does not advocate simply inventing things about history, but he does not rule out the fruitful relationship between history and literary invention. This is a fascinating theory for a historian, and one that the writers I analyse here would seem to subscribe to, as their texts are part of a desire to provoke questions and challenge their readers to consider what they are saying. Ginzburg seems to be very much part of the Manzonian tradition of cross-pollination between historical writing and literature. This dialogue and borrowing between the disciplines of history and fiction has clearly continued into the twenty-first century.

Interestingly, Ginzburg, like Wu Ming and other Italian writers and critics, displays a wariness towards postmodernism, whilst simultaneously absorbing elements of it. He deeply mistrusted postmodernist relativism, and he and Giovanni Levi spoke out against depriving historiography of cognitive value (Ginzburg 2006: 264–65). He insisted instead on being able to access historical truth through the use of evidence. However, he does suggest that the way in which the literary narration of microhistory admits to a lack of total knowledge of the past mirrors the literary production of the twentieth century. Just as novels have moved away from the omniscient narrator of the nineteenth century, narrative history has not shied away from revealing the incompleteness of historical knowledge. He argues that our sensibilities as readers began to be changed not only with changing historiography, but also with the work of writers like Marcel Proust and Robert Musil, or even with Fellini's film *8 1/2*, so that, today: 'Il rapporto tra chi narra e la realtà appare più incerto, più problematico [...] l'intreccio tra realtà e finzione, tra verità e possibilità è al centro delle elaborazioni artistiche di questo secolo' [The relationship between who narrates and reality appears more uncertain, more problematic [...] the intertwining of reality and fiction, of truth and possibility, is at the centre of the artistic elaborations of this century] (Ginzburg 2006: 313–14). This seems to align him with a postmodernist climate of ontological questions and uncertainty.

In many ways, his ideas were not dissimilar to those of White in *The Content of the Form*, in which the American theorist argued that accounts of history are a type of narration, that 'what distinguishes "historical" from "fictional" stories is first and foremost their content, rather than their form' (1987: 27). Pisani (2007) has insightfully pointed out that there are more overlaps and fewer oppositions than the two thinkers tended to realise between their approaches to historical knowledge. Although Ginzburg, in his essay 'Unus testis' (in Ginzburg 2006), criticises White's theories for leaving open the possibility for historical accounts like those of the Holocaust-denier Robert Faurisson, White's insistence on moving away from understanding narrative history as a science was not a descent into complete doubt; he states that, even if the truths that narrative history offers are different from those of the social sciences, 'this is no reason to rule them out as merely imaginary constructions. To do so would entail the denial that literature and poetry have anything valid to teach us about reality' (White 1987: 44). His conception of the role of storytelling, of creating a plot between different human actions in order to understand the past is also useful for understanding recent Italian literature. Like Ginzburg, and recent Italian writers, White emphasises the value of storytelling that draws on literary tools whilst addressing real-life events to create meaning and deepen understanding.

Della Colletta rightly asserts that Manzoni's *I promessi sposi* and 'Del romanzo storico' established 'the problematic and contradictory parameters that influenced the development of historical fiction in Italy' (1996: 198). As we have seen, Manzoni's approach also influenced the development of microhistory, which ran alongside comparable developments in theories of history from beyond Italy's borders. However, I would also suggest that it is unsurprising that this focus on the interplay between reality and fiction has continued to play a role in Italian historical fiction in the twenty-first century when so many of the events of the nation's recent history remain shadowy or misrepresented. Memory wars over the events of the *anni di piombo* continue to be played out on the public stage, not to mention the questions still being raised over fascist Italy, as shown by the controversy surrounding the monument in Affile to Rodolfo Graziani in 2012.[8] It is no coincidence that

Scrittura industriale collettiva named their collectively written novel about the much-contested Italian Resistance *In territorio nemico*. The past in Italy is enemy territory, it is contested territory, and it is a territory we can never truly access. Recent Italian writers have explored such ideas, at the same time trying to make the past less inimical, or in L. P. Hartley's famous wording in *The Go Between*, less of a foreign country, without ignoring the role of doubt, and possibility, in historical knowledge, in line with a practice dating back to Manzoni.

Una storia romantica by Antonio Scurati

In Scurati's *Una storia romantica* (2007b), we encounter an ageing and neurotic Manzoni, peeping fearfully out of his window at the revolutionaries he will not join during the *Cinque giornate* [Five Days] in Milan in 1848, more or less demanding they get out of his back yard: 'Più in là, più in là, dì loro di andare a farla più in là questa rivoluzione. Perché la devono dare proprio davanti alla porta di casa mia?' [Further, further, tell them to go and have this revolution further away. Why do they have to have it right outside my front door?] (261). Through the elderly Manzoni's refusal to be actively involved in the insurrection, Scurati raises questions over the writer's role in society and what literature can do, questions that, as we have seen, Manzoni himself struggled with. Like *I promessi sposi*, *Una storia romantica* revolves around a manuscript, here sent to the main protagonist Italo 37 years after the *Cinque giornate*, in which he reads about his then betrothed, Aspasia, and her infidelity to him with his friend Jacopo. Italo aptly frames the discovery of the truth about his past as one of digging up bodies years later, evoking the ghosts of the past — 'che idea romantica!' [what a romantic idea!] (16) — which is what the text itself seems to do by evoking nineteenth-century Italy. This operation invites reflection across temporal divides and expresses ideas about history and Italy's present that have far wider implications that the text's simple title suggests.

Una storia romantica is not the only UNO in Scurati's oeuvre, which very much reflects on the ideas I explore throughout this study, although, like other writers who were included in the NIE nebula — Wu Ming 1 references Scurati's historical novel in the Memorandum (Wu Ming 1 2009a: 13) and Scurati responded favourably to the concept of the NIE in an article in the newspaper *La Stampa* (Scurati 2009) — this is done very much through a male lens, with *Una storia romantica* as an exception to this in the sections focalised through the character of Aspasia, which also reflect on so-called women's issues.[9] It is no coincidence that the two protagonists of *Una storia romantica* are both orphans, as, apart from experimenting with the historical novel form,[10] Scurati has shown a particular interest in exploring questions of inheritance and the kind of generational problems I explored in chapter 2: *Il sopravvissuto* [*The Survivor*] (2007a) is the story of a boy who walks into his final school exam and shoots all of his teachers except one; *Il padre infedele* [*The Unfaithful Father*] (2013) addresses fatherhood, and Di Martino (2016) has examined it in terms of Recalcati's theories; in *Il bambino che sognava la fine del mondo* [*The Child who Dreamed the End of the World*] (2010), which could also have been one of the primary texts chosen for chapter 4 in its combination of reportage and autofiction, Scurati's girlfriend discovers she is pregnant much to his chagrin, as he did not want to have children, and his explorations of a case of paedophilia are intertwined with troubled recollections from his own childhood. Significantly, he describes *Il bambino che sognava la fine del mondo* in its foreword echoing the subtitle of Manzoni's essay on the historical novel: 'Questo romanzo appartiene al genere dei componimenti misti di cronaca e d'invenzione' [This novel belongs to the genre of mixed works of news and invention] (Scurati 2010).[11] Like other writers and critics in the twenty-first century, Scurati believes that this generation needs to engage and push forward change to combat the shortcomings of a time that he characterises as one of inexperience in his essay *La letteratura dell'inesperienza* [*Literature of Inexperience*] (2006a) (which I address later in this chapter and again in the following one). He enacts this change through his experimental novels that aim to give a sense of depth to what he perceives to be the shallowness of the present; he concludes *La letteratura dell'inesperienza* by stating: 'Ciò di cui in futuro si dovrà tenere conto è che oggi, in piena esplosione dell'*inesperienza*, qualsiasi romanzo si scriva, anche il più ferocemente autobiografico, il più ingenuamente attuale, lo si scrive come un romanzo storico' [What we must keep in mind is that today, in the full explosion of inexperience, any novel that is written, even the most ferociously autobiographical, the most ingenuously current, is written as a historical novel.] (Scurati 2006a: 78)

Despite seeming to be a classical example of the historical novel genre harking back to the nineteenth century, *Una storia romantica* is in fact a complex hybrid with allegorical aims. By imitating the nineteenth-century historical novel, Scurati returns to a time of ideals and a struggle for freedom, when literature was used in Italy as a vehicle for political ideology (Ganeri 1999: 31), just as recent Italian writers have advocated a return to literary *impegno* or commitment. The nineteenth century Scurati depicts also has other parallels with the climate of twenty-first-century Italy. It was a time that pitted classical tradition and rhetoric against new and innovative approaches to art. Camilletti has pointed out that the tensions of the Classicist versus Romanticist quarrel in the nineteenth century seemed to be re-posed by the debate surrounding the NIE phenomenon, 'showing again how the dichotomies between tradition and newness, preservation and avant-garde, national heritage and foreign inspiration, still form a tensive core within Italian culture and society' (Camilletti 2013: 18). Camilletti also underlines the way in which both debates centred on generational conflict, 'issues of parenthood, legitimacy and usurpation' (2013: 18), as writers were wrestling with the after-effects of what came before, just as those today are reassessing the legacy of the twentieth century.

This tensive core can be detected within *Una storia romantica* too, which combines the old and the new, serious political considerations and playful postmodern experimentation. Scurati employs some of the tropes of the Romantic novel, with the exaggerated love story relying on clichés, such as love in the time of war, and the female adulterer's forbidden love recalling that of other novelistic examples of the time, such as Madame Bovary, Anna Karenina or Effie Briest. The text also frequently draws attention to its own fictionality, for example likening Jacopo to a Foscolo hero (40) and Aspasia to the heroine of a popular serialised novel (52). These aspects could encourage us to see the novel as parody, yet it contains deep reflection on the issues at stake. The grim horrors of the conflict are constantly played out alongside the romance between Jacopo and Aspasia. The fighting on the barricades mimicking Hugo's *Les Misérables* is portrayed in all seriousness, and at moments it has a real sense of pathos, for example when the kidnapped girl Lucia Mattioli is returned to her father after being abused and raped, made to crawl back to safety in her broken state, 'come accecata dalle violenze subite' [as if blinded from the violence suffered] (209).

Yet, Scurati is also employing tools that could be associated with postmodernism, as we realise at the end of the text, where we encounter the 'Tabula gratulatoria', in which he lists the extensive variety of borrowings and inspiration that went into the text, followed by the 'Tabula mistificatoria', in which he indicates the historical sources. In the former section, the list of this huge range of influences shows the text to be almost a collage or cut-up made up of parts taken from films, songs, philosophy, outright borrowing of situations and characters from other texts, and pop culture, to create what he calls '[un']opera di bracconaggio' [[a] work of poaching] (547). This seems to highlight that the way in which we understand history is filtered or remediated through other accounts and narratives. It recalls Glynn's work on Eco's *Il nome della rosa* [*The Name of the Rose*] and other 'anti-illusionist historical novels', which seek to 'present a plurality of histories, or at least *a* contingent history, rather than *the* history' (Glynn 2005: 27). Indeed, although Eco's seminal historical novel has been seen as a quintessential example of postmodernist play that recent writers may have tried to move away from — it is criticised by Wu Ming 1 in the Memorandum for its tongue-in-cheek parody and citationism (Wu Ming 1 2009a: 16 n. 10), which would be lost on the 'lettore ingenuo' [ingenuous reader] that Eco refers to in the postscript (Eco 2005: 525), and Genna's review of *Una storia romantica* similarly maintains a distance from Eco in his statement that Scurati is not smiling at us from behind the mask of history as Eco did (Genna 2007b) — *Il nome della rosa* did have a sense of *impegno*, as Serkowska has argued,[12] and it is in fact comparable to Scurati's historical novel, which, like other recent Italian novels, can be read on different levels, hiding its inner workings on a more superficial reading.[13] The key difference between Eco's and Scurati's historical novels could be seen in the fact that, in *Una storia romantica*, we might remain the ingenuous reader for much of the text, but Scurati ensures that we understand the mechanics and sense of *impegno* behind the text by explaining himself in detail in these final sections. Eco's postscript, on the other hand, was not initially appended to the novel, but appeared in *Alfabeta* three years after the novel first appeared (Eco 2005: 505), and Eco is arguably not as open in explaining the workings of the text as Scurati is. Scurati states: 'Il mio intento non era quello del gioco intellettuale' [My intention was not an intellectual game] (547), again implying a distancing from the kind of postmodernist play that Eco was seen as engaging in. He says that he wanted to harness the power of these other artistic products and encourage his readers to go and read, listen to and watch the sources for *Una storia romantica*, in order to gain a powerful sense of what he wanted to convey. He lays out the workings of his novel because he wants his readers to re-engage with a history he feels has lost its power. This is a belief that he put forward in *Letteratura dell'inesperienza* and re-states in *Una storia romantica*: 'Nell'epoca in cui viviamo, non migliore né peggiore di altre, il passato sembra aver perso la sua forza' [In the age we live in, no better or worse than others, the past seems to have lost its strength] (547).

This questionable view suggests what Antonello has described as 'one of the formulaic elements which allegedly define postmodern epistemology', that is 'the flattening of any temporal perspective into an everlasting present, effacing memory, recovering the past only for parodic purposes' (Antonello 2009: 235). Scurati sees himself working against this in *Una storia romantica* by giving a sense of depth to the present. This view has also been implied by other critics, including Amici, who states when discussing the NIE that 'working on the past is a natural form of resistance because of its capacity to exalt that which the techno-communicative transition tends to undermine from within: the profundity of the present, its roots in the past, the complexity of history' (2010: 14). Yet, I would echo Antonello's scepticism about this alleged perpetual present. As I argued in the introduction to this study, the Digital Age has brought with it new methods for interacting with the past and archival material. Antonello (2009: 236) rightly points out that the growth in interest in cultural memory studies indicates that we have formulated new ways of understanding how history and identity work.[14] Our relationship with history is complex and varied in the twenty-first century, and we are not simply overwhelmed with a 'deluge of information concerning the here and now' (Amici 2010: 14).

Like Eco's, Scurati's approach to his subject matter is metaphorical, using the past to reflect on the present, in common with a series of other recent novelists. *Una storia romantica* can be placed in a broader constellation of allegorical historical novels that examine the subject of normal people taking action and resisting authority, frequently followed by disenchantment and a sense of the pendulum of history swinging back the other way. This can be seen, for example, in Luther Blissett's *Q*, which portrays the Reformation in Europe and the struggle for religious freedom,[15] Alessandro Bertante's *Al diavul*, in which the main character Errico goes to Spain to join the civil war in the 1930s,[16] Scrittura industriale collettiva's *In territorio nemico*, about the Italian Resistance in the Second World War,[17] or Wu Ming's *L'Armata dei Sonnambuli*, about the French Revolution.[18] All of these novels portray disillusionment with the final result of their conflicts, and a need to continue fighting for their ideals. This is implied by the epigraph to Wu Ming's historical novel *54*: 'Non c'è nessun dopoguerra' [There is no post-war] (Wu Ming 2002), which described the way in which the Second World War did not truly come to an end but simply morphed into the Cold War, but has allegorical possibilities beyond, particularly in light of the fact that the text was being written in 2001 against the backdrop of 9/11 and, closer to home, the G8 in Genoa (Wu Ming 1 2009a: 5), seen by some as a type of oppression that recalled previous armed struggles against the authorities (see chapter 1). Errico's father states of Mussolini's rise in *Al Diavul*: 'È la Storia che si ripropone' [It is History that is repeating itself] (Bertante 2008: 64); we see the *topos* of the failed revolution repeat itself again and again in recent Italian historical fiction, particularly those texts that have examined the Risorgimento. Italy's battle for independence in the nineteenth century has been held up by writers including Scurati on the eve of its 150th anniversary as encapsulating these ideas of betrayed ideals, as shown by the title of De Cataldo's Risorgimento novel *I traditori* [*The Traitors*], or the statement on the cover of Evanglisti and Moresco's *Controinsurrezioni* dubbing it 'una rivoluzione tradita' [a betrayed revolution],[19] or Italo's allusion in *Una storia romantica* to Garibaldi as the 'eroe tradito' [betrayed hero] (16).

Indeed, Scurati's and others' depictions of the Risorgimento demonstrate the memorial processes that Erll (2009) has described as 'premediation' and 'remediation'. The fight for Italian independence has become the object of premediation, in that it provides a schema — in this case the failed revolution — that can be used for other experiences and their representation (Erll 2009: 111). In terms of remediation, the Risorgimento has been repeatedly represented over time in different media, so that the term 'Risorgimento' has become like the sites of memory Erll discuses: it 'seems to refer not so much to what one might cautiously call the "actual event", but instead to a canon of existent medial constructions, to the narratives, images and myths circulating in a memory culture' (2009: 111). Erll's processes of memory are foregrounded by Scurati in various ways, provoking reflection on the idea that, as the narrator of *Una storia romantica* states: 'Il disastro del presente trascina anche con se il passato' [The disaster of the present also drags the past along with it] (474). The *Cinque giornate* resulted in victory, but only for a short while, and ultimately the monarchy remained. In the sections set in 1885, we see the aftermath of this insurrection, with Italo as a corrupt politician who prefers to read the newspapers from cover to cover rather than actively take part in political life in this brave new world they created. This brings to mind Scurati's description in *La letteratura dell'inesperienza* of people nowadays passively watching war and conflict on TV 'sorseggiando birra fresca' [sipping cool beer] (Scurati 2006a: 63). Indeed, in that essay, he describes our modern age as being characterised by a lack of engagement with reality and the end of humanism (Scurati 2006a: 14), which he associates with nineteenth-century nationalist ideas. By returning to that time, he seems to be trying to show how these ideas were eroded to arrive at the present situation. Scurati also deepens the allegorical layers of the novel through references to the Second World War: we are told that the death of Aspasia's friend Berta deliberately recalls that of Anna Magnani's character Pina in Roberto Rossellini's neorealist classic *Roma città aperta* [*Rome Open City*] (552), and Jacopo's words when he describes how they should fight the Austrians echo those of Milanese partisans (566), tapping into the conception of the Italian Resistance as a second Risorgimento (see Cooke 2012). In addition, Scurati tells us that Radetsky's threats to the protestors echo those of the Bosnian Serb General Stanislav Galić during the siege of Sarajevo in 1992 (565), and he later mentions that he re-employed the words of Joseph Stalin and Osama Bin Laden too, saying that he did so in order to show that they reoccur in the same way across eras (564). Indeed, the final sections of the text outlining its citations and intertextual references clearly demonstrate the ways in which *Una storia romantica* moves between past and present, provoking reflection across time periods through this multidirectional memory (Rothberg 2009) and recalibrating today's relationship with the past.

Concerns about history and memory can also be seen within the *fabula* at the exhibition about the Risorgimento in the 1885 section. Italo is not able to recognise his real experience in the events that are lifelessly and meaninglessly arranged for tourists' consumption into 'un'agghiacente sincronia' [a chilling synchronism] (491). This text seems to be working against such a way of remembering the past; instead of neatly flattening out the Risorgimento, Scurati aims to communicate a real sense of what it was like to live through those momentous events. At the exhibition, crowds of people file through to look at the exploits of those who fought and died, stomping all over this dead and mythologised past. Italo reflects: 'Quella massa di visitatori alla ricerca della propria identità nella storia [...] avrebbe finito per ridurla a una polvere senza significato' [That mass of visitors looking for their identity in history [...] would end up reducing it to a meaningless dust] (494). He ironically observes that this is probably just another piece of entertainment for these visitors 'tra uno spettacolo di fuochi pirotecnici e una bicchierata in osteria' [between a fireworks display and a drink in a tavern] (493). Yet, there is far more at stake for a country that has moved away from a dream of complete independence, just as today's readers can see the need truly to reflect on the past and on their national identity created by historiography, rather than pursuing a romantic idea of history, to play on the words of the title. By attempting to bring something relegated to the history books back to life, Scurati seeks to combat this and close the distance between us and what Ricoeur calls 'the uncanniness of the historical past' (2006: 394).

Italo describes the manuscript, interestingly entitled 'La vera storia' [The true story], in a way that could be applied to this and other recent UNOs: 'Era una finzione di tipo diverso [...] a Italo il poter distinguere tra realtà e finzione appariva non soltanto impossibile, ma addirittura irrilevante' [It was a fiction of a different kind [...] being able to distinguish between reality and fiction seemed to Italo not only impossible, but irrelevant] (296). When reading Scurati's novel, the distinction between true and verisimilar is generally difficult to detect, although he later goes on to clarify in the 'Tabula mistificatoria' the ways in which he amended real historical events, people and places in order to fill any lacunae. He tells us that this hybrid mixture of reality and fiction is his literary vision of a possible truth, bringing to mind Wu Ming 1's potential uchronias (Wu Ming 1 2009a: 34) or Ginzburg's (2006: 298–99) distinction between reality and possibilities rather than between true and invented: 'ho raccontato le cose non come siamo certi che siano accadute ma come sarebbero potute accadere' [I narrated things not how we are sure that they happened but how they could have happened] (563).

Timira. Romanzo meticcio by Antar Mohamed and Wu Ming 2

'Questa è una storia vera... comprese le parti che non lo sono' [This is a true story... including the parts that are not]. This is the epigraph to Mohamed and Wu Ming 2's *Timira. Romanzo meticcio* [*Timira: Mestizo Novel*] (2012), suggesting another text that does not offer an absolute, empirically verifiable truth, but rather a literary one by embellishing on the past and imagining its possibilities. While Scurati's novel aims to examine a period of history that has been extensively commemorated, the authors of *Timira* conversely choose to examine an aspect of Italian history that has been under-represented by mainstream historiography: Italian colonialism. Scurati's novel can be seen as part of a strand of texts that reimagine mythologised moments of popular resistance, whereas *Timira*, like a series of recent historical novels, explores the forgotten/overlooked and darker aspects of Italy's past. Italian colonialism has begun to receive greater attention in recent years from both writers and scholars, although its treatment by writers related to the NIE has largely focused on white, male, Italian experience (as pointed out by Lombardi-Diop and Romeo 2012: 9), which could also be linked to the NIE's tendency to overlook so-called migrant writing (as I argued in chapter 1); this is particularly surprising in the light of the NIE's focus on alternative histories and subaltern subjects, whose voices are largely silent in its corpus, with *Timira* representing a rare exception. Despite the difference in subject matter, there are several parallels that can be drawn between Scurati's Risorgimento cut-up and Mohamed and Wu Ming 2's unusual biofiction, which also draws on the rich Italian tradition of merging and problematising history and fiction. This disrupts and shows the limitations of historical discourse, and it is particularly well suited to postcolonial reconsiderations of a traditionally Euro-centric narrative of History. When discussing postcolonial approaches to history in fiction, Ashcroft describes a method of political contestation that could be compared to the approach of *Timira*: 'it is one that works through, in the interstices of, in the fringes of, rather than in simple opposition to, history' (Ashcroft 2001: 102).

Published in 2012, *Timira* tells the life story of Isabella Marincola, a half-Somali half-Italian woman born in 1925, who grew up in Italy under the impression that she was the legitimate daughter of her Italian father and stepmother, before discovering the truth about her parentage. We follow her life, moving forwards and backwards between time planes and locations, from her difficult childhood in Italy, her return as an adult to Somalia to meet her mother, and her flight from Mogadishu during the civil war in the early 1990s. The story was based on recorded interviews with Isabella, who was to be the third co-author but died before the text was completed. It is a self-proclaimed 'mestizo novel', as it is written by Isabella's son, Antar Mohamed, a Somali exile living in Italy, and Wu Ming 2, an Italian writer with a Chinese name. This mestizo quality is also present in the style of the text, which incorporates different types of text — letters, diary entries, newspaper articles, official documents, photographs and poems — alongside its literary narrative. It also has a transmedial extension through a Pinterest board online containing videos, photographs and documents related to the life of Isabella and about Italian colonialism that readers can interact with, as well as including readers' responses to the text.[20] These elements both anchor the story in history and encourage readers to engage with the text, as we shall see.

As Lombardi-Diop and Romeo (2012: 7) have pointed out, Italy has only recently begun to examine its colonial era and the lasting effects it has had on Italian society. *Timira* responds to an urgent need to reconsider the past, in common with the urgency Scurati and others have expressed in reconsidering mythologised aspects of Italy's history like the Resistance or Risorgimento. Isabella's story shows how one woman's life can be completely defined by the effects of the Italian colonial project, from growing up as an outsider stared at by strangers, to being sexualised as an exotic nude model as a young woman, to belonging nowhere when she has to flee Somalia but is not supported by the Italian state. She reflects that still today in Italy: 'Se sei italiano e hai la pelle scura, sei una contraddizione vivente' [If you are Italian and have dark skin, you are a living contradiction] (449). Mohamed and Wu Ming 2 do not simply portray the reality of a Somali-Italian woman, but also interrogate Italian colonial memory. We see Isabella as a girl being made to learn the 'official' version of the past, pinning Italian flags on the map where important battles were won for control of Ethiopia (90). Later, on returning to Italy in the 1990s, she tries to have her brother's efforts as a partisan who fought and died for Italy officially recognised, but realises that his life has been glossed over — it is 'una traccia sottile, nella polvere degli archivi. Impronte di formica' [a subtle trace in the dust of the archives. Ant prints] (150) — whereas there is a monument in Mogadishu to the Italian soldiers who died in Somalia. The various archival documents throughout the story also contain reflection on ways of remembering, as in some cases these *reperti* [exhibits], as they are called, juxtapose different versions of the same event, such as the vitriolic anti-Italian poem written by Timiro Ukash, a poet and militant of the Somali Youth League, preceding the transcript of an Italian newsreel from 1960 describing Somalis and Italians joyfully celebrating Somalia's independence together (349–50). Like *Una storia romantica* and other recent historical novels, *Timira* thus aims to explore modes of understanding history.

By re-examining national historiography, the authors call into question a version of the past in which Italians still see themselves as having been 'colonialisti buoni' [good colonialists] (420), the myth that is commonly referred to as *Italiani, brava gente* [Italians nice people], overlooking the violence that was perpetrated in Italy's colonies. In *Timira*'s 'twin' (Wu Ming 2013) *Point Lenana* by Wu Ming 1 and Roberto Santachiara, which also explores Italy's colonial project in Africa, this 'pseudo-historiography' is framed in more explicit and angry terms: 'Rassicurazione dopo rassicurazione, cliché dopo cliché, il nostro passato proto-nazionale e nazionale diventa una pappa indifferenziata su cui gli italiani galleggiano da "brava gente"' [Reassurance after reassurance, cliché after cliché, our proto-national and national past becomes an undifferentiated mush with Italians floating on it as 'nice people'] (Wu Ming 1 and Santachiara 2013: 15–16). Like Scurati, these writers feel that there is a need to address and dislodge such clichés or accepted truths in order to truly understand the past and gain a better understanding of events happening now too. This is enacted in Ghermandi's *Regina di fiori e di perle* [Queen of Flowers and Pearls]

(2007) by the main protagonist, Mahlet, listening to and narrating people's stories about her native Ethiopia, in a text that displays many characteristics of the NIE but fails to be mentioned in the first version of the Memorandum and is then relegated to a footnote in later versions (Wu Ming 1 2009a: 13 n. 5), representing another example of a migrant writer who is overlooked by the NIE. The stories range from the Ethiopian resistance to Italian rule in the 1930s to the experience of being an Ethiopian immigrant in today's Italy, where Mahlet repeatedly hears from Italians that they helped improve her country by building roads and schools, being unaware of the Ethiopian version of what happened (Ghermandi 2007: 237); she realises that they will not see themselves from the outside, that they need to look through the eyes of others in order to understand the truth: 'Si sentivano superiori, e non accettavano di guardarsi dall'esterno, con gli occhi degli altri' [They felt superior, and refused to look at themselves from the outside, through the eyes of others] (Ghermandi 2007: 153). Looking at the past and present through the eyes of others is often what recent writers of UNOs seek to do. In a comparable way to Scego's work analysed in chapter 4, *Timira* is an attempt to undermine simplistic views on immigrants and colonisation that are held in the present, the views that Antar's girlfriend Celeste expresses: 'che c'entro io se nell'Ottocento sono venuti a casa vostra e vi hanno portato via tutto, e che c'entro io se a Mogadiscio avete deciso di spararvi uno contro l'altro?' [What has it got to do with me if in the nineteenth century they came to where you lived and took everything away, and what has it got to do with me if in Mogadishu you've decided to shoot each other?] (286). The text shows instead how these events are relevant, that they do have something to do with us, tracing back the roots of today's problems to events of the past.

Written after the Memorandum but by a member of Wu Ming, *Timira* can be seen as being part of the nebula, although I would argue that it is one of the more successful examples of NIE texts that look at colonialism and its after-effects. It is not a perfect attempt; here too, there is a lack of acknowledgement of the influence of writers who are not ethnically Italian. Specifically, Scego is not listed in the final section outlining the authors' sources for *Timira*, but her work is clearly an intertextual reference when Isabella says 'la mia patria era l'Italia, mentre la Somalia era la mia *matria*' [my fatherland was Italy, whilst Somalia was my *motherland*] (403), recalling Scego's short story 'Dismatria', which explores how 'qualcuno — forse per sempre — aveva tagliato il cordone ombelicale che ci legava alla nostra *matria*, alla Somalia' [someone — maybe for good — had cut the umbilical cord that linked us to our *motherland*, to Somalia] (Scego 2005: 11).[21] However, there is a more sensitive investigation of non-white experience in *Timira* than can be found in the work of NIE writers such as Lucarelli[22] or Camilleri.[23] This is partly due to the collaboration between Wu Ming 2, Mohamed and Isabella, as well as the text's female subject. Wu Ming 2 is deliberately sensitive to his role in the text, saying in a letter to Isabella that he did not wish to colonise her memories, despite his original suggestion that he rewrite them in the role of a biographer rather than collaborating equally: 'sono venuto alle tue coste come un europeo d'altri tempi, per trasformare le tue terre nella mia colonia' [I came to your shores like a European of yesteryear, to turn your lands into my colony] (344). He recognises that this was wrong and that a joint effort is the best way of addressing their subject matter. He is deliberately self-conscious and self-critical, aware of the fact that his status as a successful, white, male intellectual compromises him ethically to an extent, because it endows him with a certain kind of power, but he attempts to undermine this power by calling the readers' critical attention to it, and inviting them to 'disempower' him, in effect. Moreover, although it was ultimately written by men, *Timira* has what Gargani (1984) has called 'la voce femminile' [the female voice]. I am borrowing this idea from Re's article (1993) comparing Morante's *La storia* [*History*] — another key precursor to recent Italian historical novels, although it is not mentioned by Wu Ming 1 in relation to the NIE — with Manzoni's *I promessi sposi*, as Re's reading of the two texts is relevant to *Timira* too. This female voice is not dependent on the gender of the writers, but the way in which they represent protagonists at the mercy of a history that has traditionally marginalised and forgotten them. Mohamed and Wu Ming 2 give a powerful sense of this in the text, and do not shy away from so-called women's issues either, as shown by the sexism Isabella is often the victim of, or the harrowing scene of her home abortion (312). They explore issues across gender and race lines and paint a vivid portrait that she collaborated with them to create. There is certainly a sense that, as Wu Ming 2 puts it in one of his letters to Isabella, she prepared the meal with them and they are left to dish it up (346).

This sense of participation from Isabella is also created through the transmediality of the text, which includes videos and photographs of her alongside the narrative. The text's Pinterest board contains a pin that links to a YouTube clip of Isabella talking about her life: the low-quality video, which seems to have been made by a non-professional, shows her speaking in a cluttered domestic setting, at times looking directly into the camera, addressing it like an interlocutor and creating a sense of intimacy.[24] Like the recordings of Genna reading *Medium* that I discussed in the previous chapter, this personal video gives voice and embodiment to the subject of the text, which deepens both the reality effect and the readers'/users' engagement with it. This is also achieved through the photographs of Isabella and other protagonists of the story that we are offered online and that are peppered throughout the book. The photographs are particularly interesting in terms of exploring colonisation, as photography was used in the colonial period as a means of documenting and cataloguing the 'objects' of the colonial enterprise in such a way as to appear to be scientific or anthropological enquiry, whilst also possessing the exoticising and pleasure-giving possibilities afforded by visual spectacle (Hight and Sampson 2004: 3). During Mussolini's rule, photography was used to mass produce orientalist pornographic images of colonial subjects, which were sent home as postcards or published in magazines (Ponzanesi 2005: 173; Burdett 2007: 137; Clò 2010: 28). In *Timira*, Isabella remembers that people recognised in her 'l'icona dell'aventura colonial [...] questa "bella abissina" [...] la Venere nera' [the icon of the colonial adventure [...] the 'beautiful Abyssinian' [...] the Black Venus] (169); yet, the photographs of her in the text and online subvert this exoticisation by resembling the kind of everyday images that would be found in any family photograph album, as seen, for example, in the childhood picture of her and her brother (12), or the older pictures of Isabella (170 and 248). By including prints in *Timira* that are black and white, worn and creased, and speak of the archive — that are, literally and metaphorically, 'dated' — the authors seem to hark back to the colonial use of photography, but juxtapose it with the more fluid and impermanent visual technology of the text's Pinterest board online, provoking reflection on different forms of history and memory.

Aside from its 'female voice' and its interaction with documentation, the novel is in keeping with the Manzonian/microhistorical model outlined earlier in other ways too. Isabella as an eternal refugee is at the mercy of larger forces throughout her life, displaced from Somalia to Italy, then travelling back to settle in Mogadishu, only to have to flee again. There is in fact a nod to Manzoni in *Timira*, when Isabella's departure during the civil war in the 1990s ironically echoes Lucia's famous 'Addio ai monti' [Farewell to the mountains]: 'Giunti sulla rotonda del "Kilometro 4", persino la paccottiglia dell'Arco di Trionfo Popolare ti strappa un addio in stile Lucia Mondella' [Reaching the 'Kilometro 4' roundabout, even the shoddy Arch of the People's Triumph wrings a Lucia Mondella-style farewell from you] (59). The authors give a strong sense of what it was like to experience historical developments on an everyday level and Isabella, as a woman of colour in Mussolini's Italy, and later in a society that does not recognise her as Italian, could be seen as the exceptional normal that microhistorical studies tend to focus on; that is, someone seen as an outsider according to the system of power, but whose story can express something revealing about that very system. Wu Ming 2 strikingly uses a map metaphor when discussing Isabella's story: 'eravamo entrambi convinti che la tua terra avesse diritto a un posto sul mappamondo' [we were both convinced that your land had a right to a place on the world map] (345). This brings to mind Manzoni's topographic map, which would be fleshed out by the private stories of individuals like Isabella; in the twenty-first century, the map can also be fleshed out by transmedial elements alongside the historical novel itself, which, in the case of *Timira*, literally bring more colour in the form of the photographs and videos online that help reanimate the past. Micro- and macro-history are put into sharp relief throughout the text and on its Pinterest board, which juxtaposes personal history (family photographs and the video of Isabella) and History with a capital 'H' (newspapers, newsreel footage). A similar operation takes place in the narrative, starting from Wu Ming 2's run-down of historical events that have been happening since he last saw Isabella in his letter that opens the narrative: 'un anno e mezzo pieno di rivolta e di quello che si usa chiamare la Storia, per poi convincersi che sia un pezzo di carta, o di marmo, e non di vita' [a year and a half full of revolt and of what we are in the habit of calling History, to then convince ourselves that it is a piece of paper, or marble, and not life] (7). This recalls both Manzoni's opening to *I promessi sposi* that evokes 'L'historia' and his similarly ironic reference later in the book to 'Many important events', quoted earlier.[25] This opening letter from Wu Ming 2 to Isabella also underlines how this historical novel was constructed. Like *I promessi sposi* and *Una storia romantica*, *Timira* foregrounds the way in which it was based on historical documentation, the red folder (9) that Antar had brought to Wu Ming 2 eight years before. The documents inside the folder are then presented like clues, listed one by one, but remaining obscure to the reader at this point, marking the beginning of his search to understand her micro(hi)story and bring it to us. In *Timira*, once again, we see the historical operation brought to the fore.

Combined with this commitment to unearth the overlooked aspects of Italy's past, we can detect some elements that could be seen as postmodern, as shown by its tongue-in-cheek epigraph: 'This is a true story... including the parts that are not'. It is again reminiscent of Eco's *Il nome della rosa*, this time in its epigraph — 'Naturalmente, un manoscritto' [Naturally, a manuscript] (Eco 2005) — which gives a similar dual sense of being both literary and based on real evidence. Mohamed and Wu Ming 2 explain the epigraph in the postscript by saying that they did not aim to depict an absolute truth, but what they call 'più modestamente la verità-di-Isabella' [more modestly the truth-of-Isabella] (505). This suggests that, for all the novel's inclusion of real documentation and historical fact, we can only truly engage with history through subjective and 'modest' means. Parts of Isabella's life need to be imagined, such as her journey to Italy as a toddler in the care of nuns. The narrative's lack of authority is frequently underlined, for example in the sections using a second-person singular narrative voice, which highlights the role of conjecture: 'Ti immagino in camera, alla luce di due candele, davanti all'armadio spalancato e ai cassetti aperti' [I imagine you in the room, in the light of two candles, in front of the wide open wardrobe and open drawers] (43). Wu Ming 2 states in a letter to Isabella that he wanted to weave together the episodes she remembers 'col filo del dubbio' [with the thread of doubt] (344). Thus, the poetic licence that the authors employed is foregrounded, just as Scurati underlined his insertions of the verisimilar into history. Some of the documents included in *Timira* were modified or even falsified, as we find out in the postscript. Isabella's birth certificate (46–47) was reconstructed by combining elements of other documents belonging to her and her brother, as she did not have the original certificate (508), and the extract from Siad Barre's revolutionary speech (382–85) was created from the text of the original with the addition of a final part taken from a longer speech he made only to the armed forces a few weeks later (518). Again, there is a combination of political aims with textual experimentation and playfulness, casting doubt on the status of this historical knowledge, which, at the same time, casts doubt on the rejection of postmodernism we have seen from recent writers like Wu Ming 1.

Like other texts written by the Wu Ming collective, *Timira* comes to a close with the filmically titled 'Titoli di coda' [Credits], in which the authors list the various sources and inspiration that contributed to the writing of the narrative. Using similar wording to Scurati, Mohamed and Wu Ming 2 explain that this is to encourage readers to engage with the material and develop the text beyond the pages of the book: 'grazie ai lettori il testo acquista nuovi significati e genera poi discorso, passaparola, commenti, recensioni, riscritture, trasposizioni' [thanks to the readers, the text gains new meanings and then generates conversation, word of mouth, comments, reviews, rewritings, transpositions] (503). In *Timira*, the text does not end with the paper copy: as well as the 'Titoli di coda' and Pinterest board, *Timira* is part of the same story world as the 2008 historical text about Giorgio Marincola's life by Carlo Costa and Lorenzo Teodonio, which was made into a theatre performance set to music with Wu Ming 2, and later released as an audio CD.[26] This 'Progetto Transmediale Multiautore' [Multi-Author Transmedial Project][27] gives readers the opportunity to assess and digest various accounts of history, rather than simply accepting one version, in an attempt to give the past back the force that Scurati desires. However, it should also be noted that the Pinterest board in particular can be seen as an effective marketing tool to attract readers to the text, as it is created by both Einaudi and Wu Ming, and Einaudi have also created Pinterest boards for other books they have published,[28] showing that it is not unique to the narrative strategy of *Timira*, even if it is an effective extension of the text's life-writing. The internet also played a key role in the construction of the text, as shown by the authors' references in the final section to their use of tools such as Google Earth, Flickr, YouTube and Facebook in imagining the spaces and people depicted (509). The internet is frequently present throughout *Point Lenana* too (which also has a Pinterest board extension),[29] helping Wu Ming 1 in his function as 'il disseppellitore di storie' [the unearther of stories] (Wu Ming 1 and Santachiara 2013: 14). His quest to discover the author of *Fuga sul Kenya* [*No Picnic on Mount Kenya*] started with: 'La cosa più normale del mondo: digitare "Felice Benuzzi" su un motore di ricerca' [The most normal thing in the world: typing 'Felice Benuzzi' into a search engine] (Wu Ming 1 and Santachiara 2013: 17). This reflects the way that nowadays we can encounter history in a wider variety of ways than ever before, given that from a personal computer it is possible to view film footage, access archives, read documents, or simply encounter straightforward historical accounts. History no longer appears purely as text written by historians, and the advent of new technologies entails 'the co-existing of previously more distinct modes of cultural memory, for instance: the "private" and the "public"' (Hoskins 2009: 101). Recent historical novels such as *Timira* and *Point Lenana* reflect this changing landscape of how we access the past, and how anybody can dig up personal or national (hi)stories, although they also demonstrate Jenkins's (2006a: 18) observation that corporate interests are still present in convergence culture.

As with Scurati's text, we see in *Timira* the dynamics of cultural memory as described by Erll and Rigney:

> an ongoing process of remembrance and forgetting in which individuals and groups continue to reconfigure their relationship to the past and hence reposition themselves in relation to established and emergent memory sites. As the word itself suggests, 'remembering' is better seen as an active engagement with the past, as performative rather than as reproductive. (Erll and Rigney 2009: 2)

The book performs this reconfiguration by sharing and reflecting on different versions of the past, and encouraging their readers to engage with this memory too. As a 'mestizo novel', it combines different types of memory and different forms of discourse and media, always reminding its readers that it is not a singular, definitive version of history, but a hybrid that poses questions, showing that: 'Qualsiasi narrazione è un'opera collettiva' [Every narrative is a collective work] (504).

Le rondini di Montecassino by Helena Janeczek

Janeczek has particularly examined the workings of memory and how the past reflects on and endures in the present, although she is another female author who is a surprising omission from the NIE nebula: Wu Ming 1 states in a footnote of the Memorandum that Janeczek's 2002 text *Cibo* [*Food*] is a UNO but not part of the NIE (Wu Ming 1 2009a: 44 n. 37). Perhaps she was not seen as Italian enough for the NIE — she was born in Germany to Polish-Jewish parents, but has lived in Italy since the 1980s and writes in Italian — or perhaps her insistence throughout her work on doubt and fragmentation could be seen as incompatible with the epic label. Janeczek's 2010 text *Le rondini di Montecassino* came shortly after the Memorandum, and it can undoubtedly be aligned with the concerns that Wu Ming 1 outlined (as Piga 2012 has also pointed out), as can her other texts, *Lezioni di tenebra* (1997), *Cibo* (2002), and *La ragazza con la Leica* (2017), given her exploration of history, memory, generational issues and inheritance through unusual combinations of life-writing and fiction.[30] As Wu Ming 1 (2009a: 44) points out, Janeczek's work also undoubtedly influenced Saviano and she is his editor; we will see some interesting affinities and differences between the two writers in their approach to testimony through literature in this chapter and the next.[31] Yet, the NIE label once again can be seen as problematic when applied to *Le rondini di Montecassino*: whilst Janeczek's subject matter might be seen as epic in choosing to focus on the battle in the Second World War that led to the destruction of the abbey of Monte Cassino, her approach is through a narrative that she describes within it as 'una "collezione di piccole epopee" confuse e frammentarie, simili forse a qualche pezzo dei mosaici trovati fra le rovine dell'abbazia' [a 'collection of small epics' that are confused and fragmentary, similar perhaps to some of the pieces of mosaics found among the ruins of the abbey] (344). Unlike Saviano in *Gomorra* (as we will see in the following chapter), Janeczek does not claim to achieve any sense of completion in reconstructing the mosaics or hide the ways in which she has manipulated or embellished the material that she addresses, explicitly reflecting on both the contradictions and the responsibilities of examining real-life events in an approach that might be seen as anti-epic.

Like the other historical novels that we have seen in this chapter and like many other UNOs in this study, *Le rondini di Montecassino* brings to the fore questions about the kind of knowledge that the storyteller can offer. The opening sentence of the text states: 'Mio padre è stato a Montecassino, ha combattuto nel Secondo Corpo d'Armata polacco, con il generale Anders' [My father was at Monte Cassino, he fought in the Polish Second Army Corps with General Anders] (11). Janeczek goes on to explain how her father met and married an Italian woman, and says that she is telling this story to a taxi driver, who is Polish. Yet, on the following page, it transpires that she did not talk to the taxi driver about Monte Cassino, but simply invented an Italian mother to excuse her inability to speak Polish. She then tells her readers that her father did not in fact fight at Monte Cassino. She explains that her surname is not her father's real surname, but one he assumed during the war to hide his Jewishness, something she holds back from the taxi driver. The book thus opens with a series of false statements and corrections, leaving the reader confused as to what is real and what is not. This leads her to ask a series of questions about the nature of truth and testimony:

> Che cos'è una finzione quando si incarna, quando detiene il vero potere di modificare il corso della storia, quando agisce sulla realtà e ne viene trasformata a sua volta? Cosa diventa la menzogna quando è salvifica?
> E quali storie, mi domando infine, posso narrare io di fronte a questo? A quale invenzione posso ricorrere essendo testimone in carne e ossa che fra il vero e il falso, fra realtà e finzione, corre talvolta il confine labile che separa la vita dalla morte? (13–14)

> [What is a fiction when it becomes incarnate, when it possesses the true power to change the course of history, when it acts on reality and in turn is transformed by it? What becomes of a lie when it brings salvation?
> And what stories, I finally ask myself, can I narrate faced with this? What invention can I resort to, being a witness in flesh and blood who, between true and false, reality and fiction, sometimes runs along the fine line that separates life from death?]

Here, she underlines the responsibility of her role as storyteller, but also the value of fiction, or even of lies, of false testimony. She situates the author as someone who is on the borders, who is in between, who can never completely find herself on one side or the other of the binaries true/false, reality/fiction. This in-between-ness is what we have seen foregrounded and explored in the unidentified genre that I address in this study.

The answer to Janeczek's question about what she can narrate when faced with these contradictions is, as she describes it in the quotation mentioned earlier, a mosaic of stories. She constantly draws links between the past and the present, between history and History, as do the other historical novels that we have seen here, moving between fictional and non-fictional elements and between the present day and historical reconstructions based on documentary research. She takes the battle as a starting point for the different microstories she narrates, inserting the personal into the historical and collective. The book is divided into sections focalised through the different protagonists she chooses to portray, who are both real and imagined people — a Texan sergeant, the grandson of a Maori veteran, teenagers from Rome of Indian and Polish descent, and herself in search of the experiences of her ancestors — and each larger section begins with pages that resemble memorials with their dates and quotations (9, 17, 31, 147, 275), anchoring individual stories, whether invented or not, in a sense of official memory. By voicing these different transnational stories, she builds up a more complex picture of this watershed event than the history books provide and shows how the battle reverberated afterwards and continues to reverberate today, in what Piga (2012) rightly points out is enacting Rothberg's (2009) multidirectional memory, as we saw too with Scurati's *Una storia romantica*. For example, the story of Janeczek's

Polish ancestors' escape from a Gulag to join Anders's army runs alongside the present-day story of the teenagers Anand and Edoardo, who are in the cemetery at Monte Cassino to raise awareness about Poles who have disappeared in Italy, linking forgotten stories of the past to forgotten stories of the present, reflecting on migration and persecution across the years. Janeczek's image of her stories forming mosaics is comparable to Manzoni's more colourful maps, as her piecing together of fragments with the tools of fiction is an attempt to render the past more nuanced, vivid and relevant, although this operation causes Janeczek's mother the kind of discomfort that Manzoni explored when she asks her daughter: ' "Ma tu sei uno storico o stai scrivendo un romanzo?" ' ['But are you a historian or are you writing a novel?'] (191).

The narrative thus raises questions about historiography and memory, about what we remember and what we forget, and why. The theme of commemoration is particularly a feature of the present microstory of Rapata, who travels from New Zealand to the cemetery at Monte Cassino to remember his grandfather. He gradually realises the unstable nature of his grandfather's tales about the past, which reveal themselves to be 'così friabili' [so crumbly] when he goes to explore them in Monte Cassino; as stated earlier, Janeczek does not downplay the doubtful nature of our knowledge about the past. Nevertheless, Rapata decides to continue to believe in his and his grandfather's memory: 'Doveva fidarsi di suo nonno e di se stesso, fare un atto di fede in quella trama creata a quattro mani' [He had to trust his grandfather and himself, to have faith in that jointly created plot] (105). Storytelling is shown to be important when creating a sense of identity, but the memory it is based on is once more shown to be a collective work, something that can be reconfigured rather than set in stone. Rapata also comes to realise the biased nature of history through visiting the *lieu de mémoire* of the cemetery. He observes:

> l'allestimento del sacrario militare non era soltanto classista e razzista, ma soprattutto falso. Il cimitero trasmetteva il messaggio che gli uomini caduti in quelle battaglie fossero per maggior parte native della Gran Bretagna, gli altri presenze trascurabili da relegare in fondo, dove restavano invisibili a chi non fosse andato a cercarli apposta.

> [the layout of the military memorial was not only classist and racist, but above all false. The cemetery conveyed the message that the men who fell in those battles were mostly British natives, the others insignificant presences to be relegated to the bottom, where they remained invisible to those who had not gone to look for them deliberately.] (92)

It is these other presences that Janeczek's stories make more visible, bringing to light forgotten perspectives on the past through showing the range of different participants in the battle. We see this approach again later when she discusses the soldiers who raped women in Ciociaria: after the war, these rapes are known about but not discussed, whereas Janeczek breaks this silence about these women's experiences. When we do see the famous destruction of the abbey (59), Piga points out that it is narrated from the kind of oblique viewpoint that Wu Ming 1 describes in the Memorandum:

il precipitare delle bombe sul monastero è narrato dal punto di vista di chi è assediato e inerme: i rifugiati e gli sfollati riparati nell'abbazia, nelle grotte, nei costoni, nei bunker. [...] I loro punti di vista vanno a convergere in un unico punto di vista descrivibile come 'obliquo'. (Piga 2012)

[the falling of the bombs on the monastery is narrated from the viewpoint of those who are besieged and defenceless: refugees and displaced people sheltering in the abbey, in the caves, in the ridges, in the bunkers. [...] Their viewpoints converge into a single viewpoint that can be described as 'oblique'.]

However, I would argue that Janeczek's text is more successful than many others in Wu Ming 1's nebula in working against the bias of history books to focus on the actions of important white men and in focusing instead on other subaltern stories and on her-story, in what can be seen as another example of a text that has Gargani's female voice (1984).

Also significant in terms of history and memory is the choice to include multiple perspectives in the narrative, as Scurati and Wu Ming 2 and Mohamed do too, as well as many other recent historical novels, particularly those written collectively by Wu Ming.[32] Neumann argues:

Texts with a multi-perspectival narration or focalization provide insight into the memories of several narrative instances or figures and in this way they can reveal the functioning and problems of collective memory-creation. [...] By giving voice to those previously silenced fictions of memory, they constitute an imaginative counter-memory, thereby challenging the hegemonic memory culture and questioning the socially established boundary between remembering and forgetting. (Neumann 2010: 338–39)

Certainly, Janeczek's approach to the famous battle, remembered as an Allied assault to break through enemy lines to reach Rome, brings to the fore marginal and forgotten experiences, emphasising the transnational dimension of the events through the range of participants we encounter, as well as the diverse effects that continue to be felt in the present, in what can certainly be described as an imaginative counter-memory.

Alongside these microstories, Janeczek includes interjections about herself, concerning both her writing of the text and her investigations of her relatives who, unlike her father, were directly involved in the battle. These metafictional interjections clearly break the illusion of the narration, showing that the text is based on writerly work, and filtered through Janeczek's own understanding. This can be seen when she reflects on the difficulties of writing about Rapata; she tells us of her months of research on New Zealand, where she has never actually been (137), but also emphasises the role of imagination in reaching understanding, significantly stating:

Importa l'urgenza di conoscere [...] che non si illude di poter colmare i vuoti né tantomeno sostituirsi all'esperienza, ma è soprattutto un movimento verso, una tensione con cui cerchi di accorciare una distanza che non riguarda più soltanto quello che sai, ma quel che senti e immagini. In questa prospettiva non esiste nulla di distintamente inutile, soltanto il sogno di una realtà che ti tocca inseguire anche a casaccio, perché tu riesca a fartela passare dentro e renderla vera sulla pagina. (138)

> [What is important is the urgency to know [...] which is not deluded about being able to fill the gaps or even replace the experience, but it is above all a movement towards, a tension with which you try to shorten a distance that no longer only affects what you know, but what you feel and imagine. From this perspective, there is nothing distinctly useless, only the dream of a reality that you must pursue even haphazardly, so that you can make it go inside you and make it true on the page.]

A movement *towards* knowledge is cast as the work of the writer, who employs imagination and feelings, in work that is rife with tensions and often based on chance, but that also springs from reality. Unlike Saviano, whom we will see in the next chapter downplaying the embellishments in his account in *Gomorra*, Janeczek highlights the gaps in her knowledge, as she did in her previous texts too, particularly in *Lezioni di tenebra*, in which there is a profusion of language denoting uncertainty about her family's past.[33] Throughout her work, Janeczek tends to move away from the kind of certainty we will see in Saviano and towards the more tentative approach to knowledge that we will see in Jones's text in the next chapter.

The metafictional moments in *Le rondini di Montecassino* are comparable to the postscripts to *Una storia romantica* and *Timira*, as Janeczek similarly guards against her reader being Eco's ingenuous reader. They are also reminiscent of Ginzburg's microhistorical approach described earlier, in which 'le ipotesi, i dubbi, le incertezze diventavano parte della narrazione; la ricerca della verità diventava parte dell'esposizione della (necessariamente incompleta) verità raggiunta' [the hypotheses, the doubts, the uncertainties became part of the narrative; the search for truth became part of the exposition of the (necessarily incomplete) truth reached] (Ginzburg 2006: 256). We see Janeczek weigh up different versions of what happened, as when she notes the differences in British, French and Indian historiography, in which each country takes any possible credit and downplays any mistakes, or emphasises the mistakes of others (311). She is reflecting on the various possibilities about the past, recalling Wu Ming 1's 'potential uchronias' (Wu Ming 1 2009a: 34). This can be seen most obviously in her series of 'what ifs' about the battle: 'Se il generale Tuker non si fosse ammalato, se il generale Tuker, già febbricitante, non avesse avuto l'idea di mandare un suo ufficiale a rovistare nelle biblioteche e nelle librerie napoletane' [If General Tuker had not been ill, if General Tuker, already feverish, had not had the idea of sending one of his officers to rummage in the Neapolitan libraries and bookstores] (56); these conditionals then continue over the following pages (56–58), as she imagines how history could have been otherwise. There is also a sense of alternative history fiction in the opening of the text, when she tells different versions of her family's past and reflects on her false surname that survived the Second World War in contrast to 'una vertigine di nomi veri, di nomi dimenticati, di nomi perduti, di nomi scomparsi' [a dizzying array of real names, forgotten names, lost names, missing names] (14); these reflections spark off her explorations of these other names alongside her own. There is a sense once more that the author's imagination can help illuminate the past in new ways that more straightforward historical accounts do not, and this is again done through foregrounding the historical operation rather than hiding it.

As in her previous texts, there are constant connections drawn in *Le rondini di Montecassino* between Janeczek's personal history, the microstories she tells and a wider sense of History with a capital 'H', and these connections are explored through the prisms of the various real and imagined characters that criss-cross the text, whose stories bring up ideas about bearing witness. Her investigation of her family's involvement in the battle takes her on a journey to Israel, where she speaks to Irka, the wife of her mother's cousin, about what happened. As in her exploration of her mother's experience of the Second World War in *Lezioni di tenebra*, in which she journeys to Auschwitz with her, there is a strong sense of the limits of what she can discover, due not only to a reticence about asking certain painful questions, but also to some unreliability in the accounts she receives. In *Le rondini di Montecassino*, for example, Irka says that her own mother was taken to Treblinka when she was thirty; Janeczek doubts she was so young but, instead of asking more, she goes to verify the account through research, discovering that Irka's mother was in fact thirty-eight when she died in Treblinka (181–82). Irka also does not clarify the details of her escape with Janeczek's mother's cousins from the gulag to which they had been deported, simply saying they left on a train, although Janeczek is aware that this restraint may be because the memory is too traumatic, stating: 'Molti polacchi [...] raccontano che quel viaggio era stato la cosa peggiore, molto peggio della deportazione' [Many Poles [...] say that the journey had been the worst thing, much worse than the deportation] (238). Testimony is thus supplemented with research, but remains incomplete. Janeczek's texts (as we will see too with Jones's text in chapter 4) recall Agamben's work on the essential aporia in testimony in *Quel che resta di Auschwitz* [*Remnants of Auschwitz*], which he explored through the life-writing of Primo Levi. Like other Holocaust survivors, Levi could not bear witness for those who did not survive the concentration camps; Agamben states: 'I "veri" testimoni, i "testimoni integrali" sono coloro che non hanno testimoniato né avrebbero potuto farlo. [...] I superstiti, come pseudotestimoni, parlano in vece loro, per delega: testimoniano di una testimonianza mancante' ['The 'true' witnesses, the 'complete witnesses' are those who did not bear witness and could not bear witness. [...] The survivors, as pseudo-witnesses, speak in their place, by proxy; they bear witness to a missing testimony] (Agamben 1998: 31–32).

As a second-generation narrative, Janeczek's work multiplies this sense of aporia, as she is bearing witness for her family members or for others, and must negotiate gaps, silences and even lies in what she knows of the experiences she attempts to narrate. Janeczek's work deals with what Hirsch has termed 'postmemory':

> 'Postmemory' describes the relationship that the 'generation after' bears to the personal, collective, and cultural trauma of those who came before — to experiences they 'remember' only by means of the stories, images, and behaviors among which they grew up. [...] These events happened in the past, but their effects continue into the present. (Hirsch 2012: 5)

We can see the generation of postmemory in the key role that her parents' history as Holocaust survivors plays throughout Janeczek's texts, in which she traces how her own memories and identity interact with past experiences. Postmemory can also be seen in many recent Italian novels, particularly in those that insistently return to the *anni di piombo*, to events the authors did not experience first-hand, as I discussed in chapter 1. Not coincidentally, Hirsch (2012: 5) underlines the influence of 'the era of "posts"' on postmemory, which can be linked to a postmodernist questioning of sources of knowledge, and Hirsch's era of posts also recalls the statement from Bhabha that I quoted in the introduction to this study, when he describes the turn of the millennium as being characterised by 'the current and controversial shiftiness of the prefix "post"' (Bhabha 1994: 1). Janeczek's UNOs could be seen as part of the questioning atmosphere of Bhabha's 'beyond' where new narrative strategies are sought, but postmodernism once again has not been overcome.

Janeczek's original interest in the Battle of Monte Cassino sprang from the experience of a family friend who fought there, Milek. However, Milek chose never to tell anyone about his experiences, and Janeczek therefore finds herself having to discover what happened to him, saying: 'ho tentato di colmare le memorie perse con quelle raccolte e conservate: testimonianze di deportati e militari che nei punti dove si incrociano con la storia di Milek, diventano in grado di illuminarla' [I tried to fill the lost memories with those that had been gathered and preserved: testimonies of deportees and soldiers which, when they coincided with Milek's story, were able to illuminate it] (344). This indirect illumination is reminiscent of Cercas's in *The Anatomy of a Moment* quoted in the introduction to this chapter, as well as Scurati's sewing together of what is true and what is verisimilar. Janeczek then realises that even this is not enough, and that she can tell only a few of the many transnational stories that converge on this battle. Milek's story was appropriated by her own father, who was jealous of his friend and used to pretend that he had fought in the battle instead, when in reality he was alone trying to escape the Nazis in Poland at the time. She tells us: 'Milek [...] era quel che mio padre avrebbe voluto essere, il suo doppio immaginario' [Milek [...] was what my father would have wanted to be, his imaginary double] (361). It is interesting that she seems to have transmitted this lie again with the taxi driver at the beginning of the text. She reflects on all the things she could have asked her father when he was alive but did not, leaving blanks in the story. She dedicates the book to him — whom she calls 'mio soldato immaginario' [my imaginary soldier] (362) — before stating in the final lines:

> Ai nostri padri non possiamo più domandare niente. Possiamo solo ricordare le loro vite e le loro verità, anche quando assumono la forma della diceria inverificabile, o si ricoprono della pietà mai abbastanza grande, mai abbastanza impermeabile, della menzogna. (362)

> [We can no longer ask our fathers anything. We can only remember their lives and their truths, even when they take the form of unverifiable rumours, or become covered by the never big enough, never impenetrable enough, mercy of a lie.]

The text thus comes back round to another lie, just as it began, and, indeed, it ends precisely on the word 'lie'. The fathers' truths that Janeczek refers to are not coincidentally in the plural, rather than being one definitive truth, yet they remain truths despite their plurality, despite the lies with which they are interspersed.

We have seen that twenty-first-century Italian historical novels have aimed to rethink both the remembered and the forgotten aspects of recent history, displaying a distrust of grand narratives, a desire to insert the personal into the collective, and a foregrounding of the ways in which we apprehend the past. *Una storia romantica*, *Timira* and *Le rondini di Montecassino* all merge existing accounts with literary invention, and combine postmodern experimentation with political aims, playing with different ideas and versions of what the 'truth' about the past might be. The overarching ambition of these writers is to do what Manzoni imagined his readers demanded of the historical novelist: 'volete che vi dia, non una mera e nuda storia, ma qualcosa di più ricco, di più compito; volete che rifaccia in certo modo le polpe a quel carcame, che è, in così grand parte, la storia' [you want him to give you not just the bare bones of history but something richer, more complete; in a way, you want him to put some flesh back on the skeleton that history largely is] (1973: 1730). Yet, in bringing history 'back to life', these authors are self-reflexive and even self-critical at times, as they use this apparition to help us reconsider the past in the light of the present and future.

Notes to Chapter 3

1. These French novels also show that there have been various returns to the Second World War in twenty-first-century European literature, which we can also see in recent Italian historical novels, such as Giorgio Falco's *La gemella H* [*Twin H*], Genna's *Hitler* (2008a), or Janeczek's work analysed in this chapter.
2. However, Boscolo argues that the difference between the NIE and the texts Elias analyses is that the NIE 'does not display the postmodernist traces Elias identifies' (Boscolo 2010b: 26); again, I would argue that, on the contrary, we can certainly detect postmodernist traces.
3. This idea has been taken by Erll and Rigney (2009) from media studies — in particular, from *Remediation: Understanding New Media* (1999) by Jay Bolter and Richard Grusin — and employed in cultural memory studies to describe the way in which we remember historical events. It will be more fully developed in the section of this chapter on Scurati's *Una storia romantica*.
4. The Italian title plays on the dual sense of the word 'storia', which could be translated as 'history' or 'story'.
5. This climate is reflected in Wu Ming's project *La prima volta che ho visto i fascisti* [*The First Time I Saw the Fascists*], which collected testimony from various people on the occasion of the 60th anniversary of 25 April. The text, freely available to download online, contains: 'pagine di diario, frammenti, racconti, reminiscenze, visioni febbrili. Testi curati o tenuti per anni in un cassetto della mente, rovesciati sulla pagina d'istinto, di getto, senza preoccupazioni di estetica o di stile' [pages of diaries, fragments, stories, reminiscences, feverish visions. Edited texts or texts kept for years in a drawer of the mind, poured onto the page instinctively, in one go, with no worries about aesthetics or style] (Wu Ming 2005: 8).
6. Another example of Manzoni resurfacing in recent literature is in De Michele's trilogy, where the character Cristiano in prison spends his time reading and re-reading Manzoni (De Michele 2004: 55).
7. The quartet consists of *L'amica geniale* [*My Brilliant Friend*] (2011), *Storia del nuovo cognome* [*Story of a New Name*] (2012), *Storia di chi fugge e di chi resta* [*Those Who Leave and Those Who Stay*] (2013) and *Storia della bambina perduta* [*The Story of the Lost Child*] (2014).
8. For more on this controversy, see the section on Scego in chapter 4.
9. For example: Aspasia comes into contact with the real-life figure of Cristina di Belgiojoso, who writes her a letter about the condition of women (72–75). The period of fighting for women is

shown to be one of living in fear of rape (134), and Aspasia points out that women will never be free even if they win the fight (277).

10. Apart from *Una storia romantica*, he has written *Il rumore sordo della battaglia* [*The Muffled Sound of the Battle*] (2006b), and the biofictional *Il tempo migliore della nostra vita* [*The Best Time of Our Lives*] (2015) and *M. Il figlio del secolo* [*M: The Son of the Century*] (2018).

11. The full title of Manzoni's essay is 'Del romanzo storico e, in genere, de' componimenti misti di storia e invenzione' [On the historical novel and, in general, on mixed works of history and invention].

12. Serkowska rightly sees a sense of *impegno*, although concealed, in *Il nome della rosa*, and also in Eco's later text *La misteriosa fiamma della Regina Loana* [*The Mysterious Flame of Queen Loana*] (Serkowska 2012: 372). She points to an ethical underpinning to the way in which Eco invites his readers to scrutinise the past and confront memories. Eco himself stated in the postscript to *Il nome della rosa* that talking about the medieval period was simply a mask (Eco 2005: 512), and, as Serkowska points out, he embedded references to the *anni di piombo* in the plot of his novel (Serkowska 2012: 377). He was reflecting on the present by using the past as metaphor, just as we see recent writers doing.

13. I am thinking, for example, of the outcry about the parts of *Gomorra* that Saviano invented (discussed in the following chapter), which surprised readers who read it as a non-fictional journalistic investigation. Luther Blissett's *Q* could also be read as a more straightforward, illusionist historical novel (Glynn 2005), if it were not for the final section of images and captions, suggesting allegorical possibilities for interpretation. It is no coincidence that, when *Q* first appeared with an anonymous author, some suggested that it had been written by Eco (Arie and Ezard 2003). Wu Ming themselves cannot seem to resist knowing winks to their readers in their historical novels, suggesting they are smiling from behind the mask of history just as Eco did. For example, in *Q*, the main protagonist is unconvinced that an energising drink from Arabia, made from beans and called *quahvé*, will take off in Europe (Blissett 1999: 617–18). In *54*, Cary Grant and David Niven discuss 'un libro ridicolo e disgustoso, scritto da un certo Fleming. Il protagonista è un agente MI6 di nome "James Bond". [...] Ecco un libro da cui non trarranno mai un film!' [A ridiculous and disgusting book written by a certain Fleming. The protagonist is an MI6 agent named 'James Bond'. [...] Here's a book that will never be made into a film!] (Wu Ming 2002: 215).

14. Antonello (2009) discusses recent ideas of *impegno* as expressed in theatrical storytelling, which has many overlaps with the approaches of recent novels. Indeed, he considers Ginzburg's evidential paradigm in relation to this type of storytelling (Antonello 2009: 244–46), and likens their approach to justice to recent Italian *noir* by Carlotto and De Cataldo (Antonello 2009: 247), as well as to Saviano's approach inspired by Pasolini in *Gomorra* (Antonello 2009: 250).

15. When the name-changing main protagonist and his fellow Protestants win the fight for freedom in Munster, it is only to find a new source of oppression at the hands of corrupt leaders. *Q* has been seen as an allegory for Bologna's Movimento del '77 (Genna 2007b), but it also makes wider points about how Europe today was shaped and the beginnings of the capitalist system, as hinted at by the final section in which the historical images are captioned by a press communiqué from Luther Blissett about the NATO bombings of Yugoslavia in 1999 and a quote from Marx and Engels's *Manifesto of the Communist Party*.

16. It is no coincidence that Bertante mentions Scurati in the acknowledgements (Bertante 2008: 245), as there are several similarities with *Una storia romantica*, which was published only a year before Bertante's historical novel. Errico finds that as he fights he loses his sense of humanity, until at the end nobody celebrates their victory, because: 'Non siamo eroi' [We aren't heroes] (Bertante 2008: 224). This sentiment is not dissimilar to that of Jacopo in his later incarnation as Antonio in Scurati's novel, who points out to Italo in the 1885 section: 'non è più tempo di eroi' [the time of heroes is over] (453). Whilst Wu Ming 1 at the time of writing the Memorandum saw *Al diavul* as being an allegory for the way in which Italy viewed Spain under Zapatero as more enlightened and culturally superior to their own nation (Wu Ming 1 2009a: 81), there are wider resonances in this text. Bertante shows how countries can sleepwalk into oppression in a way that could be seen as referring to any number of conflicts that spill blood in the name of ideals that later descend into hatred and corruption.

17. Two of the main characters, Adele and her brother Matteo, join the partisan struggle and actively fight the Nazis, but the text also depicts Adele's husband Aldo, whose fear leads him to hide in his mother's loft and eventually descend into madness in a stark depiction of a lack of *impegno*. The text thus reflects on bravery and cowardice, sacrifice and self-preservation. It closes with presentiments that the end of the war may not bring real change for the people, that whilst they are feeling satisfied with the victory, it may be premature to stop imagining as Matteo does in the final line 'sogni di città e mondi ideali' [dreams of ideal cities and worlds] (Scrittura industriale collettiva 2013: 308). From the point of view of allegory, Adele's experience in particular has almost anachronistic elements, reminiscent of the terrorist activities of the Red Brigades in the *anni di piombo*, which one of the authors has pointed out was part of their aim to 'indagare le origini del contemporaneo' [investigate the origins of the contemporary] (Galimberti 2013).

18. The French Revolution is obviously a key foundational moment for exploring such ideas. In the fourth part of Wu Ming's text, entitled 'Termidoro' [Thermidor], D'Amblanc looks at the people around him and thinks: 'sembravano voler dire: "Siamo ancora qui, guardate i nostri candidi colli, guardate le nostre testacce ancora bene attaccate, siamo vivi, siamo sopravvissuti al Terrore e adesso il Terrore siamo noi"' [they seemed to want to say: 'We are still here, look at our white necks, look at our heads still well attached, we are alive, we survived the Terror and now the Terror is us'] (Wu Ming 2014a: 655).

19. Interestingly, in the story that Moresco contributed to *Controinsurrezioni*, we can see a direct connection made between the Risorgimento and the G8 in Genoa, when his story splices modern scenes of war and devastation into his depiction of nineteenth-century Italy and includes: 'Inquadratura degli scontri, delle devastazioni e dei bestiali pestaggi di Genova e del sangue sui pavimenti' [Shot of the clashes, devastation and savage beatings in Genoa and of blood on the ground] (Evangelisti and Moresco 2008: 118).

20. A review on a blog and a tweet: see <http://www.pinterest.com/einaudieditore/timira/>.

21. For more on Scego, see chapter 4.

22. Lucarelli's *L'ottava vibrazione* [*The Eighth Vibration*] has come under fire for not being seen to take a critical enough attitude towards the stereotypes it invokes (Stefani 2010: 51 and Triulzi 2012: 108). Whilst there are defences for Lucarelli's approach, as argued by Sabelli (2013), it is difficult to stomach his exoticising gaze and animalistic depictions of colonial subjects in his reimagining of the Battle of Adwa, even if his aim was to overturn these tropes of colonial discourse.

23. Camilleri takes two sharply contrasting approaches to the issues surrounding Italian colonialism during the fascist period. *Il nipote del Negus* [*The Negus's Nephew*], inspired by a true story although very much embellished (as Camilleri explains in the postscript), tells the story of the Ethiopian prince studying in Italy not from his point of view, but from that of various Sicilians involved and through documents (letters, reports, newspaper articles). It has a comic feel, reflecting what Camilleri describes in the notes at the end as 'il clima di autentica stupidità generale, tra farsa e tragedia, che segnò purtroppo un'epoca' [the climate of authentic general stupidity, between farce and tragedy, which unfortunately marked an era] (2010: 277). *La presa di Macallé* [*The Conquest of Mek'ele*] (Camilleri 2003), on the other hand, is an extremely disturbing text about a boy called Michelino during the war with Ethiopia, who is exploited or abused by all of those around him, a victim of the same fascist and Catholic rhetoric that is used to justify the colonial war. However, in both cases, we can again see the focus on white, male experience that critics have seen as characterising the NIE's approach to Italy's colonial past.

24. See https://www.youtube.com/watch/?v=ivqZeYkMCmo.

25. We discover in the 'Titoli di coda' [Credits] at the end of the narrative that it was actually adapted from Carlo Levi's opening words in *Cristo si è fermato a Eboli* [*Christ Stopped at Eboli*] (505–06). Whilst Levi's text could provide another interesting precursor for the NIE *exposés* of injustice that we will see in the next chapter, Mohamed and Wu Ming 2 explain that it was used in relation to Roberto Derobertis's postcolonial reading of Levi at a conference (506).

26. The information for this project is collated on the website www.razzapartigiana.it. See also Wu Ming's blog *Giap*: <http://www.wumingfoundation.com/giap/?cat=455>.

27. As it is referred to here: <http://www.einaudi.it/speciali/Wu-Ming-2-Antar-Mohamed-Timira>.

28. See www.pinterest.com/einaudieditore/.

29. See www.pinterest.com/einaudieditore/point-lenana/.

30. *Lezioni di tenebra* explores her parents' experiences as Holocaust survivors, whilst in *Cibo* she examines her eating habits and those of people she meets in her everyday life, containing a striking change of tone in the final section, an impassioned piece of hybrid reportage on the BSE epidemic. Her most recent Strega prize-winning text, *La ragazza con la Leica* [*The Girl with the Leica*] (2017), is a work of biofiction that explores the life of Gerda Taro, a Polish Jew and the first female photojournalist to die on the front lines, in the Spanish Civil War in 1937.

31. Not coincidentally, the front cover of *Le rondini di Montecassino* has a quotation from Saviano from a review in *La Repubblica*: 'Helena Janeczek scrive un romanzo potentissimo... Montecassino diviene la guerra di tutti, il luogo da cui tutti veniamo' [Helena Janeczek writes a very powerful novel... Monte Cassino becomes everyone's war, the place everyone comes from]. Janeczek also thanks Saviano in her acknowledgements (363).

32. See, in particular, *54* (2002), in which Wu Ming even narrated from the point of view of a television.

33. For example, Janeczek points out that 'non so pressoché niente: quasi niente della mia storia familiare, niente delle singole vicende' [I know nearly nothing: almost nothing of my family history, nothing of the individual events] (Janeczek 2011: 22); later, she says that she knows that her mother suffered from anxiety attacks before she was born and had been sent to a psychologist, but adds: 'non so per quanto tempo ci sia andata, né cosa abbiano scoperto insieme' [I don't know how long she went there for, or what they discovered together] (Janeczek 2011: 94). As she states near the beginning of the text: 'so di avere a che fare con un mistero irrisolvibile' [I know I am dealing with an unsolvable mystery] (Janeczek 2011: 16).

CHAPTER 4

Literature of Experience:
Representing Reality in the Digital Age

In 2008, the same year as Wu Ming 1's Memorandum on the New Italian Epic (NIE) appeared, the online journal *Allegoria* published an issue on the theme: 'Ritorno alla realtà? Narrativa e cinema alla fine del postmoderno' [Return to reality? Narrative and cinema at the end of the postmodern].[1] It put forward the argument that there had been a return to an engagement with the current reality in film and literature in the twenty-first century (Donnarumma 2008b: 7). Recent work by Italian intellectuals was framed as a reaction against 'la derealizzazione postmoderna' [postmodern derealisation] (Donnarumma 2008c: 28), which was seen as a postmodernist tendency for narrators to shy away from portraying the present situation and instead rely on inwardness and self-referentiality. Such ideas are not dissimilar to those that we have seen Wu Ming 1 discuss in the Memorandum on the NIE, where he also referred to realism in his corpus of unidentified narrative objects (UNOs), but saw it as being combined with epic, allegorical qualities (Wu Ming 1 2009a: 68–72). Donnarumma (2008c: 48), however, insists on a postmodernist crisis of experience, a problem that had been previously discussed at length by Scurati in two essays (2003, 2006a), in which he explored the difficulties of authentic experience in the highly mediated modern world that Baudrillard (1994) has described as hyperreal. Instead of actively participating in what is happening, we are, according to Scurati and others, reduced to being simply passive spectators in front of our televisions; events such as war have become 'una realtà deprivata della sua esperienza. Una serata di morte comodamente adagiati sul divano del salotto sorseggiando birra fresca' [a reality deprived of its experience. An evening of death lying comfortably on the living-room sofa sipping cool beer] (Scurati 2006a: 62). This passivity and lack of engagement is what the contributors to *Allegoria* see recent writers as working against, particularly through the use of first-person narratives according to Donnarumma, who states that they have been using their personal subjectivity to combat 'la disgregazione dell'esperienza' [the disintegration of experience] (Donnarumma 2008c: 49) and to denounce the urgent problems facing Italy and the wider world in the twenty-first century.

The assertions in *Allegoria* on this alleged return to reality led to a heated debate, chiefly on the blog *Nazione indiana*, where Cortellessa (2008), among others, took issue with many of the points raised. As he pointed out, many of the writers and film-makers interviewed by *Allegoria* as part of the issue did not subscribe to Donnarumma's views either;[2] indeed, many of them had what Ganeri (2011) has described as allergic reactions to such labelling of their work.[3] Yet despite such controversy, the issue of *Allegoria* also marked the beginning of a series of edited volumes based on the subject, such as those of Spinazzola (2010), Santoro (2010), Serkowska (2011), and Somigli (2013).[4] This indicates that *Allegoria*'s issue 57 brought to the fore a need to describe what was happening both within Italy and further afield, a tendency comparable to what was labelled *Reality Hunger* by David Shields in his 2010 text.

This chapter begins by unpicking the various strands of this debate to interrogate the approaches of Donnarumma, Scurati, Wu Ming and others to what has been called 'new realism'. It will also analyse the relationship between text and reality in the light of the Digital Age and trace the origins of UNOs that employ literary journalism. It will then focus on a close reading of recent texts that fall under this category and consider the implications of considering such work to be 'neo/realist/ic'. Saviano's *Gomorra* [*Gomorrah*], although being held up as the archetypal return to reality by *Allegoria*, relies heavily on fictionalising in an exposé of the Neapolitan mafia known as the Camorra. Jones takes the conflicts in the Balkans as her subject matter in *Sappiano le mie parole di sangue* [*My Words Be Bloody*], exploring the possibilities and limitations of the writer as witness. Scego and Bianchi's *Roma negata* [*Denied Rome*] works creatively across media to show the endurance of colonialism in today's Italy and raise issues related to migration and racism. All three of these authors use a personal approach to communicate political messages, seeking to combat the shortcomings of the mainstream media in reporting on their subject matter without overlooking the tensions of portraying experience and processing reality in today's world.

Reality, Representation, Reportage

The description of the return to reality in *Allegoria* contains both fruitful observations and erroneous assertions about the climate of twenty-first-century Italian literature. Aside from substantial reservations about the putative end of postmodernism, which I have discussed in detail earlier (see chapter 1 in particular), I would also point out that the writers of the articles in *Allegoria* 57 and other critics discussing the topic problematically tend to conflate and to use with little theoretical grounding ideas such as 'reality', 'realism', 'realistic' and 'real'. It is difficult to dissociate realism from the conventions of the nineteenth-century novel, which, as we shall see, are certainly not present in these texts. Moreover, as Cortellessa (2008) argued, the concept of the 'Real' has been shown to be unreachable and problematic since Lacan. Along similar lines, Nove pointed out in his interview in *Allegoria*: 'Dopo Freud, dopo lo strutturalismo e dopo Lacan parlare di realismo in buona fede mi sembra impossibile senza accettare che si tratta della convenzione di un'altra *fiction*' [After Freud, after structuralism and after Lacan, talking about realism in good faith seems impossible to me without accepting that it is the convention of another fiction] (Donnarumma and Policastro 2008: 19). At times, the return to reality is also understood by those interviewed as a return to neorealism, which the film-makers overwhelmingly reject (as pointed out by Taviani 2008: 86). Genna expresses a similar feeling that this debate seems in many ways out of date, stating that these questions of how literature can influence reality 'si poteva porre negli anni cinquanta a Vittorini, esistente il Partito Comunista Italiano' [could have been posed to Vittorini in the fifties, when the Italian Communist Party existed] (Donnarumma and Policastro 2008: 14).

This lack of theoretical clarity could go some way towards explaining the opposition expressed by those interviewed on the proposition of a return to reality, which on closer examination of the articles is less controversial than it would initially seem. The issue seems not to be devoted to discussing mimetic realism, and indeed Donnarumma makes a distinction towards the end of his article between what he is discussing and (what he again slightly vaguely terms) 'un realismo di scuola' [a school realism] (Donnarumma 2008c: 54). Rather, he describes the restoration of a dialectic between realism and modernism that was interrupted by postmodernism: 'Gli scrittori che si impongono dagli anni Novanta, in un certo senso [...] dimostrano come fra realismo e modernismo, fra volontà di parlare del mondo e consapevolezza autoriflessiva della letteratura esiste una conciliazione produttiva' [The writers who have dominated since the nineties, in a certain sense [...] demonstrate that there is a productive conciliation between realism and modernism, between the will to speak about the world and the self-reflexive awareness of literature] (Donnarumma 2008b: 27). He does not ignore tensions in trying to portray a reality that can be problematic and elude representation, but one that he believes needs constant interrogation to gain meaning through literature (Donnarumma 2008b: 54). Neither does Vicari subscribe to mimetic realism in his article, instead underlining the strongly subjective nature of recent film-making, which he feels would require referring to the depiction of plural realities rather than one reality (Vicari 2008: 78). Taviani describes this return to reality in a way that similarly does not overlook the complexities of realism today: 'Si può (si deve) stare addosso alla realtà [...] *raccontando una storia*, attraverso uno sguardo personale che non esclude il ricorso all'ibridazione dei generi' [One can (one must) stay close to reality [...] *telling a story*, through a personal gaze that does not exclude employing the hybridization of genres] (2008: 87). She does not advocate a return to neorealism either, but puts forward the view that these recent narrators and film-makers have been influenced by a neorealist heritage, and are thus 'Riallacciando il filo con i Padri' [Reconnecting the link with the Fathers] (2008: 90). This reference to paternity resonates strongly with the issues discussed in chapter 2, and, indeed, the insistence on ideas of return surrounding the debate on 'new realism' could be understood in terms of a desire for a return to order after the waywardness of postmodernist experimentation, which could once again be read psychoanalytically. Overall, instead of advocating a classically (neo)realist mode, the authors of *Allegoria* 57 seem to be saying, in common with Wu Ming 1 in some ways, that there has been a renewed sense of *impegno* or commitment among intellectuals, who have sought to engage with the present situation in Italy, doing what Donnarumma describes as 'pronunciamento sui temi della vita pubblica' [pronouncement on the topics of public life] (2008c: 44).[5]

It is, however, difficult to subscribe to Donnarumma's and Scurati's conception of a crisis in experience in the modern world, or what Giglioli (2011) has characterised as a lack of trauma. Scurati opens his essay *La letteratura dell'inesperienza* [*The Literature of Inexperience*] by contrasting precisely the fertile neorealist literary explosion after the Second World War with the climate facing his literary generation (Scurati 2006a: 10), making the sweeping statement that, nowadays, 'l'idea del futuro è divenuta oscena, il culto del passato perversione macabra, l'umanesimo letterario un'idea estinta' [the idea of the future has become obscene, the cult of the past macabre perversion, literary humanism an extinct idea] (Scurati 2006a: 14). In *Senza trauma* [*Without Trauma*], Giglioli links his ideas to those of Scurati — 'In quella che Antonio Scurati ha chiamato l'età della compiuta "inesperienza", la realtà si dissolve tra le dita di chiunque voglia raccontarla' [In what Antonio Scurati called the age of complete 'inexperience', reality slips through the fingers of anyone who wants to narrate it] (Giglioli 2011: 15) — and he attributes recent Italian writers' unease about the relationship between literature and the world to the fact that they live without conflict on home soil: 'Niente più guerre qui da noi, carestie, epidemie, conflitti religiosi' [No more wars here, famines, epidemics, religious conflicts] (Giglioi 2011: 8). For Scurati and Giglioli, this generation seems to be waiting for a watershed moment to happen so they can write about it in the same way as Calvino and Vittorini were able to do in the post-war years. Donnarumma expresses comparable ideas, although he takes this beyond the Second World War to the *anni di piombo*. In his discussion of the constant return to the 1960s and 1970s that is particularly present in recent *noir* fiction, he states: 'Dal tedio del presente, quel passato acquista il colore dell'età degli eroi, dei grandi intrighi, della possibilità di essere dentro la Storia come protagonisti o vittime, anziché come semplici spettatori' [From the tedium of the present, that past takes on the colour of the age of the heroes, of great intrigues, of the possibility of being part of History as protagonists or victims, rather than as simple spectators] (Donnarumma 2008c: 37). There is a similar sense of missing a crucial moment and being relegated to an inability to participate actively in something meaningful in the twenty-first century.

Scurati's view of the period following the Second World War as being superior to the situation today is limited. As Burns has argued, the post-war conception of *impegno* quickly fragmented, but literary work thereafter was by no means bereft of a sense of political and ethical commitment. Starting in the 1960s, there was both an 'erosion of faith' in the role of politically committed literature, but also 'freedom from the stylistic straitjacket of neorealism' (Burns 2001: 37). Therefore, a return to the characteristics of this post-war period would not necessarily be a positive development. Seeing it as a golden age implies viewing it through the lens of a 'good old days' mentality, suggesting that Scurati is displaying nothing more than a nostalgia for a time when writers were not necessarily better off than they are today. Casadei rightly questions Scurati's views on the myth of the experience of war, and points out that direct experience was not the starting point of stories in the past, making the point that Tolstoy was narrating events in *War and Peace* that had happened before he was born (Casadei 2007: 25). This also brings us to a clear shortcoming in Giglioli's text, that is, the role of what Hirsch has called 'postmemory', the transmission of memories of traumatic events that took place before your lifetime.[6] The symptomatic return to the Second World War and the *anni di piombo* by recent Italian writers is testament to the enduring power of events that have not been directly experienced. Jansen points out that, rather than the desire to hear extreme stories in the absence of lived experience that Giglioli describes, we can detect in texts like Janeczek's analysed in the previous chapter 'un autentico bisogno di "guarire" dal trauma e di trovare una dimensione comune' [a genuine need to 'heal' from the trauma and find a common dimension] (Jansen 2012).

Scurati's particularly apocalyptic descriptions of what a highly mediated reality has done to cognitive experience also need interrogating. He draws heavily on Baudrillard's work, particularly in his 2003 essay addressing television and the Gulf War, in which Scurati describes the passivity of a television audience watching war unfold and being unable to participate or understand it as real: 'Trasformandola in spettacolo, la Tv inquadra la guerra nella cornice di una finzione generalizzata' [Turning it into a show, TV frames war as a generalized fiction] (2003: 13). As Somigli (2013: xiii) points out, anxiety about the role of television in our lives now seems somewhat dated in the light of the Internet Age, and he states that we are fully able to distinguish what is reality and what is not. Perhaps Scurati's aversion to television could be part of the tendency among these writers and critics to reject postmodernism, television being seen as the postmodernist medium *par excellence*. Casadei (2007: 26) rightly points out that an alleged loss of experience risks becoming a (post)modern myth, and that, although we have lost some types of direct experience, we have also gained others through more complex forms of perception. Antonello (2012: 84–85) highlights the fact that television has become more sophisticated in recent years, offering new narrative possibilities and, rather than being a passive activity, can be educational and constructive. The fact that NIE texts such as *Romanzo criminale* and *Gomorra* have been made into hugely successful and high-quality television series further calls into question television's negative influence.

Indeed, in the twenty-first century, reality might be highly mediated, but this has led to a world in which people are more connected and empowered to comment on events, in some cases effecting change, in what Jenkins (2006a) has described as a convergence culture. Viewers/users nowadays have developed a sophisticated understanding of the techniques and tropes of recreating realities of various kinds on screen, and they may well be creators of such images themselves on personal devices, rather than passive spectators. Many of the technological advances affecting literature, such as online collaborative writing, fan fiction and hypertexts, are based on interactions between writers and readers in the real world, always relating back to a materiality and connectedness that have not disappeared since the digital revolution, but have strengthened in some cases. Antonello (2012: 69) has described a common mistrust of, and failure to engage critically with, the mass media among Italian intellectuals, aside from a few exceptions such as Eco, who astutely identified an artificial binary in pitting the humanist novel against the barbaric mass media, and instead foresaw a rhizomatic, collective intelligence resulting from interactions with the mass media in his text *Apocalittici e integrati* [*Apocalypse Postponed*] (1988). In terms of the writers analysed in this study, we see that they employ transmediality to develop their written texts, connect more closely with their readers and push them to engage with their stories. We must be wary of being too optimistic when discussing cultural changes as a result of the Digital Age, as I outlined in the introduction to this study. However, despite some drawbacks to the internet environment, it is difficult to see today's world in Scurati's and others' apocalyptic terms.

Scurati's (2006a: 77) answer to what he perceives to be a crisis in our relationship with reality is to write historical novels, in order to exit what he sees as an eternal present — another postmodern myth, as I analysed in the previous chapter — whereas Donnarumma and Giglioli see first-person narratives as the counterpoint to our everyday lack of experience, which the latter believes explains the popularity of books like *Gomorra* (Giglioli 2011: 61). However, many of the recent texts that can be associated with the so-called 'new realism' might be called autofiction rather than autobiography, as we have seen in the work of Genna (chapter 2) and Janeczek (chapter 3). In an interview with Genna (2007a), Jones quoted William S. Burroughs, who stated of his work: ' "Every word is autobiographical and every word is fiction" ' (quoted in Morgan 1988: 539). If readers see this as approaching reality as closely as possible, they would certainly be mistaken. These works could in fact be described using the epigraph to David O. Russell's 2013 film *American Hustle*: 'Some of this actually happened'. We will see that, whereas Saviano engages with the ambiguities of real and fictional experience under the surface of his text, Jones particularly brings to the fore meditations on the difficulties of representation and on her narrative's unreliability, while Scego plays with her personal story in different ways across her various texts. This suggests that these first-person narratives are more complex than a simple desire for something 'real' to engage with, but indicate, once again, a combination of postmodernism and *impegno*.

This sense of *impegno* often comes from an emotional, embodied engagement, in contrast to more traditional forms of *impegno*.[7] Focused through the first-person and on individuals, these texts seek emotion through communicating experience; yet, simultaneously, they often call for an investment of imagination by not insisting on the reliability of the author/witness, which has caused some anxiety surrounding their reception, as we shall see. The political importance of communicating embodied experience for Jones, Saviano, Scego and other recent Italian writers recalls feminist theory and practice, such as Luisa Muraro's emphasis on the importance of experience and subjectivity in the light of the effacement of the female subject by post-structuralism; she has given a talk on the subject that is not coincidentally entitled 'Il pensiero dell'esperienza' [The Thought of Experience] (Muraro 2006).

Similarly, Cavarero's *Tu che mi guardi, tu che mi racconti* [*Storytelling and Selfhood*] (1997) explored the ethical power of self-narration, which is also shown by the practice of *autocoscienza* [consciousness-raising] that characterized Italian feminism in the 1970s.[8] As I have discussed elsewhere, feminist concerns do not tend to enter into the NIE discussion, and they seem to be absent too from discussions of the return to reality,[9] but there are striking and fruitful parallels in considering them, not only in terms of recent texts that examine parental legacies as we saw in chapter 2, but also in relation to recent Italian life-writing, and we will see Jones seeming to allude to feminist principles when communicating her experiences and those of the women she encounters. Significantly, much recent Italian autofiction is by women writers and also by so-called migrant writers,[10] suggesting the potential of hybrid life-writing for addressing questions of gender, race and belonging, in contrast to the very much male-dominated writing collectives attempting to eliminate the figure of the author through more impersonal forms of writing.[11]

Genna pointed out in his interview in *Allegoria* 57 that these questions about how to narrate reality were similar to those that were being asked of writers like Tom Wolfe and Norman Mailer in the 1960s (Donnarumma and Policastro 2008: 13). Indeed, there are fascinating echoes between the discussions surrounding the role of Italian literature in the twenty-first century and those that greeted the beginnings of New Journalism. The New Journalists were similarly critical of the interests that controlled the news media and saw their work as bringing greater depth to the stories addressed (Hollowell 1977: 22–23). Wolfe described New Journalism's mixture of reportage with literary techniques as being part of a search for a new way to reflect the contemporary reality: 'So help me, this is the way people live now!' (1975: 68). The insistence in the twenty-first century on moving away from the classical novel form has a similar drive to engage with the present world, in which some feel that pure fiction 'has become culturally irrelevant' (Siegel 2010); Philippe Forest has asked: 'Un roman est-il possible aujourd'hui?' [Is a novel possible today?] (2007: 53); Will Self has proclaimed 'The novel is dead (this time it's for real)' (2014); and Shields has said of the unselfconscious contemporary novel: 'it's not clear to me how such a book could convey what it feels like to be alive right now' (2010: 71). Although the playing field has changed somewhat in recent years due to technological developments, there are unresolved tensions related to ideas about truth and authenticity that writers continue to wrestle with in a similar way to their counterparts in the 1960s and 1970s. These recent Italian writers' desire to go beyond what they see as a lack of engagement with contemporary issues in postmodernist narratives echoes the New Journalists' reaction against the lack of realism they perceived in the neo-fabulists (Wolfe 1975: 56). Just as New Journalism was greeted by accusations of being dishonest — 'The bastards are making it up!' (Wolfe 1975: 24), or as Gore Vidal famously said of Capote, 'Truman made lying an art form'[12] — and written off as not being highbrow literature (Wolfe 1975: 52–53), so too has *Gomorra* come under fire for its unstable truth status, as we shall see, and many of the texts I refer to have been relegated to what Ferroni has labelled *Scritture a perdere* [*Throwaway Writing*] in his 2010 text (see introduction). We have seen that twenty-first-century Italian literature often demonstrates continuity with postmodernist experimentation; at times, this is specifically with a combination of journalism with literature and the associated blurring of the lines between fiction and nonfiction that American New Journalists in many ways pioneered years before.

Yet, hybrid mixtures of fiction and non-fiction have a tradition in Italy that goes further back than the non-fiction novels associated with New Journalism.[13] I return, again, to Manzoni, as I did in the previous chapter, although in this case to his investigation into the miscarriage of justice surrounding the torture and execution of the *untori* accused of spreading the plague in 'Storia della colonna infame' [History of the Infamous Column] (Manzoni 1987). I hazard that this essay must have not only influenced later works like Sciascia's 1978 text *L'affaire Moro* (Sciascia 1994), but also more recent exposés of the workings of power and injustice.[14] This includes the texts analysed in this chapter, but also Carlotto's *noir*-ish *Perdas de Fogu* (2008) written with the collective Mama Sabot about the harmful effects of military testing in Sardinia; Evangelisti, Genna, Wu Ming and others' *Il caso Battisti* [*The Battisti Case*] (Evangelisti and others 2004), a compilation of reflections on the controversial case surrounding the attempted extradition of Cesare Battisti; Giovanni Maria Bellu's *I fantasmi di Portopalo* [*The Ghosts of Portopalo*] (2004) investigating the death of approximately 300 migrants trying to reach Italy in 1996; or Scurati's *Il bambino che sognava la fine del mondo* [*The Child who Dreamed the End of the World*], in which Scurati seems to refer to 'Storia della colonna infame' when describing the spread of gossip about the paedophile ring in Bergamo he is investigating: 'Il tempo delle voci, della diceria dell'untore, sarebbe venuto poi' [The time of rumours, of gossip about the plague-spreader, would come later] (Scurati 2009: 115). Manzoni's work, first published in 1840 and, like Janeczek's 'epilogo morale' [moral epilogue] to *Cibo* [*Food*] on the BSE epidemic (Janeczek 2002: 231), originally an appendix to a longer fictional work, incorporated the tools of fact with those of fiction. The result could be called a UNO and would pave the way for later writers' investigations combining history, reportage and literary techniques. Manzoni's depiction of 'cose che in un romanzo sarebbero tacciate d'inverisimili' [things that would be accused of being unrealistic in a novel] (Manzoni 1987: 837), despite its clinical examination of historical documentation, also relies on vivid, emotive descriptions of the experiences of its protagonists and rhetorical questions to draw in its readers. Through necessity, Manzoni had to resort to conjecture at times when the facts were silent, for example about the meeting between Piazza and the auditor; he points out that nobody knows what happened so we must each imagine it (Manzoni 1987: 873). Indeed, he goes on to imagine what happened, reflecting on Piazza's possible psychological state as he struggled with what to do, a description embellished with vivid detail. Manzoni asks rhetorically before answering his own question: 'chi può immaginarsi i combattimenti di quell'animo' [who can imagine the struggles of that soul] (1987: 873). It is precisely a writer like Manzoni who can imagine such things, just as Sciascia could read and interpret the strange events surrounding Moro's kidnapping and death from a different standpoint, uncovering hidden meanings and offering insights that are at once 'politiche, psicologiche, psichanalitiche' [political, psychological, psychoanalytical] (Sciascia 1994: 184).

Another Italian writer speaking of endemic corruption in politics when journalists would not do so, despite not having all the evidence at his fingertips, famously stated:

> Io so. Ma non ho le prove. Non ho nemmeno indizi.
>
> Io so perché sono un intellettuale, uno scrittore, che cerca di seguire tutto ciò che succede, di conoscere tutto ciò che se ne scrive, di immaginare tutto ciò che non si sa o che si tace; che coordina fatti anche lontani, che mette insieme i pezzi disorganizzati e frammentari di un intero coerente quadro politico, che ristabilisce la logica là dove sembrano regnare l'arbitrarietà, la follia e il mistero. (Pasolini 1974)

> [I know. But I don't have the proof. I don't even have the clues.
>
> I know because I am an intellectual, a writer, who tries to follow everything that happens, to know everything that is written about, to imagine everything that is unknown or unsaid; who coordinates even distant events, who puts together disorganised and fragmentary pieces into a complete coherent political picture, who re-establishes logic where arbitrariness, madness and mystery seem to reign.]

This belief in the writer's ability to assemble and make sense of reality's 'disorganised and fragmentary pieces' is precisely what many of the writers of this journalistic 'new realism' feel they have the privileged ability to do, and, like Pasolini, or Sciascia or Manzoni before him, this only partly relies on proof. Significantly, we shall see that Pasolini's famous statement is echoed and modified by both Saviano and Jones, and it has also resurfaced in Genna's *Dies irae*[15] and in the introduction to a selection of Antonio Tabucchi's journalistic output.[16] We can thus trace Italian writers over time who combine evidence with conjecture, to try to understand human motivations, writing what Scurati (2010) describes in a note at the beginning of *Il bambino che sognava la fine del mondo*, in another nod to Manzoni, as 'componimenti misti di cronaca e d'invenzione' [mixed works of news and invention].

These Italian texts are not unique in their mix of fact and fiction, although such UNOs seem to be particularly widespread in Italy. There are myriad examples of comparable works in the contemporary literary landscape, as I have argued elsewhere (Willman 2017), and as Mosca (2014) has pointed out. Crossovers between literature and journalism have become increasingly common, with novels frequently co-opting reportage — Pellini (2011: 148) also points this out — and newspaper features tending towards being literary in tone. Saviano states that the difference between literature and journalism is not a question of style or subject matter, but that literature is unique in 'questa possibilità di creare parole che non comunicano ma esprimono, in grado di sussurrare o urlare, di mettere sotto pelle al lettore che ciò che sta leggendo lo riguarda' [this possibility to create words that do not communicate but express, that are able to whisper or scream, to get under the readers' skin that what they are reading is about them] (Saviano 2009: 241); other writers seem to be of a similar view about the power of a more literary mode of writing.[17] Moreover, many of these hybrid journalistic texts from across the globe — François Bon's *Daewoo* (2004) about factory closures in France or Dave Eggers's *Zeitoun* (2009) about Hurricane Katrina, for example — are attempts to combat a lack of attention in the mainstream media to the issues they address through their humanising stories, as well as to help process the deluge of (mis)information we are bombarded with today, in a world where news reporting continues to be influenced by corporate or political interests. In Italy, this was keenly felt given Berlusconi's power over the telecommunications sector through his company Fininvest, which was a source of concern for many writers. Not coincidentally, Wu Ming started as part of the Luther Blissett project engaging in media pranks to unmask the limitations in the ways in which the press and television report information, before the era of widespread discussion about 'fake news'.[18] Mosca points out that there has been a sense of a need to bridge the gap between literature, which was seen to have disengaged with real events, and journalism, which was seen as lacking in depth and in need of a more critical analysis of events; by combining the two, these writers can use their UNOs to create 'un nuovo patto con il lettore, chiamato di volta in volta a farsi toccare da ciò che legge, e coscientemente decidere di prolungare gli effetti della lettura anche al di fuori dei ristretti confini del privato' [a new pact with the reader, called on from time to time to be touched by what is being read, and consciously to decide to extend the effects of reading also outside the narrow confines of the private] (Mosca 2009: 322).

Overall, the texts related to the so-called return to reality — like the other UNOs addressed in this study — are not indicative of a straightforward move from anti-realist/unrealistic postmodernist experimentation to neo/realist/ic *impegno*, but instead demonstrate elements of, and crossovers between, all of these components. They explore interactions between reality and fiction, between testimony and journalism, between technology and tradition, and between different media. This is more complex than a simple shift from one mode to another; it is rather characterised by a range of interactions, as these writers both push literature forward and draw on what came before. The results make for interesting, unusual and even uncomfortable reading.

Gomorra by Roberto Saviano

The book chosen as the focus for issue 57 of *Allegoria* was *Gomorra. Viaggio nell'impero economico e nel sogno di dominio della camorra* [*Gomorrah: A Journey Into the Camorra's Economic Empire and Dream of Domination*].[19] Saviano's first-person account of the nefarious influence of the Neapolitan mafia known as the Camorra, ostensibly springing both from his investigative journalism and personal experience, was seen as a prime example of the return to reality, a view that my analysis will call into question. The text was a sensation when it was first published in 2006, as many Italians were unaware of the extent of the corruption and violence that was taking place in Naples and its surrounding areas (Pocci 2011: 245). Saviano had to go into hiding as a result of writing it after death threats from the mafia, although, as we will see, he has also been accused of fabricating parts of his account. Despite this, *Gomorra* made Saviano a celebrity, both at home and abroad, where it has been translated into many different languages. Subsequent to *Gomorra*, Saviano has written a book-length exposé of the cocaine trade entitled *ZeroZeroZero* (2013), which was also polemical due to accusations of plagiarism and again of fabricating parts, from which Saviano defended himself by pointing out that it is a nonfiction novel (see Moynihan 2015), although, as we will see in the case of *Gomorra* too, the English edition has been marketed as nonfiction, which raises ethical questions about UNOs when they are not open about their generic hybridity.[20]

Gomorra centres on the microstories of various people Saviano tells us he has encountered in and around Naples. These are fragmented, everyday stories of people who work for or are affected by the Camorra, including Saviano himself, with frequent moments of poetic licence. He furnishes his readers with real or imagined details to bring the various characters related to the vast network of the Camorra's activities to life. Gallippi (2013: 511) makes the point that this is what distinguishes the characters in the text from the faceless victims of the mafia that we encounter in newspaper reports. Saviano's narrator often focuses on seemingly minor, human details, such as the fact that Don Ciro, one of the so-called submarines who distribute monthly allowances to the wives and girlfriends of imprisoned *camorristi*, has 'i baffi gialli, laccati dalla nicotina così come l'indice e il medio della mano destra' [a yellow moustache, coloured by nicotine just like the index and middle finger of his right hand] (155). These are small, simple, almost banal details of people who do not spend their lives killing or on the run, but simply operate in a web of organised crime. Yet, these microstories also open up to wider points about Italian and indeed global issues, including Russia, Scotland, the United States and China among other countries in narrating this web. Tricomi (2008: 190) states that what *Gomorra* reveals is not only the workings of the Camorra 'system', but of the entire world economic system.[21] There are shifts from the local to the global as we see the micro- and macro-dimensions of the subject brought into relief.

The text seemingly aims for a greater level of realism than other portrayals of both the mafia and the situation in Naples. Saviano considers existing filmic representations of organised crime, highlighting the influence of the cinema industry on the behaviour of the Camorra in the 'Hollywood' section of *Gomorra*, whether it is the clan boss Walter Schiavone's house modelled on that in *Scarface* (267), Cosimo Di Lauro dressing like Brandon Lee in *The Crow* (274), or the lasting effects of Tornatore's *Il camorrista* on the imaginary of organised crime in Naples (275). However, he also portrays the phenomenon in deliberately stark contrast to these familiar visions, insisting instead on the grim truth of organised crime. This is shown most clearly by the deaths of two micro-characters Giuseppe and Romeo, whose fate is described with allusion to the mafia films the boys had so admired: 'Lasciarono che le mani dei cadaveri dei ragazzini fossero beccate dai gabbiani e le labbra e i nasi mangiucchiati dai randagi che circolavano sulle spiagge di spazzatura. Ma questo i film non lo raccontano, si fermano un attimo prima' [They let the hands of the boys' corpses be pecked by the seagulls and their lips and noses eaten up by the stray dogs that were roaming the rubbish-covered beaches. But they don't show this in films, they stop a moment before] (280). Saviano both interacts with popular mythology and overturns it, refusing to stop his recording of events in an attempt to work against the tendency of the cinematic gaze to glorify or sensationalise organised crime.

Previous representations in film may have fallen short of exposing the truth about the mafia, but so have representations in the media. Saviano portrays other journalists in *Gomorra* as underestimating the situation in Naples, 'dove si credeva esistessero ormai solo bande e scippatori' [where it was believed there now only existed gangs and bag-snatchers] (136), and as being more interested in conveying the aesthetics of the poorer Neapolitan neighbourhoods (139), rather than in unearthing the truth. They keep their distance from the action, only getting involved once it is over (95). They are even tricked by officials into photographing police officers pretending to be drug pushers (138). The narrator, on the other hand, is among the gangs and drug pushers, riding across town on his Vespa and observing murder scenes. He displays a strong sense of urgency to delve into his subject matter, going undercover at great risk to get under the skin of the Camorra, and it has been widely publicised that he had to go into hiding and has lived under police protection since writing the text.

Given such a desire to expose the reality in Naples, it is perhaps surprising that he chooses a highly literary and subjective style. On opening the text, we encounter a description of the port of Naples, alternatively described as 'una ferita' [a wound] (12), 'il buco nel mappamondo' [the hole in the world map] (12), 'un ano di mare che si allarga con grande dolore degli sfinteri' [an anus of sea that widens with great pain of the sphincters] (14), 'Un'appendice infetta mai degenerata in peritonite' [An infected appendix ever degenerated into peritonitis] (16) and 'Un anfibio di terra, una metamorfosi marina' [A land amphibian, a marine metamorphosis] (16). This abundance of metaphors is not what a reader would immediately associate with reportage, or a text with an overt aim for greater realism. Casadei argues that this bodily element in *Gomorra*, combined with the presence of Saviano as witness, was why the text had such an effect on its readers, more so than Antonio Franchini's *L'abusivo* [*The Unauthorised*] (2001) or Nanni Balestrini's *Sandokan* (2004), which were published around the same time, examined similar subject matter, and merged fact and fiction, but lacked the emotional power of Saviano's text (Casadei 2010: 107–11). This is also an instance of the bodily engagement discussed earlier, which we will see in Jones's and Scego's texts too.

After these descriptions of the port, the narrative then moves very quickly to Saviano's narrating 'I': 'Al porto ci andavo spesso per mangiare il pesce' [I often went to the port to eat fish] (17). Throughout the text, this 'I' partly serves to legitimise his occasionally rather far-fetched narration, part of what Casadei (2010: 110) calls a process of 'authentication', as if to show that Saviano 'really' did experience these things, but he also uses it to seek empathy by drawing us into his personal story. His experience of the Camorra did not start with the writing of this text, but in his childhood, as is evident from the way in which memories interact with what he relates. When describing a crime scene, he tells us: 'La prima volta che ho visto un morto ammazzato avrò tredici anni' [The first time that I saw someone who had been killed I must have been thirteen] (112). Later, when he introduces the story of Don Peppino Diana, a priest who was killed by the Camorra after speaking out against them, he starts with his personal recollection of the day of his funeral: 'Avevo sedici anni [...] Mi svegliò mia zia, come sempre, ma con una violenza strana [...] non disse niente e camminava facendo un rumore fortissimo, come se sfogasse tutto il nervosismo sui talloni' [I was sixteen. [...] My aunt woke me as usual that morning, but strangely roughly [...] she didn't say a word and was walking around noisily, as if she were venting all her irritation through her heels] (241). He also describes how his father, a doctor, was beaten up by the Camorra for helping a boy who had been shot: 'Per i successivi quattro [mesi] non riuscì a guardare in faccia nessuno' [For the following four [months] he couldn't look anyone in the eye] (190). Saviano's childhood and his family have been personally affected by the violence he depicts in the text, and he uses these stories to invite deeper emotional identification from his readers. Saviano himself, then, is the main microstory of *Gomorra*, appearing in almost every paragraph of the text, yet these autobiographical elements are included in order to explore collective issues. His own experience of the Camorra adds to the power of what he says, showing the way in which organised crime affects everyone who lives in the Naples area. Once again, this use of autobiographical elements shows what Wu Ming 1 describes as 'introspezione e autofiction per narrare un fatto pubblico e "storico"' [introspection and autofiction to narrate a public and 'historic' event] (2009a: 15 n. 9).

In including so many personal elements, Saviano casts himself as something of a hero, both intra- and extra-diegetically. Within the text, his crusade to expose the truth at all costs is mirrored by the character of Don Peppino. Saviano strongly aligns himself with this heroic figure, who used the power of the word to try to change his time (251). This mirroring manifests itself on a textual level too when the narrator quotes from Don Peppino's text condemning the Camorra — entitled 'Per amore del mio popolo non tacerò' [For love of my people I will not stay silent] (244) — whilst giving his own running commentary alongside it, weaving his own words into the priest's to bind the two of them together. Don Peppino's condemnation echoes the rhetorical quality of much of Saviano's text, using accumulation and repetition to hammer home what he is saying.

Outside the text, Saviano has employed different media to communicate his message further in what Jenkins would call 'content streaming', a shift 'from media-specific content toward content that flows across multiple media channels' (Jenkins 2006a: 243). He writes newspaper articles on similar subjects, does frequent interviews, has made a television series entitled *Vieni via con me* [*Come Away With Me*] dealing with Italian social issues, has created a website, regularly posts on Facebook and tweets to over one and a half million followers. He has also been involved in adapting *Gomorra* for Garrone's 2008 film adaptation and the Sky television series starting in 2014. Pocci states: 'Saviano has become not only a public figure but a living symbol, nationally and internationally, of the intellectual actively and directly involved in the fight against organised crime' (Pocci 2011:

225). Dal Lago is more damning in his assessment of this phenomenon, caustically referring to 'Santo Saviano' [Saint Saviano] (Dal Lago 2010: 106), and arguing that he absolves the state of responsibility by framing his fight against organised crime in absolutist, moral terms (Dal Lago 2010: 19–20), as demonstrated by *Gomorra*'s biblical title, as well as the title chosen for Saviano's collection of essays, *La bellezza e l'inferno* [*Beauty and the Inferno*].

Certainly, there are limitations to Saviano's heroic and self-sacrificing approach to denouncing organised crime, not only due to the danger it has put him in. Unlike other writers of UNOs who are open about the role of fictionalising in their texts, Saviano at times insists on the truth status of what he recounts, despite including invented elements, which could be seen as undermining his commitment to combating misinformation about these issues, reinforcing a 'post-truth' culture rather than greater realism. When Saviano's narrator goes to visit Pasolini's grave, he becomes angry thinking of all these things that he knows about the Camorra's activities, and turns Pasolini's famous words around, repeatedly maintaining 'Io so e ho le prove' [I know and I have the proof] (repeated over pages 233–40), 'Io so e ho le prove. E quindi racconto. Di queste verità' [I know and I have the proof. And so I tell them. These truths] (234). Yet, parts of the text are based on his imagination, which he does not always openly admit. His description of the funeral of Annalisa Durante has particularly come under fire from others who were also present and have disputed various aspects of his testimony (as pointed out by Dal Lago 2010: 59–61, Pocci 2011: 230 and Policastro 2008: 188). Saviano changes or adds details without openly declaring it to the reader, such as Annalisa's friends ringing her mobile phone that is lying on her coffin as it is carried out of the church: 'Squilla sul feretro: è il nuovo requiem. Un trillo continuo, poi musicale, accenna una melodia dolce. Nessuno risponde' [It rings on the coffin: it is the new requiem. A continuous ring, then becoming musical, a sweet melody. No one answers] (173). This adds to the pathos of the scene, the funeral of a teenage girl who had nothing to do with the Camorra, and, yet, died at their hands. Interestingly, these embellishments recall those of Capote in *In Cold Blood*, as I have pointed out elsewhere (Willman 2017: 7), showing an affinity with New Journalism. Although in many cases Saviano does offer up 'proof' — figures, statistics, quotations from intercepted phone calls — in other cases, he either does not have such proof or chooses to move away from nonfiction into fiction. It is significant that *Gomorra* does not have a reference section at the end, or a bibliography, and that the film and television series based on the text are not documentaries, but fictional. Saviano may try to move away from Pasolini's words to make 'l'io so del mio tempo' [The 'I know' of my time] (233), but the knowledge *Gomorra* offers is frequently literary, gaining power not from cold evidence, but from poetic licence and the writer's passion to bring these things to light, as was the case for Pasolini.

Yet, Cortellessa (2011a: 510–11) points out that Saviano's pronouncements about *Gomorra* have gradually mutated, from a more circumspect attitude to the truth status of his book on its publication[22] to recasting it as a battle for truth. Cortellessa (2011a: 511) suggests that this could be linked both to the strong identification he has experienced from readers and to the threats he has received from the Camorra, forcing him to leave behind both his home and the realms of literature. There are moments in *Gomorra* when Saviano suggests the role of literary tools and imagination in his text. Near the beginning, we meet Pasquale, an impoverished but highly skilful tailor working for the Camorra, whose disappointment at seeing Angelina Jolie sporting one of his creations leads him to quit and become one of the Camorra's truck drivers instead. The narrator imagines how he must still think of his success, in a passage that gives an insight into Saviano's liberal use of poetic licence to embellish his narrative to invite identification through fictionalising:

> Sono sicuro che Pasquale, da solo, qualche volta, magari quando ha finito di mangiare, quando a casa i bambini si addormentano sfiancati dal gioco a pancia sotto sul divano, quando la moglie prima di lavare i piatti si mette al telefono con la madre, proprio in quel momento gli viene in mente di aprire il portafogli e fissare quella pagina di giornale. E sono sicuro che, guardando quel capolavoro che ha creato con le sue mani, Pasquale è felice. Una felicità rabbiosa. Ma questo non lo saprà mai nessuno. (46–47)

> [I am sure that Pasquale, alone, sometimes, maybe when he has finished eating, at home, when the children exhausted by playing have fallen asleep on their stomachs downstairs on the sofa, when his wife phones her mother before washing the dishes, just at that moment he thinks of opening his wallet and staring at that page from the newspaper. And I am sure that, looking at the masterpiece he created with his own hands, Pasquale is happy. An angry happiness. But nobody will ever know this.]

The narrator's repetition of 'I am sure that' asserts a certainty that does not exist for such imagined details. He insists on this certainty and simultaneously flags up the role of literary imagination in his narrative. He does this again at various points throughout the text, such as his flight of imagination about how another couple affected by the Camorra, Gelsomina and Gennaro, first met: 'Se mi fermo e prendo fiato riesco facilmente a immaginare il loro incontro, anche se non conosco neanche il tratto dei visi' [If I stop and take a breath, I can easily imagine their meeting, even if I do not even know what their faces look like] (98). When he describes Giuseppe and Romeo's last moments, he starts from what facts we have about them, and then uses what Chimenti (2010: 47) describes as 'a literary operation as a springboard — to throw the reader into a reality'. This is indicated by phrases such as: 'Me li immaginavo sui motorini' [I imagined them on their mopeds] (279), or: 'immagino la scena che hanno raccontato i giornali' [I imagine the scene described by the newspapers] (279). Again, there is a combination of painting a verisimilar picture of his protagonists and simultaneously underlining that it is based on personal conviction more than objective evidence. The phrase that most clearly emphasises what type of knowledge he is offering us in imagining the young boys' thoughts when they met their end could be applied to many aspects of the stories recounted in *Gomorra*: 'sono sicuro di una certezza che non potrà mai avere alcun tipo di conferma' [I am sure with a certainty that will never be able to have any kind of confirmation] (279–80). As he suggests in the final sentence of the passage on Pasquale — 'But nobody will ever know this' — nobody can *know* such things, just as Manzoni could not know all the details about the *untori*, or Sciascia could not know about Moro's mental state, but they believe that their research combined with their imaginings as writers have weight.

Aside from Pasolini, another important precursor to *Gomorra*, which similarly calls into question the newness of the 'realism' that Saviano is engaging with, is Michael Herr's *Dispatches*. In an essay in which Saviano describes what he so admires about Herr's *exposé* on the Vietnam War, we can see parallels with what he wanted to do in *Gomorra*. Herr can be associated with the New Journalism discussed earlier, and many aspects of *Dispatches* arguably make it a UNO, in which the author mixed fact and fiction to say something about the Vietnam War that the then mass media were ignoring. It worked against the mythology surrounding what Herr refers to as 'movie-fed war fantasies' (Herr 1978: 157), just as Saviano seeks to break open Hollywood stereotypes of the mafia. Herr felt that his subject matter somehow required a new form to address it; as he states in the text: 'Conventional journalism could no more reveal this war than conventional firepower could win it' (Herr 1978: 175). Like other recent UNOs, *Dispatches* is a collage or cut-up of literary and pop culture references, memoir, reportage, splices of conversation and fragmentary images of lived experience. Saviano imagines a moment in which Herr must have decided to abandon objectivity and rigorous distance in his account of the conflict: '"Chi se ne frega. Non mi interessa se sbaglio [...] Racconto come funziona, racconto il puzzo delle scarpe coi piedi marciti dentro"' ['Who gives a damn. I don't care if I'm wrong. [...] I narrate how it works, I narrate the stink of shoes with rotting feet inside them'] (Saviano 2009: 175). This is exactly what Saviano himself does in *Gomorra*, diluting facts with vivid and emotive description to bring home to the reader what is truly happening. Saviano's words in a speech reveal the visceral quality of what he aims to do with such writing: 'la letteratura mette paura al crimine quando ne svela il meccanismo, ma non come accade nella cronaca. Fa paura quando lo svela al cuore, allo stomaco, alla testa dei lettori' [literature scares crime when it reveals its mechanism, but not as it happens in the news. It is scary when it reveals it to the readers' heart, stomach, head] (Saviano 2009: 197).

What is also relevant about Herr's text is the fact that it is not simply about the Vietnam War, but foregrounds the experience of being a war reporter, just as Saviano — and Jones and Scego, as we shall see — foreground their experiences in investigating their subject matter. Saviano says of Herr: 'trascina il lettore in guerra' [he drags the reader to war] (Saviano 2009: 174); this is precisely what Saviano does too. He feels that one needs to be thrown into things in order to fully understand them, telling us of his decision to follow the war in Secondigliano: 'comprendere significava almeno farne parte. Non c'è scelta, e non credo vi fosse altro modo per capire le cose. La neutralità e la distanza oggettiva sono luoghi che non sono mai riuscito a trovare' [understanding meant at least being part of it. There is no choice, and I don't think there was another way to understand things. Neutrality and objective distance are places I have never been able to find] (86). Santoro emphasises the narrator's belief in direct observation of events in *Gomorra*, calling it 'un vero e proprio pathos della presenza' [a true pathos of presence] (Santoro 2010: 41). This statement could also be applied to Herr's need to go to Vietnam, and also to Jones's narrator, although Santoro surprisingly overlooks Jones's text. It is difficult not to think of *Sappiano le mie parole di sangue* particularly in what Santoro goes on to say about Saviano offering 'il proprio corpo e il proprio sangue alla parola' [his own body and his own blood to words] (Santoro 2010: 41) in order to act on reality and the reader. Experience, in an age that is supposed to be one of inexperience, is what these writers insist on, to add power to what they describe and to take their readers with them, even if the journey — indeed, Saviano calls his text a *viaggio* in its subtitle — is not necessarily into events precisely as they happened.[23]

Pocci describes *Gomorra* as performative in two senses: in the author constructing and performing an identity as a protagonist in his own text, and in its 'actional force [...] to involve the readers, ethically and emotionally' (2011: 240), which partly springs from its generic hybridity.[24] The section on the Kalashnikov is typical of the unsettling fusion of genres we see at work in *Gomorra*. It opens with an elusive description of Saviano running his finger around something that eventually transpires to be a bullet hole from an AK-47, leading on to a brief history of the weapon complete with facts and figures. Spliced into the narrative is his recollection of bumping into his estranged father with his new family, provoking personal thoughts about their relationship: 'Mio padre mi guardò con la solita delusa espressione, come dire che ormai neanche scherzando mi avrebbe sentito dire ciò che avrebbe voluto ascoltare' [My father looked at me with the usual disappointed expression, as if to say that I never said what he wanted to hear, even when I was joking] (187). This is subsequently interrupted by a flashback to his childhood, when his father was beaten up by the Camorra. Then there is the apocryphal account of Mariano, a *camorrista* and gun enthusiast, going to Russia to meet the inventor, supported by a narration of what he filmed on his camcorder in Mikhail Kalashnikov's house: 'Il video saltava, le immagini si agitavano, i volti ballavano, le zoomate deformavano occhi e oggetti, l'obiettivo sbatacchiava contro pollici e polsi' [The video was jumping, the images were shaky, the faces dancing, the zooms deforming eyes and objects, the lens banging against thumbs and wrists] (192). The jumping around and skewed angles of this video are inscribed onto the narrative of this section. It is exemplary of Saviano's desire to 'wake up' his readers through a combination of elements that require different types of reading and reflection. As he said of *Gomorra* in an interview: 'Volevo essere "bastardo" perché sapevo che questa materia, se non fosse stata trattata in un modo diverso, sarebbe rimasta relegata o negli ambiti del genere *thriller*, o cose del genere, o nella saggistica, per così dire, più specialista' [I wanted to 'bastardise' because I knew that this subject, if it had not been treated in a different way, would have been written off either as part of the thriller genre, or something similar, or as more specialist nonfiction, so to speak] (quoted in Pocci 2011: 243).

However, the blurring of fiction and nonfiction is ethically problematic when it is hidden from the reader. Wu Ming 1 divides readers of Saviano's text into two groups: inattentive readers, who simply take it to be a straightforward mafia exposé, and attentive readers, who realise that what they are encountering is something uniquely powerful, asking questions such as: 'Dove diavolo era Saviano per aver visto questa roba? Chi è l'io narrante? [...] Sto leggendo un reportage giornalistico o sto leggendo un romanzo travestito da reportage giornalistico?' [Where the hell was Saviano to have seen this stuff? Who is the narrating I? [...] Am I reading journalistic reportage or am I reading a novel disguised as journalistic reportage?] (Wu Ming 1 2009b: 113). Once the latter group come to terms with the uncanniness of what they are reading, Wu Ming 1 believes that they can better engage with the text, taking an active role in interpreting it. Yet, where does that leave the inattentive readers of *Gomorra*, who take it to be factual, particularly readers of the English edition, which is labelled nonfiction on the back cover (Saviano 2008)? There is a fascinating echo in Wu Ming 1's words of Eco's description in the postscript of *Il nome della rosa* [*The Name of the Rose*] of the 'ingenuous reader' (Eco 2005: 525) who could read Eco's text as a straightforward historical detective novel without noticing its complexities, as discussed in the previous chapter, again showing postmodern play and doubt to have crossed over into more recent texts claiming greater realism and more serious engagement with today's reality.

What we encounter in *Gomorra* is unquestionably a hybrid reading experience. Saviano communicates a powerful message, and the book's huge success has increased awareness about the issues raised, fulfilling Saviano's stated aim: 'quello di incidere con le mie parole, di dimostrare che la parola letteraria può ancora avere un peso e il potere di cambiare la realtà' [that of influencing with my words, of demonstrating that literature can still have weight and the power to change reality] (2009: 15). However, we must be attentive to the role of fiction in what we are reading, which is far from a return to reality.

Sappiano le mie parole di sangue by Babsi Jones

Like *Gomorra*, which appeared a year before it, Jones's text is a response to what the author perceives to be shortcomings in public knowledge about her subject matter. *Sappiano le mie parole di sangue* (2007) depicts the seven days she spent as a reporter in Mitrovica in Kosovo, during violent clashes between Serbs and Albanians, although this 'quasiromanzo' [quasi-novel] (255) is more broadly about the ongoing conflicts in the Balkans, and the way in which other countries, and in particular 'quell'Europa smemorata' [that forgetful Europe] (45), have turned a blind eye to what has been happening. Jones has also worked as a music journalist, and *Sappiano le mie parole di sangue* is her first and last book; she has since disappeared from the public eye, as I will explore later in this section, and she is thus a much more marginal cultural figure than Saviano, despite her approach to reportage in her UNO being similarly original and thought-provoking. In the book and in blog extensions online that have now disappeared, she narrates what happens in Mitrovica, in what she calls 'Tempo reale' [Real time],[25] alongside periodic flashbacks to some of the narrator's other experiences in the former Yugoslavia, as well as to incidents in history as far back as the fourteenth century that help explain how this situation came about.

Despite her constant reflections on her inability to represent the situation truly, Jones's narrator has a similarly strong sense of commitment to Saviano to bring her readers' attention to what has been happening — 'come se io fossi l'ultima Cassandra disponibile' [as if I were the last Cassandra available] (27) — but manages to avoid the rhetoric of heroism that can be detected in *Gomorra*.

Sappiano le mie parole di sangue centres loosely round letters that the narrator is ostensibly sending to her boss at the newspaper for which she is reporting. She directly addresses her interlocutor, Direttore, imploring him to hear her words. Like Saviano, she puts herself at personal risk in order to find out what is going on, getting into the thick of events in order to let others know about them, and ideally, although perhaps, she realises, not realistically — she is more circumspect than Saviano in this — to effect change through the power of her words. She tells us: 'non ho vissuto in questo pogrom, ho *scritto*. E ogni giorno, con l'illusione di cambiare qualcosa, qualsiasi cosa, ho afferrato una matita e ho ricominciato' [I have not lived in this pogrom, I have *written*. And every day, with the illusion of changing something, anything, I have grabbed a pencil and started again] (199). She too fights against the official version of events, undermining those who speak of 'i *liberatori* [...] i *delegates* [...] è *finita la guerra*' [the *liberators* [...] the *delegates* [...] *the war is over*] (42), NATO's rhetoric of 'albanesi dentro, serbi fuori' [Albanians in, Serbs out] (111), and an unscrupulous press that puts the speed of circulating news above its veracity (52).[26] Although these events are taking place on foreign soil, she also shows their relevance to Italy, highlighting her country's involvement in the NATO bombings in 1999, even though the Direttore prefers her to focus more on the drama of the violence and deaths than on the uncomfortable truth of how they happened, seeming to support Mosca's (2009: 322) observation, discussed earlier, that the Italian press tends to shy away from critical depth. The narrator asks him: 'non hai il desiderio di sapere *come* accade, quel che accade in Serbia a causa dei *nostri* bombardimenti, Direttore?' [don't you want to know *how* it happens, what happens in Serbia because of *our* bombing, Director?] (189). This is what she wants to know, as she uncovers the truth about the illegal cluster bombs that were used, rather than simply adhering to the sort of stories the rest of the press prefers.

Part of this fight against these versions of the story is the way in which the narrator constantly attempts to bring the readers into her experience, to make us breathe the air she breathes, as well as see what she sees, in the same vein as Saviano. Like the narrator of *Gomorra*, she resorts to intertextuality to illustrate more clearly what she encounters, seeking identification from her readers through references to films — *Dogville* (152), *Matrix Reloaded* (147), *Apocalypse Now* (203) — or other literary texts — the work of Kerouac (83), Büchner's *Woyzeck* (110), Joyce's *Ulysses* (166). There is also frequent interference from other media, whether it is the songs that find their way into the narrative through being played in the background (16–17, 23, 203), or the slogans of advertisements on the radio (237–38). This gives the narrative a sense of immediacy, as the reader takes in the cacophony of layers that make up this reality. At one point, the narrator differentiates between the work of a war reporter who, like Saviano's journalists, stays at a safe distance from the action in a comfortable hotel, and a writer like her:

> Il percorso dello scrittore è diverso [...] le sue frasi affiorano lentamente, come ascessi; il tempo per ripensarle, nelle stanze scelte a caso, di notte, è un tempo rischioso; parola per parola per parola per parola: una monotona emorragia semantica mi consuma.

> [The writer's path is different [...] her sentences emerge slowly, like abscesses; the time to rethink them, in rooms chosen at random, at night, is a risky time; word by word by word by word: a monotonous semantic haemorrhage consumes me.] (65)

These are her words of blood from the frontlines.

The text's title is based on a quote from *Hamlet* — 'O, from this time forth, | My thoughts be bloody, or be nothing worth!' (IV. 4. 65–66) — although the translation into Italian raises different possible meanings. She may be exhorting her words to be bloody, or 'know' of blood, or even 'taste' or 'smell' of blood, bringing to the fore the visceral quality of her writing, which is comparable to how Saviano describes Herr's depiction of the smell of the soldiers' shoes in Vietnam. The title could also be exhorting her readers to know her bloody words. Without knowing the title's provenance, its effect is almost like a curse or reminiscent of the Old Testament, imbuing the text with an epic seriousness similar to that bestowed on *Gomorra* by its biblical title. The slippage from 'thoughts' in the original *Hamlet* quote to 'words' in the text's title suggests a desire to connect lived experience and language, to create a short circuit between her cognitive awareness of these events and what we are reading on the page. However, this is impossible; such direct communication is only a dream, like the one she relates to the Direttore: 'ho sognato un cavo USB che inserito nella mia nuca si collegasse alla tua, Direttore. Un cavo che attraversasse il Mediterraneo placido, e lasciasse fluire interi blocchi di vissuto, integrali e disorganizzati, nella tua testa' [I dreamed of a USB cable that plugged into my head and connected to yours, Director. A cable that would cross the placid Mediterranean and let whole disorganized blocks of experience flow into your head] (99). Such reflections also bring to mind the gap between signifier and signified at the centre of post-structuralist theory, again undermining an alleged end of postmodernism by bringing to the fore the unbridgeable gap between language and reality.

Sappiano le mie parole di sangue, like *Gomorra*, is a book that deliberately resists easy categorisation. Jones told Genna (2007a) in an interview: 'ho intrecciato fatti reali e fiction [...] Volevo un testo denso, tachicardico, che mandasse in frantumi le regole del gioco, che potesse innestare epica, storia medievale e reportage, autobiografismo, narrazione, finzione' [I intertwined real facts and fiction [...] I wanted a dense, tachycardic text that shattered the rules of the game, that could graft epic, medieval history and reportage, autobiography, narration, fiction]. The narrator highlights again and again throughout the narrative that it is not a straightforward novel, often using conditionals, the subjunctive mood underlining its doubtful status: 'Se questo fosse un libro' [If this were a book], she repeats over several pages (99–102), then: 'Se queste pagine fossero un reportage, un romanzo o un saggio, se fossero un libro' [If these pages were reportage, a novel or an essay, if they were a book] (102). Jones seems to share Saviano's desire to avoid the text being relegated to a single genre, choosing the medium of a UNO in order to create what she later defined as 'un testo che scatena domande' [a text that provokes questions] (Genna 2007a). Besides the genres mentioned above, there is also the stylistically abstract final section, entitled 'Amletario', drawing on *Hamlet*, which comes after the main body of the text. It consists of six surreal monologues that move between Elsinore and Mitrovica to show the tragedy of events, searching for ways to work through and represent the horror. To return to Pocci's analysis of the performative function of language in *Gomorra*, here too the 'interdiscursive hybridity' (Pocci 2011: 232) of the text appears to be a way of making what Jones is saying act in the world, attracting attention to the situation in order to change it. Jones refers to herself as 'il narrA(t)tore' [narrA[c]tor] (246) in the 'Amletario', and she is both trying to display something in front of her readers, her 'spettatori' [spectators] (250), but also trying to act on what has been happening in Kosovo, using literature to elevate the suffering she witnesses to something that will reach and affect a wider audience.

Interestingly, the narrator carries Primo Levi's *I sommersi e i salvati* [*The Drowned and the Saved*] around with her, among other books. Antonello (2012: 123) suggests that Levi could be seen as another model, in combination with Pasolini, for twenty-first-century engaged writers. Jones has Levi's powerful drive to communicate these horrors — at one point, her repetition of the words 'Non dimenticarti' [Don't forget] (190) has incantatory resonances of Levi's poem 'Shemà' at the beginning of *Se questo è un uomo* [*If This Is a Man*] — but she also has an awareness of the limitations of her gaze. She compares her snapshots — which are both literal photographs (although we never see them) and literary pictures of the situations she experiences — to Levi's tendency to depict the details at the extremes of human experience. She says of her camera:

> Mi piaceva la funzione macro: si sposta attraverso i dettagli, inquadra microcosmi che si separano in fotogrammi più specifici, l'universo si scinde: quello che si dilata sul visore è una specie di esistenza all'estremo. Pensavo a Primo Levi: ne *I sommersi e i salvati*, spiega che i lager non erano un buon osservatorio; era raro, sostiene, che i prigionieri potessero acquisire una visione d'insieme di quel che stava accadendo; talvolta non conoscevano nemmeno il nome del campo in cui erano stati condotti, né conoscevano gli altri campi, anche se posti a poca distanza; non erano in grado di valutare la misura della strage che si stava svolgendo. Noi siamo nella stessa condizione. All'inizio adottavo la funzione macro per questo: per vedere, della guerra, solo gli elementi particolari spinti al limite ultimo; se non posso avere uno sguardo d'insieme, restringo fino al dettaglio più inumano. (114)

> [I liked the macro function: it moves through the details, frames the microcosms that separate into more specific frames, the universe splits: what expands on the viewfinder is a sort of existence at the extreme. I thought of Primo Levi: in *The Drowned and the Saved*, he explains that the concentration camps weren't a good observatory; he says that it was rare for the prisoners to be able to get an overview of what was happening; sometimes they didn't even know the name

of the camp they'd been taken to, nor did they know the other camps, even if they were a short distance away; they weren't able to assess the extent of the massacre that was taking place. We're in the same condition. At the beginning, I used the macro function for this reason: to see only the particular elements of the war pushed to the absolute limit; if I can't have a gaze over everything, I restrict myself to the most inhuman detail.]

As we saw with Janeczek in the previous chapter, Jones is engaging with the aporia of historical knowledge that Agamben discussed in reference to Levi, Auschwitz and testimony: 'la non-coincidenza fra fatti e verità, fra costatazione e comprensione' [the non-coincidence between facts and truths, between verification and comprehension] (Agamben 1998: 8). She may only be able to capture fragments of what she sees, but these can be pieced together and illuminate something more general both about the nature of this conflict and also about the difficulties of representation, recalling Janeczek's mosaic of stories that do not eliminate doubt in *Le rondini di Montecassino*. Indeed, like many other UNOs, Jones's text focuses on micro-details, but simultaneously opens out to considerations on a macro-scale.

The 'indicibilità' [unsayability] (179) of what the narrator witnesses is a constant trope of the text, as she repeatedly comes up against the limits of words and testimony. She comments, for example: 'Raccontarlo, però, è impossibile' [Narrating it, however, is impossible] (31), or 'Cerco parole' [I search for words] (38). There is an ever-present sense of disintegration, fragmentation, even what could be called a balkanisation of language, as the narrative seems to be an attempt to describe the conflict with her words, and, at the same time, inscribe it onto them. At the beginning of each of the seven days in Mitrovica, there is a page of a notebook, showing barely legible handwriting, crossed out and underlined, where we can find traces of what we are about to read. The presence of these pages of course brings the physical act of writing to our attention, partly perhaps as a piece of evidence that she 'really' did go there and write about it (although we have no guarantee that this is her notebook from the time or if it was fabricated afterwards), but it also demonstrates the way such writing can be edited, transcribed and transformed into the neater printed version. Yet, even the printed version indicates the difficulty of communication, at times with crossed out words — 'J̶a̶s̶e̶n̶o̶v̶a̶c̶ ̶/̶ ̶M̶a̶r̶i̶j̶a̶ ̶B̶i̶s̶t̶r̶i̶c̶a̶ ̶(̶C̶r̶o̶a̶z̶i̶a̶)̶ ̶/̶ Kosovo' (220) — or a lack of punctuation — 'Mitrovica è una città priva di caffè zucchero farina riso sapone detersivi cerotti quaderni a righe e a quadretti lacci da scarpe biscotti burro sigarette' [Mitrovica is a city lacking coffee sugar flour rice soap detergent plasters lined and squared notebooks shoelaces biscuits butter cigarettes] (134) — or contamination from other languages: Russian, English, Serbian, Arabic. The main body of the book ends by illustrating the difficulties of representing Jones's subject matter with a final unfinished sentence that stops mid-word (239). Like the black pages in Genna's *Hitler* (2008a) bringing to the fore reflections on what a writer can, or should, imagine, Jones's text employs physical indicators of the problems and limitations of the word in accessing the truth.

Fulginiti rightly states in relation to *Sappiano le mie parole di sangue*: 'se il NIE rappresenta il ritorno a una fiducia nel linguaggio, e nella capacità di fare cose con le parole, si tratta di una fiducia pur sempre provvisoria, e tutt'altro che trionfalistica' [if the NIE represents the return to a faith in language, and in the ability to do things with words, it is a faith that is still provisional, and far from being triumphalistic] (Fulginiti 2009: 3). Perhaps this is why Wu Ming 1 insists in the Memorandum on calling Jones's text a failure — although a useful one: 'Ringraziamo Babsi Jones per "averci provato", e anche per aver "fallito". La sfera pubblica ha bisogno di "fallimenti" come questo' [We thank Babsi Jones for 'having tried', and also for having 'failed'. The public sphere needs 'failures' like this] (Wu Ming 1 2009a: 43 n. 36) — given that he desires contemporary writers to take up responsibility, rather than insist on a failure to communicate fully the reality around us as Jones does again and again. Yet, as my reference above to Genna's *Hitler* and Janeczek's *Le rondini di Montecassino* suggests, Jones is not the only UNO writer, or the only writer associated with the NIE, who highlights the limitations of language and literature, whilst also choosing to employ words to try to address national and global problems. In *H. P. L'ultimo autista di Lady Diana* [*H. P. Lady Diana's Last Driver*], a first-person investigation combining vigorous research and testimony with flights of imagination and reflection about the life of Henri Paul, who died at the wheel of Lady Diana and Dodi Al Fayed's car, Sebaste discusses a 'poetica del fallimento' [poetics of failure] (2007: 193) to show the doubtful status of his investigation, as I have explored in more detail elsewhere (Willman 2017). This sense of failure is in stark contrast to Saviano's heroic approach, which at times relies on readers being attentive to its contradictions despite its truth claims, and it is also in contrast to what Wu Ming 1 seems to desire of twenty-first-century Italian literature in its response to current problems. The unidentified aspect of the label UNO suggests the provisional, uncertain quality that underlies these texts, which we have seen throughout this study, as they seem to break free of the literary project Wu Ming 1 envisages.

Whilst Jones's narrator engages with documentation, which she carefully footnotes at the end of each fragment, she tells us when introducing the bibliography at the end that the secondary material 'è invocato medianicamente o inserito con metodo burroughsiano' [is invoked psychically or inserted with the Burroughsian method] (255).[27] The text is thus a cut-up of different elements, jumping between styles and media as it jumps between different time frames, recalling another famous *Hamlet* quote: 'The time is out of joint' (I. 5. 188). Readers must sometimes work hard to follow the narrator's disjointed flow of words. We are invited in the footnotes to follow links to further information online, another instance of Jenkins's 'content streaming' (2006a: 243) — although it is unfortunate that we can no longer follow these links that have now disappeared — and, at one point, there are even swathes of code for the reader to decipher (120–25). As with the other UNOs I have analysed, the author pushes us to participate actively in interpreting and constructing the narrative, rather than simply sitting back and relaxing as the narrator reveals a fixed and already deciphered reality, although, as we saw in chapter 2 with Genna's *Medium*, the instability of digital material limits how many readers/users are able to engage fully with the text.

Despite a strong sense of *impegno* to talk about what is happening, Jones undermines the truth status of her narrative in a much starker way than Saviano's narrator in *Gomorra*. She asks questions such as: 'cosa è vero e cosa è falso' [what is true and what is false] (16). Before the book even starts, at the bottom of the publication information page and so small readers could almost miss it, there is the familiar caveat that these events are 'frutto dell'immaginazione dell'autore' [fruit of the author's imagination], but she goes on to say: 'si riferiscono [...] a un "ambito mitologico" che nulla ha a che vedere con la "verità storica", intorno alla quale questo romanzo elabora una pura fantasia' [they refer [...] to a 'mythological setting' that has nothing to do with 'historical truth', around which this novel elaborates a pure fantasy]. Then, on the page opposite the dedication and quotation from *Hamlet*, there is a table of contents in which Jones quantifies elements such as 'Immaginazione personale' [Personal imagination] (29 per cent), 'Incubi / Sogni / Allucinazioni' [Nightmares / Dreams / Hallucinations] (3 per cent), 'Ricordi d'infanzia' [Childhood memories] (68) and 'Pagine tagliate in fase di editing' [Pages cut in the editing phase] (1511). 'Verità' [Truth] only makes up 12 per cent. Whilst such questioning of the type of knowledge the text can give its readers is also present in *Gomorra*, there it is largely hidden or downplayed, whereas Jones is overt in bringing epistemological questions to the fore of her quasi-novel.

She is also telling a personal story, as once again we have Wu Ming 1's formulation of 'introspezione e autofiction per narrare un fatto pubblico e "storico"' [introspection and autofiction to narrate a public and 'historic' event] (Wu Ming 1 2009a: 15 n. 9). Jones's narrator says more than once that this is *her* war (61, 82, 187). We hear personal details about her dreams and her menstruation, and, arguably, we are encouraged to imagine that she might be the naked woman whose wrists are bleeding on the text's front cover. This suggests the ethical drive behind communicating experience that feminist theorists have explored, and Simonari (2008) points out that the bloody words of the title could be related to Cixous's idea of *écriture féminine*, transforming female experience into writing. It is interesting that Jones chooses to focus mainly on the women she is holed up with in Mitrovica; as in many of the other texts I have addressed, these are marginalised characters, 'dalla parte sbagliata della Storia' [from the wrong side of History], as the blurb of Wu Ming's *Manituana* (2007b) puts it, or as Jones puts it: 'Sbalzati fuori dalla Storia' [Hurled out by History] (37). Indeed, in an interview, she framed her protagonists precisely in terms of subalternity: 'Voglio scrivere di quel che non si scrive, di quel che raramente si può dire: i mutilati, i paria, gli esclusi, i caduti. E le donne' [I want to write about what isn't written about, what can rarely be spoken about: the mutilated, the pariahs, the excluded, the fallen. And women] (Genna 2007a). Cixous (1985: 251) states that a woman 'writes in white ink', relating female discourse to mother's milk, but Jones's text drips with blood, her own and that of the women whose suffering she depicts.

Such straying from objectivity puts Jones's text at risk of the type of controversy Saviano has experienced, although her more tentative attitude to the realism of her narrative would seem to sidestep this. Significantly, in contrast to the narrator of *Gomorra*, Jones's narrator reformulates Pasolini's famous words into a series of emphatic negatives: 'Io non lo so. Io *non* so i nomi dei responsabili, e *non* li so perché *non* sono un intellettuale' [I don't know. I *don't* know the names of those responsible, and I *don't* know them because I'm *not* an intellectual] (89, emphasis in original). This difference in approach to Saviano can be explained partly by her more openly problematised attitude to language and its ability to expose what is happening. It could also be explained by the nature of the conflicts in the Balkans, which, like much (post)modern warfare, were characterised by disinformation and cover-ups to leave no trace of the violence. There is a clear example of this in the text when the narrator describes the Serbs who have disappeared:

> Sono desaparecidos. Serbi scomparsi. Sono quelli che le milizie rapiscono: li sfigurano con ferri arroventati, tolgono loro ogni segno di riconoscimento, e li interrano qua e là. Perché le famiglie non li trovino. Perché nessuno sporga denuncia. Perché non rimangono prove. (111)

> [They are *desaparecidos*. Disappeared Serbs. They are the ones that the militia kidnap: they disfigure them with red-hot irons, they take away every sign of recognition, and they bury them here and there. So that the families don't find them. So that nobody files complaints. So that no proof remains.]

In such a climate, it is not just the case that she does not have the proof, it is that perhaps nobody does. No wonder one of the narrator's interlocutors laughs at her mention of truth: '"La *verità* nei Balcani?"' ['*Truth* in the Balkans?'] (218, emphasis in original). Like Herr's Vietnam, this is a new type of war, one that is being fought in such a way that depictions of it must find new forms, no longer being able to rely on straightforward reportage. Moreover, the narrator might call it *her* war, but she is a foreigner in the Balkans, and thus has the limited perspective of an outsider, as she herself points out, and as illustrated by the fragmentary quality of what she relates. Thus, she may not 'know' or understand the whole truth. Another dimension of her disavowal of Pasolini's 'Io so' could be that she does not see herself as an intellectual, as she is a marginal and largely unknown figure on the cultural scene. Perhaps refusing the label of intellectual is part of a wish to encourage reflection on the masculinity that has traditionally been — and often still is — associated with it.

So who is Babsi Jones? She seems to be an elusive figure, another divergence from Saviano and his very public personal crusade. Throughout the text, she directs readers towards further fragments of narrative on a blog that has now disappeared and been replaced,[28] as has her website,[29] although traces of her remain online in videos. In the book trailer for *Sappiano le mie parole di sangue*, a handheld camera tracks the author wandering through a war-torn building and looking more like a pop star than a writer, but gradually shedding her heels and fur coat, whilst we hear her reading from the book in the voiceover. Like Genna's additional material for *Medium* (see chapter 2), the autofiction is deepened for readers through embodiment combined with illusion, here in the author's bodily presence in the video combined with its staged quality, created by her incongruous clothes and the abandoned building resembling a film set rather than a real place.[30] There are also videos related to the text on YouTube, one of which was created by Genna and is called an 'installazione audiovideo' [audio-video installation], featuring Jones's voice reading from Heiner Müller's postmodernist *Hamletmaschine* against a black-and-white film showing a match burning.[31] Another again features only her voice, this time reading part of T. S. Eliot's 'Ash Wednesday' against the backdrop of various images — a waterfall, books being thrown onto a pile as if for burning, what seems to be news footage or home videos of a war zone in the Balkans — creating a cut-up of artistic material with real footage accompanied by the author's voice, moving between fictional and nonfictional elements that are unexplained or unidentified.[32] These videos give a sense that Jones is almost a performance artist, creating the spectacle surrounding *Sappiano le mie parole di sangue* through various media that combine more or less referential elements, but then fading away into the background, like the 'lost word' of Eliot's poem. In common with Wu Ming 1 in the Memorandum (see chapter 1), or Genna in *Italia De Profundis* (see chapter 2), Jones chooses to reference Eliot, bringing to mind modernist questioning of existing forms and structures of knowledge, and, particularly relevant for us here, the desire of modernist writers to distance their work from the realism and enlightenment ideals that came before them. Eliot's poem, like *Sappiano le mie parole di sangue*, has a sense of despair both about the darkness of the world and about knowledge being able to illuminate it: 'O my people, what have I done unto thee. | Where shall the word be found, where will the word | Resound?' (Eliot 1969: 96).

Despite reflections on the limitations of language, and the author dissolving from view at the end of the text, Jones's words do still resound. In contrast to Saviano, she leaves a question mark over what literature can do. She may not be able to offer up proof in many cases, or fully communicate this reality, but she can communicate a powerful sense of experience. Significantly, Jones's narrator states: 'Non sono venuta qui per fare della poesia né dell'epica. Sono venuta qui per capire e osservare' [I didn't come here to make poetry or epic. I came here to understand and observe] (62). Once again, an approach that can be seen as anti-epic or anti-heroism may go further towards enacting the NIE's sense of political and ethical commitment, in questioning how we understand reality whilst also attempting to bring it closer to us.

Roma Negata by Igiaba Scego with Rino Bianchi

Scego's intermedial 2014 text *Roma negata*, which she created with the photographer and photojournalist Rino Bianchi, works in the same way as *Gomorra* as part of a network of activism across different types of texts and platforms, but, like Jones, Scego does not employ a rhetoric of heroism. Scego has employed various formats to raise awareness about the enduring influence of Italy's colonial past and about present issues of discrimination and racism through a personal approach that often draws on her own family history, as the daughter of Somali parents who fled Siad Barre's dictatorship and raised her in Italy. She does not have the level of fame that Saviano does, although she has enjoyed critical and commercial success in Italy and beyond: her most recent novel, *Adua*, has been translated into English. Aside from her literary output, she has worked as a scholar and journalist,[33] as well as appearing on radio and television shows and maintaining an active social media presence: in addition to her Twitter profile, she has a key role on the blog *Alzo la mano adesso!*, which self-describes as 'un collettivo di scrittura composto da scrittori, giornalisti e blogger di varie origini, residenti in Italia, che cerca di intervenire nel dibattito nazionale, alzando la mano e dicendo: "siamo qua anche noi e vogliamo dire la nostra"' [a writing collective made up of writers, journalists and bloggers of various origins, living in Italy, who try to intervene in the national debate, raising our hands and saying: 'we are here too and we want to have our say'].[34] She is thus engaged in increasing awareness about the lack of representation for migrant voices on the Italian cultural scene, an issue that we shall see is also raised by *Roma negata*, as her body of work picks up similar issues in different ways across different modes of communication to gain power and nuance.

Scego is another author who is surprisingly absent from many discussions of the NIE, given that her hybrid texts address identity, the impact of recent history and the power of storytelling with a strong sense of *impegno*. Her work was only admitted into the nebula after the Memorandum had been published, despite two of her novels and various short stories having already been available in 2008.[35] Once again, we can see a tendency to overlook female and transnational perspectives. When discussing writers such as Scego and Gabriella Ghermandi (whom I discuss in chapter 3), De Vivo rightly argues that 'the presence of African-Italian postcolonial women writers in the Italian public literary and cultural domain challenges the gender and ethnicity location embodied by the classic figure of the Italian "intellettuale impegnato"' (2015: 121). Certainly, we will see that Scego's work demonstrates an important and effective contribution to effecting change in Italy that reinvigorates the tradition of *impegno* to which Wu Ming 1's NIE still seems to adhere.

Likewise, it is worth pointing out that the special issue of *Allegoria* on the return to reality largely focused on white, ethnically Italian, male writers, a particularly questionable bias given the large number of migrant writers who have incorporated their real-life experiences into their literary output. Similarly, Scego has a tendency to incorporate autobiographical elements into her texts, as we will see in *Roma negata* too. This can be detected most obviously in her 2010 text *La mia casa è dove sono* [*My Home Is Where I Am*], in which she mapped her life story, but we can also see hints of life-writing in her 2008 multi-perspectival text *Oltre Babilonia* [*Beyond Babylon*], in which Zuhra might be seen as a sort of avatar of the author, having autobiographical details in common with her that we know from *La mia casa è dove sono*; as Brioni states: 'The mutual relationship between these two texts might not suggest that *Oltre Babilonia* is a realist novel (although it is inspired by and describes the lives of real people), but rather shows the hybrid nature of both Igiaba Scego's autobiography and fictional works, which cannot be reduced to a specific genre' (2015: 130). Once more, we are dealing with UNOs that cannot be seen purely as a return to reality and, as Brioni's comment hints, autofictional UNOs might be seen as particularly well suited to migrant writing, given the hybridity of migrant writers' backgrounds, as well as the fact that they are often expected to write about their life experience. Textual experimentation through including different modes of writing rather than more straightforward life-writing might be seen as a way of playing with this expectation, as well as an effective way of exploring multiple identities and belongings.[36] We will see that *Roma negata* draws on various different genres that are (at least seen as) more referential in character — travel writing, reportage, photojournalism, memoir, history (there is also a bibliography at the end) — but, as the physical book's unusual shape suggests, creates something different from all of these.

The subtitle of *Roma negata* is *Percorsi postcoloniali nella città* [*Postcolonial Journeys Through the City*], and the idea of *percorsi* is key to the text, which not only relates physical journeys through Rome (and beyond) to places that resound with colonial memory, but it also employs different routes to communicate its message to its readers (photography, text) and encourages readers/viewers to take different routes through it: the photographs are not dispersed throughout the textual fragments, but contained in a single section, encouraging us to move back and forth through the book to make the connections between Scego's writing and Bianchi's images. There is a sense of movement inscribed into Scego's narrative too, through references to the act of moving through the city and, at times, the use of ellipses and short paragraphs that make her text resemble steps rather than a flowing narrative, bringing the immediacy of her bodily presence in space to the fore. We see this particularly in the first section, which is entitled 'Inizio a camminare...' [I start walking...], then begins 'Cammino...' [I walk...] (13), continuing in fragmented thoughts punctuated by reminders of the physicality of wandering through the city: 'Il piede mi trema' [My foot trembles] (14), 'Nel frattempo un clacson strombazza isterico fracassandomi il timpano' [Meanwhile, a horn hysterically hoots, shattering my eardrum] (15), 'Cammino, devo pensare... | Un piede dopo l'altro, un pensiero dopo l'altro' [I walk, I have to think ... | One foot after another, one thought after another] (24). Subsequent chapters intermittently return to this act of walking, as if the textual fragments are part of one continuous journey: as she moves from the section on the fascist-era Cinema Impero to that on the Dogali obelisk commemorating Italian soldiers killed at the Battle of Dogali in Ethiopia, she tells us: 'Il cinema [...] è ormai alle mie spalle' [The cinema [...] is now behind me] (50). Like Jones and Saviano, Scego is taking us with her on this journey that is vividly depicted in all its detail, as a mental and physical journey through Italy's colonial traces that is also 'il mio viaggio emozionale' [my emotional journey] (50), and that eventually becomes '[il] nostro viaggio' [our journey] (98). This is alongside other narrative strategies or *persorsi*, such as her inclusion of personal, family memories in her wanderings through Rome, or her delving into Italy's history through a more factual style of writing that is complete with dates, quotations from other sources and footnotes. We shall see later on that the text has also continued its *percorso* into the online environment and real-life activism.

Whilst writers like De Cataldo have worked at unearthing the links between mafia and state in the Italian capital (see chapter 2), the scandal that Scego addresses is the overlooking or forgetting of Italy's fascist and colonial history, whose imprints can be detected in Rome today. As with the previous two texts analysed in this chapter, *Roma negata* is also addressing a failing of the mainstream media, which does not acknowledge the links of present events in the news with this past. This is shown in *Roma negata* in the case of the reporting of the drowning of Eritreans trying to reach Italy, which does not acknowledge that Eritrea is a former colony; Scego states: 'Sono stati pochi i giornalisti ad aver colto questa relazione tra Italia ed Eritrea. E nessuno ha inchiodato l'Italia alle sue responsabilità storiche come ex paese colonizzatore' [Few journalists have grasped this relationship between Italy and Eritrea. And nobody has nailed Italy to its historical responsibilities as a former colonising country] (36). She traces back the links of today's reality with recent history throughout the text, compensating for the media's lack of critical depth. This is not the only shortcoming of the media that Scego addresses: Jacomella (2015) has shown how migrant voices and stories are largely absent from the mainstream media in Italy, and we see this in *Roma negata* when Scego notes that the media have minimised the protests of migrants in Ponte Galeria, who have sewn their mouths shut in a visualisation of this silencing (24). Scego and Bianchi's text works against this, both in its subject matter — addressing colonial and migrant (his)stories, as well as visually giving a face to seemingly invisible migrant presences in Italy through the images — and in its authorship, given that the textual fragments are written by a Somali-Italian writer. Storytelling in the form of a UNO is once again a way of countering the shortcomings of how the press have addressed the issues at stake, in this case working against the act of denial encapsulated in the text's title.

It is Scego's personal history as someone coming from the Horn of Africa that compels her to tell these stories and speak about these things: 'Non la posso dimenticare IO questa storia. Non la voglio dimenticare. | Per questo forse, a modo mio, racconto. | Per questo forse cammino' [*I* can't forget this history. I don't want to forget it. | Perhaps because of this, in my way, I narrate. | Perhaps because of this I walk] (25). As in the cases of Saviano and Jones, Scego's journey is personal despite having collective significance, and she refers to her own experiences and impressions throughout the narrative, from meeting an older woman at a bus stop who tells her that Italians were good colonialists (19), to memories of her father singing her a fascist song that he was taught at school as a child (102), to going to a protest in Piazza Montecitorio against the way the drowning of Eritreans was dealt with by the Italian establishment (44), occupying a space traditionally associated with Italian politics to make visible the bodies of those who are so often ignored by mainstream discourse. Her narrative is filling the spaces of the city with (hi) stories, about herself and about others, stories that have been forgotten or erased, not only by the media but also by Italian education: 'Solo vuoto, solo silenzio, assenza, oblio' [Only emptiness, only silence, absence, forgetting] (18). Bianchi's involvement in the text is also connected to his personal story: Scego notes that, because he is married to a Turkish woman, 'ha compiuto nella sua vita un percorso di decolonizzazione che lo ha portato a vedere il mondo come un insieme di uguali nella differenza' [he has been on a journey of decolonisation in his life that has led him to see the world as a combination of equals in difference] (135).

Indeed, ways of seeing the world are foregrounded in the text, through attempts to decolonise the gaze of Italians, to see beyond the tourist gaze on the eternal city, or to see through the eyes of those coming to Italy from its former African colonies. These postcolonial subjects look straight into the camera's lens at the viewer in the majority of Bianchi's photographs, which are taken by monuments but are far from resembling postcards. Mohamed and Wu Ming 2's *Timira* similarly focuses on ways of seeing in its revisiting of Italian colonial history; as Wu Ming 2 (2012) has pointed out, the colonial project was predicated on ways of seeing space, a point that *Roma negata* demonstrates too through showing how different people might view and inhabit the Italian capital, and it is significant that both *Timira* and *Roma negata* address the colonial past through UNOs that combine textual and visual elements. Indeed, Bianchi's black-and-white photographs similarly recall and subvert the colonial employment of photography that I discussed in chapter 3 in my analysis of the use of photography in *Timira*, through avoiding exoticising and objectifying the people photographed. As Scego points out,

> Le foto di Rino Bianchi sono molto diverse da quelle che avrebbe potuto fare un suo collega di inizio Novecento [...] il soggetto delle fotografie di Rino non diventa mai oggetto, ma vive nella pellicola [...] rimanendo soggetto, ovvero portatore della propria storia e della propria anima.

> [Rino Bianchi's photos are very different from those that could have been taken by a photographer in the early twentieth century [...] the subject in Rino's photographs never becomes an object, but lives in the film [...] remaining a subject, or carrier of their own story and soul.] (135)

Bianchi's perspective is frequently from below — as seen, for example, in the photographs of Simon Makonnen, Ruth Gebresus or the unnamed political refugees — so that those photographed often look down at the viewer, deepening this sense of their being subjects rather than objects and of decentring the colonial gaze. Outside the former Museo africano, where the exotic spoils of colonial conquest in Africa were displayed, Jonis Bascir stares calmly back at us, smartly wrapped up in a winter coat and hat. The impact of this visual approach is shown by the use of ekphrasis in the narrative describing a photograph, shown to Scego by her friend F., of a Libyan girl called Kibra, who was the girlfriend of F.'s grandfather when he was in the colony of Libya; this leads Scego to reflect on how Italians want to forget these colonial memories, but faces like Kibra's demanded to be remembered, appealing to Italy's bad conscience 'con i suoi occhi, il suo dolore' [with her eyes, her pain] (21). This suggests a motive for the inclusion of the visual medium in *Roma negata*, as a way of demanding attention and emotional investment from the reader/viewer more powerfully than a straightforward written text.

Scego tells us in the final section of the text that she shares the gaze of the people in the photographs: 'Lo sguardo di Tztà o di Sofia Mahmoud sono anche il mio sguardo' [The gaze of Tztà or Sofia Mahmoud is also my gaze] (134). She embodies her narrative in herself — the traditionally white male *flâneur* instead becoming a woman of colour — and the text is also embodied in the people who populate Bianchi's photographs, living presences testifying to Italy's links to the

Horn of Africa. Scego explains that they are the most important part of the project: 'abbiamo tracciato in questo libro un percorso nella città. Un percorso fatto di monumenti, tracce, ma soprattutto volti' [in this book, we have traced a journey through the city. A journey made of monuments, traces, but above all faces] (134). The text gives a face to Italian history's effects in the present, and to the migrant presences in Italy, who too often end up simply as statistics of those killed crossing the Mediterranean, as the emotional, embodied engagement discussed in the first section of this chapter is enacted by Bianchi and Scego. Scego describes her approach in terms of giving physicality to the issues at stake through a focus on these bodily presences: 'Corpi che rivendicano una storia, un passato, una memoria. Corpi che vogliono giustizia. Corpi che sognano un'altra Italia più equa, giusta, nostra, antirazzista. Corpi che occupano con la loro dignità di persona i luoghi di quel colonialismo italiano dimenticato' [Bodies that claim a history, a past, a memory. Bodies that want justice. Bodies that dream of another Italy that is more equal, fair, ours, anti-racist. Bodies that occupy with their human dignity the places of that forgotten Italian colonialism] (125). Her rhetorical use of repetition here and elsewhere in the text recalls not only De Cataldo's use of anaphora in *Nelle mani giuste* that we saw in chapter 2, but also Saviano's rhetorical tone in *Gomorra*. Scego's metaphorical approach to Rome is also reminiscent of Saviano's vivid descriptions of the port of Naples: Scego personifies the city — 'Roma con i suoi segreti e i suoi deliri inconfessabili. Roma che non mi ha mai detto la verità fino in fondo' [Rome with its secrets and its unconfessable deliriums. Rome that has never told me the whole truth] (13) — and resorts at times to bodily metaphors, as when she describes the balcony of Piazza Venezia that Mussolini used to speak from as 'una ferita nella città, un cancro pronto a produrre metastasi' [a wound in the city, a cancer ready to metastasise] (126). Through bodily engagement and through emotive, rhetorical language in their UNOs, these authors seek to raise awareness and bring about change.

This political and ethical drive again starts on a personal, local level — for Scego, the city of Rome — but moves to wider considerations, like many of the UNOs I have addressed in this study, and it also works across different texts in Scego's case, which expand on or complement one another through different modes of writing. Many of the places mentioned in *Roma negata* are discussed in *La mia casa è dove sono*, whose chapters are named after places, but whose narrative is even more personal in nature, mapping Rome and Mogadishu through Scego's life story. This more autobiographical approach can be seen in the references to Piazza di Porta Capena, which she walks towards at the beginning of *Roma negata* to discuss its absence of colonial memory, but in *La mia casa è dove sono* it introduces the story of her grandfather and uncle: 'Nel mio piccolo, nella mia geografia personale, piazza di Porta Capena è legata al viso di due uomini, alle loro storie, ai lasciti indiretti che mi hanno trasmesso pur senza saperlo' [In my small, in my personal geography, Piazza di Porta Capena is linked to the faces of two men, to their stories, to the indirect legacies that they passed on to me without knowing it] (Scego 2012: 79). Whilst *Roma negata* also contains stories from Scego's life, *La mia casa è dove sono* is more firmly rooted in this personal geography, but this then opens up to collective concerns once again, as encapsulated in the text's final lines: 'Non è una mappa coerente. È centro, ma anche periferia. È Roma, ma anche Mogadiscio. | È Igiaba, ma siete anche voi' [It's not a coherent map. It's centre, but also periphery. It's Rome, but also Mogadishu. | It's Igiaba, but it's also you] (Scego 2012: 161). Whilst Saviano's moving between the local and the global was illustrating a web of organised crime that we are all caught up in, Scego's web or map highlights connections across national lines, across time periods, between centre and periphery, and between her readers and herself. As Bond states, Scego is 'tracing superimposed cartographies of interactive belonging where places intersect through memory and imagination in order to form poles of meaning within a mixed and flexible trans-national identity' (Bond 2014: 424). For Bond, this approach, which she also sees in *Roma negata*, recalls Ulrich Beck's conception of 'cosmopolitanisation', as a 'non-linear, dialectical process in which the universal and particular, the similar and the dissimilar, the global and the local, are to be conceived not as cultural polarities, but as interconnected and reciprocally interpenetrating principles' (Beck 2006: 72–73; quoted in Bond 2014: 424). This non-linear, interconnected approach also works across Scego's oeuvre, in which different texts feed into, and are in dialogue with, one another in different ways to reflect on the universal and the particular. The UNO might be seen as a privileged mode for expressing this cosmopolitanisation, through rejecting more straightforward textual strategies and connecting different styles and approaches as it moves between the local, the national and the global.

We have seen how Saviano has come to embody the causes that he first championed in *Gomorra*, and Scego too tends to combine her personal story and figure with the issues that she raises, as can be seen through her use of social media to supplement her texts, using different platforms that merge personal and collective elements. Her Twitter profile (@casamacombo) provides her thoughts and links to articles connected to the issues she explores in her literary production, regarding Somalia, Africa more widely, racism, the colonial past and migration, particularly focusing on the specificities of the Italian experience. This is connected to activism that she has engaged in, such as the campaign for the children of migrants born in Italy to be given citizenship (#italianisenzacittadinanza), or the protest about the monument in Affile built with public money in 2012 to commemorate Rodolfo Graziani, the leader of military campaigns in Africa during the fascist period. Scego started an online petition against the monument in April 2013 that attracted more than 20,000 signatures, although, as she described in a letter of protest to the Presidente della Camera dei Deputati, this only stopped public money going towards the project, but the monument remained.[37] She went on to publish *Roma negata* in 2014, which addresses the monument in Affile alongside the fascist traces she sees in Rome in a chapter entitled 'Affile: una vergogna nazionale' [Affile: a national disgrace] (117); this chapter was then reposted on the widely read literary and cultural blog *Nazione Indiana*.[38] What is interesting about this campaign is the way it works across media, moving between printed books, the online environment and real-life activism, showing a transmedial approach that takes in different modes of writing and action that circulate among various readers/viewers/users. Like Saviano's transmedial activism, it also maintains a personal focus through the figure of the author, as seen in the wording of Scego's letter to Boldrini, which begins: 'Non so come cominciare la lettera che deve accompagnare questa petizione. Sono troppo addolorata. Troppo...' [I don't know how to begin the letter that must accompany this petition. I'm too upset. Too much...]. Again, we can see a sense of *impegno* that is emotional and embodied in the figure of the writer/intellectual, as well as exploiting transmediality to gain visibility.

Unlike Jones, who appears to reject being a public intellectual through negating the 'Io so' and disappearing into anonymity, Scego seems to have taken on the role and reimagined the traditionally white, male figure for the new millennium. *Roma negata* combines different modes of writing and visuality to raise awareness about a history of colonialism and current issues facing migrants, who have been largely ignored or silenced by the mainstream media, and this drive to raise awareness has then been continued through online platforms. Scego might be seen as a figure whose transnational, transmedial and cosmopolitan approach shows a twenty-first-century *impegno* that represents a more complex reality than that conceived by certain Italian critics when envisaging the NIE or the alleged return to reality.

Saviano, Jones and Scego make an impact on their readers through their generically wayward texts combined with transmedial elements, which resist being simply labelled a 'return to reality'. They form part of a rich Italian tradition of *inchieste* combining literature and reportage, but also draw on the American tradition of New Journalism and the non-fiction novel. Their work displays emotional and bodily engagement, foregrounding individual, subjective, postmodern experience in order to make wider points about Italy and the world.

Despite the huge visibility he has brought to the issues he engages with, I would argue that Saviano's heroic approach downplaying the literary and invented elements of his work is ethically dubious in a world where fake news circulates, and new stories are distorted for corporate or political ends, or because of a desire to erase certain memories and voices. UNOs are more effective in combatting the shortcomings of mainstream discourse when openly and self-reflexively using different modes of storytelling to encourage readers/viewers/users to take an active role and to question the reality with which they are presented.

Notes to Chapter 4

1. See <http://www.allegoriaonline.it/index.php/i-numeri-precedenti/allegoria-n57.html>.
2. To mention a few of those writers who were most strongly opposed to the idea: Genna: 'Non parlerei di "ritorno alla realtà"' [I wouldn't talk about a 'return to reality'] (Donnarumma and Policastro 2008: 12); Lagioia: 'Il concetto di "ritorno alla realtà" applicato alla letteratura, a mio parere non ha senso' [The concept of a 'return to reality' applied to literature doesn't make sense in my opinion] (Donnarumma and Policastro 2008: 16); Trevisan: 'al contrario: credo si possa parlare di fuga dalla realtà' [on the contrary: I believe we could talk about an escape from reality] (Donnarumma and Policastro 2008: 23).
3. Ganeri's (2011: 67–68) controversial conclusion is that such a strongly negative reaction to an

alleged return to reality is indicative of the fact that these intellectuals have their own inward-looking and self-referential way of talking to one another instead of engaging with the wider world.

4. It is worth mentioning that Casadei had already started exploring ideas about recent literature's approach to reality before this in *Stile e tradizione nel romanzo italiano contemporaneo* [*Style and Tradition in the Contemporary Italian Novel*] (2007).

5. There are interesting parallels between the current climate in film criticism and that of literary criticism in Italy: as O'Leary and O'Rawe (2011) have pointed out, the term 'realism' tends to be used to endow films with value and seriousness, and we can see a similar operation happening in literature. There are also comparable anxieties about more popular or 'lowbrow' texts involved in the discussion of realism in film:

> The privileging of cinema's allotted role of 'mirror' of the nation has led to a downgrading of popular genres and a kind of nationalistic cinema history in the scholarship. Questions of the popular, or indeed an anxiety about the status and *appeal* of the popular, have occupied a permanent place at the heart of Italian film history. (O'Leary and O'Rawe 2011: 109)

In a similar way, *Allegoria* 57 could be interpreted as an attempt to elevate contemporary literature in the face of those critics, such as Ferroni (2010), who have condemned it as mindless entertainment.

6. For more on postmemory, see my discussion of Janeczek's *Le rondini di Montecassino* in chapter 3.

7. Mosca (2014: 165) also notes this change from previous forms of commitment.

8. For a fascinating discussion of Italian feminism's emphasis on subjectivity and experience in the light of postmodernism, see Ronchetti 2009.

9. Indeed *Allegoria* 57 has similar blind spots to the Memorandum on the NIE, given that, of the eight authors interviewed, only one is a woman (Pugno) and none of them are migrant writers.

10. For example: Fazel, Ghermandi, Janeczek, Scego. Women film-makers in Italy have also employed autofiction in interesting ways, such as Marazzi (see introduction), Asia Argento and Alice Rohrwacher.

11. Not only are Wu Ming all male writers, but so are Kai Zen and Babette Factory, while Scrittura Industriale Collettiva is headed by two male writers who oversee the collective writing process.

12. He provocatively added to this: 'a minor art form' (as quoted in Vespa 1979).

13. Mosca makes a similar argument, pointing to a tradition 'da Manzoni a Borghese, da Moravia a Pasolini, fino ai recentissimi Franchini, Desiati e Saviano' [from Manzoni to Borghese, from Moravia to Pasolini, until the very recent Franchini, Desiati and Saviano] (2013: 159).

14. D'Angelo (2013: 197–207) also draws a line from Manzoni to the 'return to reality', tracing similar tensions or 'nevrosi' [neuroses] as he calls them, in the relationship between reality in fiction for Manzoni and for writers like Siti and Saviano.

15. Genna interweaves fictional and autofictional stories around an investigation into the conspiracies surrounding death of Alfredino Rampi in the 1980s in Vermicino (mentioned in chapters 2 and 3). When Genna goes to Vermicino towards the end of the text, he moves from asserting his knowledge about these events — 'Io so. | So parti, pezze, tracce perse nella polvere poco più avanti' [I know. | I know parts, patches, traces lost in the dust just ahead] (2014: 637), 'So quel che so' [I know what I know] (2014: 638) — to realising 'Non è vero che so: io non so. [...] io non so e so che non so' [It isn't true that I know: I don't know. [...] I don't know and I know that I don't know] (2014: 639). He is thus closer to Jones's unstable relationship with knowledge than to Saviano's assertions of his authority, as we shall see.

16. After quoting from Pasolini's article, the writer states: 'Io non so se so, ma come per Pasolini "tutto ciò fa parte del mio mestiere e del instinto del mio mestiere"' [I don't know if I know, but as for Pasolini, 'all of this is part of my job and of the instinct of my job'] (Tabucchi 2006: 8). Tabucchi's collected articles in the volume address worrying developments in today's world,

which, similar to what Pasolini describes, Tabucchi has pieced together for the readers to show the connections and analogies between the events they address. Yet, Tabucchi insists on a more tentative 'I don't know if I know', and, significantly, he calls the text a sort of 'novel' (2006: 8). Tabucchi is slightly older than the writers I focus on in this study, and must have inspired them with his work as a writer and intellectual. His *Tristano muore* [*Tristano Dies*] (2004) could be analysed alongside the historical novels I look at in chapter 3, as it returns to the Italian Resistance to ask questions about how we bear witness to the past through an oral and experimental narrative.

17. For a fascinating discussion of more examples from Italy and elsewhere, see Mosca 2014.

18. For a detailed analysis of Luther Blissett's various pranks, see Deseriis 2011.

19. It has a different subtitle in the British English translation: *Italy's Other Mafia* (Saviano 2008).

20. The British paperback version has a foreword on the nonfiction novel, most likely in response to the criticism the book received (Saviano 2016: xxi–xxiv).

21. Significantly, Jameson (2009: 361–63) has seen *Gomorra* as expressing the way in which postmodernity as a historical stage of capitalism works through Saviano's descriptions of the clans' neoliberal approach to business and economics.

22. See his interview with Giovanna Zucconi in *La Stampa* in July 2006, in which he states that he wrote the book 'senza ossessione di verità' [without an obsession with truth], and describes the narrator's gaze as 'un io congetturale e deformato' [a conjectural and deformed I] (quoted in Cortellessa 2011a: 526).

23. In *ZeroZeroZero*, the hands-on experience that made his début so memorable and powerful is missing, due to the difficult conditions under which Saviano must now work. There is a poignant reminder of this in the dedication at the beginning: 'Questo libro lo dedico a tutti i carabinieri della mia scorta. Alle 38.000 ore trascorse insieme. E a quelle ancora da trascorrere' [I dedicate this book to all the police officers who have been my bodyguards. To the 38,000 hours spent together. And to those still to be spent]. It is once again a stylistically unusual text, which moves between Mexico, Colombia, Calabria, Russia, and all over the world, but Saviano is only present in the occasional asides that document his obsession with the drugs trade: 'Scrivere di cocaina è come farne uso. Vuoi sempre più notizie, più informazioni, e quelle che trovi sono succulente, non ne puoi più fare a meno. Sei *addicted*' [Writing about cocaine is like using it. You want more and more news, more and more information, and what you find is delicious, you can't do without it. You're addicted] (2013: 417). He must stay in hiding, accessing the facts second hand, through Wikileaks and the *Guardian* (2013: 335), documentaries on the History Channel (2013: 329), or, as one reviewer points out, lifting them from Wikipedia (Varese 2013).

24. Pocci's perceptive reading of *Gomorra* employs Austin's theories on the constative and performative function of language, showing the text's 'constative effect of *corresponding* to the reality under examination (the reality of the *camorra*) in an assertive rather than descriptive mode, and the performative one of *responding* to such reality with expressive force and brave civil engagement' (Pocci 2011: 243).

25. Although she does not state when this time is, we can assume she is referring to the events that began in March 2004 in Mitrovica, when the drowning of an Albanian child in the river sparked violence between the city's Albanians and Serbs.

26. Interestingly, De Michele (2009) has compared Jones's depiction of the way in which the first piece of news about an event is what counts, even if it is later disproved, to the way in which people reacted to the violent events at the G8 in Genoa which I discuss in chapter 1.

27. Not coincidentally, Burroughs is also mentioned in *Italia De Profundis* (see chapter 2), and Scurati's approach in *Una storia romantica* also recalls Burroughs's cut-up technique, as he brings disparate elements together from different media and genres in his collage novel (see chapter 3). Burroughs is clearly an important reference point for these recent writers, and his influence can be seen as another instance of postmodernist elements enduring in twenty-first-century Italian literature.

28. See slmpds.net. Jones described it as 'un'ulteriore stratificazione di livelli inediti' [a further stratification of unpublished levels] (Genna 2007a), one reviewer referred to it as 'un sito-

labirinto di oltre 100 pagine' [a site-labyrinth of more than 100 pages] (Sbancor 2007), and Cortellessa calls it 'la sua "vera" opera' [her 'true' work] (2011a: 537), but, unfortunately, it had already disappeared before I could access it.

29. See babsijones.typepad.com/babsi/.
30. See https://vimeo.com/305027.
31. See 'Babsi Jones — TRITTICO: Hamletmaschine — Amleto — Hamletmaschine', https://www.youtube.com/watch?v=YIZdw6CfpWk.
32. See 'La parola perduta_Babsi Jones_legge_Eliot', https://www.youtube.com/watch?v=ijιczGlFNxI.
33. Primarily for *Internazionale*: see https://www.internazionale.it/tag/autori/igiaba-scego.
34. See https://collettivoalma.wordpress.com/about/.
35. Wu Ming 1 stated in a 2014 interview that she was later admitted into the nebula (Brioni 2014: 280), and Scego has also engaged with his ideas, calling her own work NIE (Brioni 2013: 1).
36. Brioni's work on Somali-Italian literature (including Scego) has made a similar argument, saying that 'plural identities and multiple belongings of minor subjectivities are expressed through the subversive use of autobiographically inspired narrations' (Brioni 2015: 112).
37. See https://www.change.org/p/laura-boldrini-buttiamo-gi%C3%B9-il-muro-il-monumento-a-rodolfo-graziani.
38. See https://www.nazioneindiana.com/2014/05/28/igiaba-scego-affile-una-vergogna-nazionale-da-roma-negata-2014/.

CONCLUSIONS

We have looked at a series of unidentified narrative objects (UNOs) in recent Italian literature, starting in chapter 1 with Wu Ming 1's Memorandum on the New Italian Epic (NIE), a document filled with fascinating ideas to be explored regarding the twenty-first-century Italian cultural scene and coining the name UNO, but also containing blind spots and limitations. A more in-depth examination of Wu Ming 1's document revealed that important comparisons with, and influences from, so-called migrant and Cannibal writers have been largely overlooked, and his label of epic is more reflective of anxieties surrounding postmodernism's effects on the novel and the role of intellectuals in Italian society. These anxieties resurfaced in chapter 2 in an examination of recent texts that have explored parental legacies and taking responsibility, focusing on Genna's *Medium* and *Italia De Profundis*, De Cataldo's *Nelle mani giuste* and Pugno's *Sirene*. The insistence in the NIE on portraying fathers and sons as part of a sense of *impegno* or political and ethical commitment means that productive dimensions have been overlooked, in this case motherhood and female experience, attention to which would contribute to the wider picture of the nebula by reflecting on missing perspectives from the past — telling 'herstory' as well as history — and on some of the more pressing issues of our time. A survey of recent Italian historical novels in chapter 3 — Scurati's *Una storia romantica*, Mohamed and Wu Ming 2's *Timira* and Janeczek's *Le rondini di Montecassino* — provoked reflection on questions of identity and historiography today that also harked back to those on the relationship between history and literature that have haunted the historical novelist at least since the nineteenth century. This was followed in chapter 4 by an analysis of the way in which the so-called 'new realism' works through a focus on Saviano's *Gomorra*, Jones's *Sappiano le mie parole di sangue* and Scego and Bianchi's *Roma negata*, which all seek to remedy the failings of the mainstream media in addressing their subject matter through more literary, hybrid and personal approaches. Throughout the primary texts addressed here, we have seen unusual configurations of fiction and nonfiction, documentary 'proof' and poetic licence, words and experience, as these UNOs aim to provoke reflection and to effect change through storytelling.

In the introduction to this study, I quoted Bhabha, who described the end of the twentieth century as 'the beyond', characterised by a sense of in-between-ness as the past, present and future collide, and by 'the current and controversial shiftiness of the prefix "post"' (Bhabha 1994: 1). We have seen in UNOs from Italy at the beginning of the twenty-first century explorations of this beyond through in-between texts that attest to a 'post-'condition: in the postmodernism that has endured despite Wu Ming 1's and others' assertions of its demise (see, in particular, chapter 1); in the posthumous feeling that many Italian writers have examined through portrayals of patricide and matricide, even moving to posthuman considerations in some cases (chapter 2); in the postmemory that is often present in recent texts that have journeyed into Italy's history, as we saw in my analysis of recent historical novels (chapter 3); in the postcolonial in recent work that has begun to address the enduring influence of Italy's past, as we saw in chapter 3 in *Timira* and chapter 4 in *Roma negata*; and, finally, in the problematically postfactual nature of Saviano's insistence that he is conveying the 'truth' in *Gomorra*, despite combining fictional and nonfictional elements, raising ethical questions about the so-called 'new realism' (chapter 4). The UNO may be seen as the ideal form for exploring the shiftiness of twenty-first-century experience, with the oblique gaze that Wu Ming 1 describes offering exciting potential for processing recent history and current events in Italy and further afield. Just as Bhabha says of the beyond that it is 'neither a new horizon, nor a leaving behind of the past' (1994: 1), the UNOs that we have seen are experimental and may incorporate new technologies, although they can also be linked back to work by writers such as Manzoni, Pasolini and Sciascia, as well as to previous innovations related to migrant writing, microhistory and New Journalism. As all of my primary texts have demonstrated, we can see in recent Italian literature a combination of anti-realist postmodernist experimentation with neo/realist/ic *impegno*, as well as a tendency to slip between forms, styles and sometimes media.

Another thread running through the three key themes addressed in this study — parental legacies, history and journalism — is the presence of absences, folds or gaps. From confronting the absence of real or metaphorical parents, to considering the possibilities in the folds of history, to negotiating the gaps between words and experience when addressing the current reality, there is a sense in these UNOs of writing in or through the interstices. Tensions exist but are never firmly resolved, as these writers invite their readers to enter the gaps, or to seek out material that will help consider different possibilities for filling the gaps. Gaps also exist in Wu Ming 1's nebula concerning non-white and non-male viewpoints and experience in a phenomenon that purports to question dominant narratives. I have suggested ways of filling these gaps, and of considering these questions from different angles, whether by trying to think through concepts like epic, postmodernism, *impegno* and realism, by moving away from a focus on fatherhood to consider motherhood or even posthuman perspectives, or by considering writers whose work has been ignored or under-valued in the NIE through my analysis of texts by Pugno, Janeczek, Jones and Scego alongside those that Wu Ming 1 and others have favoured in discussions of recent Italian literature.

However, I am aware that gaps also exist in my study. Whilst I have gone some way towards remedying some of the biases of the NIE, there is more to be done in this direction. I argued in chapter 2 that Pugno's text shows the productive potential of new and unexpected perspectives in literature, but there are some that I have overlooked, such as queer perspectives, which the oblique gaze and the multiplicity of the UNO might be particularly suited to exploring. Moreover, although I allude to the presence of UNOs in other art forms in the introduction to this study through my mention of Alina Marazzi's films as UNOs, I focus on literature, whereas cinema has provided comparably hybrid work that warrants attention. Nanni Moretti might be another film-maker whose work could be compared to the UNOs I have addressed here, combining postmodernism and political concerns (as analysed by Barotsi and Antonello 2009), sometimes through an autofictional lens, and engaging with the problems raised by the end of the First Republic in films like *Palombella rossa* [*Red Wood Pigeon*] (1989) and *Il caimano* [*The Caiman*] (2006). The unusual configurations of fiction and nonfiction that we can see in the UNOs I have examined and in some of Moretti's and Marazzi's films can also be seen in other recent docufiction from outside Italy, such as: Sarah Polley's *The Stories We Tell* (2012), which explores her personal family history through real-life interviews and footage shot to look like home movies; Clio Barnard's *The Arbor* (2010), which tells the story of the late playwright Andrea Dunbar using actors lip-syncing the testimony of the people she interviewed; or Peter Jackson's *They Shall Not Grow Old* (2018), in which he colourised, transformed and added sound to original footage of the First World War to depict the soldiers' experiences more vividly. UNOs seem to be the order of the day, whether in books or films, and not only in Italy, where such mysterious and elusive portrayals of real-life events have a long and rich tradition.

Through the issues raised and discussed in this study, I have sought to establish that UNOs deserve a place on the map of Italian culture, and, indeed, of a wider twenty-first-century culture. Combining different modes of writing and, in some cases, different media formats, they offer innovative approaches to coming to terms with the past and narrating experience in the contemporary world. UNOs might provide the answer to Philippe Forest's (2007: 53) question that we encountered in chapter 4: is a novel possible today?

BIBLIOGRAPHY

AGAMBEN, GIORGIO. 1998. *Quel che resta di Auschwitz. L'archivio e il testimone (Homo sacer III)* (Turin: Bollati Boringhieri)

AMATO, LORENZO. 2009. 'Dal G8 di Genova alla sconfitta dell'intellettuale. Il New Italian Epic fra generi tradizionali e nuove forme di comunicazione', *Carmilla*, <http://www.carmillaonline.com/archives/2009/09/003186.html#003186> [accessed 30 June 2018]

AMICI, MARCO. 2010. 'Urgency and Visions of the New Italian Epic', *Journal of Romance Studies*, 10.1: 7–18

ANDERSON, PERRY. 2011. 'From Progress to Catastrophe: Perry Anderson on the Historical Novel', *London Review of Books*, 33.15 (28 July), <http://www.lrb.co.uk/v33/n15/perry-anderson/from-progress-to-catastrophe> [accessed 30 June 2018]

ANDREETTO, JADEL. 2008. 'Ho freddo. I vampiri di Gianfranco Manfredi tra storia e leggenda', *Panorama*, <http://cultura.panorama.it/libri/Ho-freddo-I-vampiri-di-Gianfranco-Manfredi-tra-storia-e-leggenda> [accessed 30 June 2018]

ANIA, GILLIAN and ANN CAESAR (eds). 2007. *Trends in Contemporary Italian Narrative 1980–2007* (Newcastle: Cambridge Scholars Publishing)

ANTONELLO, PIERPAOLO and ALAN O'LEARY. 2009. 'Sotto il segno della metafora: Una conversazione con Giancarlo De Cataldo', *The Italianist*, 29: 350–65

ANTONELLO, PIERPAOLO and FLORIAN MUSSGNUG (eds). 2009. *Postmodern Impegno: Ethics and Commitment in Contemporary Italian Culture* (Bern: Peter Lang)

ANTONELLO, PIERPAOLO. 2009. 'New Commitment in Italian "Theatrical Story-telling"', in *Postmodern Impegno: Ethics and Commitment in Contemporary Italian Culture*, ed. by Pierpaolo Antonello and Florian Mussgnug (Bern: Peter Lang), pp. 233–57

——2012. *Dimenticare Pasolini. Intellettuali e impegno nell'Italia contemporanea* (Milan: Mimesis)

ARIE, SOPHIE and JOHN EZARD. 2003. 'From Watford Striker to Top Novelist — But Only the Name's the Same', *The Guardian* (28 August), <http://www.theguardian.com/uk/2003/aug/28/football.books1> [accessed 30 June 2018]

ASHCROFT, BILL. 2001. *Post-colonial Transformation* (London and New York: Routledge)

BAIRD, ROBERT P. 2006. 'Stories Are Not All Equal: An Interview with Wu Ming', *Chicago Review*, 52.2: 250–59

BAJANI, ANDREA. 2006. *Mi spezzo ma non m'impiego. Guida di viaggio per lavoratori flessibili* (Turin: Einaudi)

——2007. *Se consideri le colpe* (Turin: Einaudi)

——2010. *Ogni promessa* (Turin: Einaudi)

BAKHTIN, M. M. 1981. *The Dialogic Imagination*, ed. by M. Holquist (Austin: University of Texas)

BALESTRINI, NANNI. 2004. Sandokan. Storia di camorra (Turin: Einaudi).

BARAŃSKI, ZYGMUNT G., and PERTILE, LINO (eds). 1993. *The New Italian Novel* (Edinburgh: Edinburgh University Press)

BAROTSI, ROSA and PIERPAOLO ANTONELLO. 2009. 'The Personal and the Political: The Cinema of Nanni Moretti', in *Postmodern Impegno: Ethics and Commitment in Contemporary Italian Culture*, ed. by Pierpaolo Antonello and Florian Mussgnug (Bern: Peter Lang), pp. 189–212

BARTHES, ROLAND. 1986. 'The Discourse of History', in *The Rustle of Language*, trans. by Richard Howard (New York: Hill and Wang), pp. 127–40

BAUDRILLARD, JEAN. 1994. *Simulacra and Simulation,* trans. by Shiela Faria Glaser (Ann Arbor: University of Michigan Press)

BAUMAN, ZYGMUNT. 2000. *Liquid Modernity* (Cambridge: Polity Press)

BECK, ULRICH. 2006. *The Cosmopolitan Vision* (Cambridge: Polity Press)

BELLU, GIOVANNI MARIA. 2004. *I fantasmi di Portopalo* (Milan: Mondadori)

——2008. *L'uomo che volle essere Perón* (Milan: Bompiani)

BENEDETTI, CARLA. 1998. *Pasolini contro Calvino* (Torino: Bollati Boringhieri)

BERMAN, SANDRA. 1984. 'Introduction', in Alessandro Manzoni, *On the Historical Novel* (Lincoln, NB and London: University of Nebraska Press), pp. 1–59

BERTANTE, ALESSANDRO. 2008. *Al diavul* (Venice: Marsilio)

BHABHA, HOMI. 1994. *The Location of Culture* (London: Routledge)

BIANCONI, GIOVANNI. 2014. 'L'americano che aiutò Cossiga. "Non dovevamo salvare Moro"', *Corriere della sera* (17 July), <http://www.corriere.it/cronache/14_luglio_17/americano-che-aiuto-cossiga-l-incompetenza-uccise-moro-0d77f9d8-0d74-11e4-9f11-cba0b313a927.shtml> [accessed 30 June 2018]

BIASINI, ROSALBA. 2010. 'Reconsidering epic: Wu Ming's 54 and Fenoglio', *Journal of Romance Studies*, 10.1: 69–82

BLISSETT, LUTHER. 1999. Q (Turin: Einaudi)

BOLTER, JAY DAVID and RICHARD GRUSIN. 1999. *Remediation: Understanding New Media* (Cambridge, MA and London: MIT Press)

BON, FRANÇOIS. 2004. *Daewoo: Roman* (Paris: Fayard)

BOND, EMMA. 2014. 'Towards a Trans-national Turn in Italian Studies?', *Italian Studies*, 69.3: 414–24

BOSCOLO, CLAUDIA. 2008. 'Scardinare il postmoderno: etica e metastoria nel New Italian Epic', *Carmilla*, <http://www.carmillaonline.com/archives/2008/04/002620.html> [accessed 30 June 2018]

——2010. 'The Idea of Epic and New Italian Epic', *Journal of Romance Studies*, 10.1: 19–35

BOURBAKI, NICOLETTA. 2014. 'Il #Giornodelricordo: dieci anni di medaglificio fascista. Un bilancio agghiacciante', *Giap*, <http://www.wumingfoundation.com/giap/?p=20954>

BOXALL, PETER. 2013. *Twenty-First Century Fiction: A Critical Introduction* (New York: Cambridge University Press)

BRAIDOTTI, ROSI. 2002. *Metamorphoses: Towards a Materialist Theory of Becoming* (Cambridge: Polity)

——2013. *The Posthuman* (Cambridge: Polity Press)

BRIONI, SIMONE. 2013. *Intervista con Igiaba Scego*, [Transcribed text] (Unpublished), Institute of Modern Languages Research, Centre for the Study of Contemporary Women's Writing E-Repository, <https://modernlanguages.sas.ac.uk/sites/default/files/files/Research%20Centres/CCWW/Scego%20Interview%20%28Brioni%29.pdf> [accessed 30 June 2018]

——2014. 'Postcolonialismo, subalternità e New Italian Epic: intervista con Wu Ming 1', *Subalternità italiane*, ed. by Valeria Deplano, Lorenzo Mari and Gabriele Proglio (Roma: Aracne), pp. 275–90

——2015. *The Somali Within: Language, Race and Belonging in 'Minor' Italian Literature* (Cambridge: Legenda)

BROLLI, DANIELE (ed.). 1996. *Gioventù cannibale. La prima antologia italiana dell'orrore estremo* (Turin: Einaudi)

BROOK, CLODAGH and EMANUELA PATTI. 2014. 'Introduzione', in *Transmedia. Storia, memoria e narrazioni attraverso i media*, ed. by Clodagh Brook and Emanuela Patti (Milan and Udine: Mimesis). Kindle ebook

BROOKS, PETER. 1984. *Reading for the Plot: Design and Intention in Narrative* (Oxford: Clarendon Press)

BUCKLEY, STEPHEN. 2018. 'Why Facebook is the Reason Fake News is Here to Stay', *The Conversation* (4 April), <http://theconversation.com/why-facebook-is-the-reason-fake-news-is-here-to-stay-94308> [accessed 30 June 2018]

BURDETT, CHARLES. 2007. *Journeys through Fascism: Italian Travel Writing between the Wars* (New York and Oxford: Berghahn Books)

BURNS, JENNIFER. 2001. *Fragments of* Impegno: *Interpretations of Commitment in Contemporary Italian Narrative 1980–2000* (Leeds: Northern Universities Press)

——2007. 'Outside Voices Within: Immigration Literature in Italian', in *Trends in Contemporary Italian Narrative 1980–2007*, ed. by Gillian Ania and Ann Hallamore Caesar (Newcastle: Cambridge Scholars Publishing), pp. 136–54

CALVINO, ITALO. 1967. *Ti con zero* (Turin: Einaudi)

CAMILLERI, ANDREA. 2003. *La presa di Macallé* (Palermo: Sellerio)

——2010. *Il nipote del Negus* (Palermo: Sellerio)

CAMILLETTI, FABIO. 2013. *Classicism and Romanticism in Italian Literature: Leopardi's Discourse on Romantic Poetry* (London: Pickering and Chatto)

CARLOTTO, MASSIMO and MAMA SABOT. 2008. *Perdas de fogu* (Rome: e/o)

CASADEI, ALBERTO. 2007. *Stile e tradizione nel romanzo italiano contemporaneo* (Bologna: Il Mulino)

——2010. '*Gomorra* e il naturalismo 2.0', in *Memoria in Noir. Un'indagine pluridisciplinare*, ed. by Monica Jansen and Yasmina Khamal (Brussels: Peter Lang), pp. 107–22

——2011. 'Realismo e allegoria nella narrativa italiana contemporanea', in *Finzione cronaca realtà. Scambi e propspettive nella narrativa italiana contemporanea*, ed. by Hanna Serkowska (Massa: Transeuropa), pp. 3–22

CAVARERO, ADRIANA. 1997. *Tu che mi guardi, tu che mi racconti* (Milan: Feltrinelli)

CECCHINI, LEONARDO. 2012. 'Ethics of Conviction vs. Ethics of Responsibility in Cinematic Representations of Italian Left-Wing Terrorism of the 1970s', in *Terrorism, Italian Style: Representations of Political Violence in Contemporary Italian Cinema*, ed. by Ruth Glynn, Giancarlo Lombardi and Alan O'Leary (London: IGRS Books), pp. 195–213

CELLULOID LIBERATION FRONT. 2013. 'Wu Ming: A Band of Militant Storytellers', *New Statesman* (29 May), <http://www.newstatesman.com/world-affairs/2013/05/wu-ming-band-militant-storytellers> [accessed 30 June 2018]

CERCAS, JAVIER. 2011. *The Anatomy of a Moment*, trans by Anne McLean (London, Berlin, New York and Sydney: Bloomsbury)

CESERANI, REMO. 2012. 'Ma maledizione degli "ismi"', *Allegoria*, 65–66: 191–213

CESARI, SEVERINO, 2003. 'Dopo i cannibali', *Carmilla*, <http://www.carmillaonline.com/2003/06/04/dopo-i-cannibali/> [accessed 30 June 2018]

CHIMENTI, DIMITRI. 2010. 'Unidentified Narrative Objects: Notes for a Rhetorical Typology', *Journal of Romance Studies*, 10.1: 37–50

CIXOUS, HÉLÈNE. 1985. 'The Laugh of Medusa', in *New French Feminisms: An Anthology*, ed. by Elaine Marks and Isabelle de Courtivron (Brighton: The Harvester Press Ltd.), pp. 245–64

CLÒ, CLARISSA. 2010. 'African Queens and Italian History: The Cultural Politics of Memory and Resistance in Testro delle Albe's *Lunga vita all'albero* and Gabriella Ghermandi's *Regina di fiori e di perle*', *Research in African Literatures*, 41.4: 26–42

CODEBÒ, MARCO. 2010. *Narrating from the Archive: Novels, Records, and Bureaucrats in the Modern Age* (Madison and Teaneck: Fairleigh Dickinson University Press)

CONTARINI, SILVIA. 2010. 'Raccontare l'azienda, il precariato, l'economia globalizzata. Modi, temi, figure', *Narrativa*, 31.2: 7–24

COOKE, PHILIP. 2012. 'La resistenza come secondo risorgimento — un topos retorico senza fine?', *Passato e presente: rivista di storia contemporanea*, 86: 62–81

CORTÁZAR, JULIO. 1966. *Hopscotch*, trans. by Gregory Rabassa (London: Collins and Harvill Press)

CORTELLESSA, ANDREA. 2008. 'Reale, troppo reale', *Nazione indiana*, <http://www.nazioneindiana.com/2008/10/29/reale-troppo-reale/> [accessed 30 June 2018]

——(ed.). 2011a. *L'illuminista. Narratori degli Anni Zero*, 31–32–33 (gennaio-dicembre) (Rome: Edizioni Ponte Sisto)

——2011b. 'TQ, fenomenologia di una generazione allo specchio', *Nazione Indiana*, <http://www.nazioneindiana.com/2011/06/07/tq-fenomenologia-di-una-generazione-allo-specchio-andrea-cortellessa/> [accessed 30 June 2018]

DAL LAGO, ALESSANDRO. 2010. *Eroi di carta. Il caso* Gomorra *e altre epopee con una postilla sul declino dello spirito critico in Italia* (Rome: Manifestolibri)

DALLA CHIESA, NANDO. 2011. 'Prefazione', in *Cittadinanza ferita e trauma psicopolitico. Dopo il G8 di Genova: il lavoro della memoria e la ricostruzione di relazioni sociali*, ed. by Adriano Zamperini and Marialuisa Menegatto (Naples: Liguori Editore), pp. xi–xiii

D'ANGELO, PAOLO. 2013. *Le nevrosi di Manzoni: Quando la storia uccise la poesia* (Bologna: Mulino)

DE CATALDO, GIANCARLO. 2007. *Nelle mani giuste* (Turin: Einaudi)

——2008. 'Raccontare l'Italia senza avere paura di sporcarsi le mani', *La Repubblica* (8 June), <http://ricerca.repubblica.it/repubblica/archivio/repubblica/2008/06/08/raccontare-italia-senza-avere-paura-di.090raccontare.html> [accessed 30 June 2018]

DE GROOT, JEROME. 2010. *The Historical Novel* (London and New York: Routledge)

DE MICHELE, GIROLAMO. 2004. *Tre uomini paradossali* (Turin: Einaudi)

——. 2008a. 'Afferare Proteo: dire l'indicibile nel Paese dei misteri', *Carmilla*, <http://www.carmillaonline.com/2008/05/19/afferrare-proteo-dire-lindicibile-nel-paese-dei-misteri/> [accessed 30 June 2018]

——2008b. *La visione del cieco* (Turin: Einaudi)

——2009. 'Simona Mammano: Assalto alla Diaz', *Carmilla*, <http://www.carmillaonline.com/2009/05/29/simona-mammano-assalto-alla-di/>

DE VIVO, BARBARA. 2015. 'Re-Mapping *Impegno* in Postcolonial Italy: Gender, Race, Class and the Question of Commitment', *Gendering Commitment: Re-Thinking Social and Ethical Engagement in Modern Italian Culture*, ed. by Alex Standen (Newcastle: Cambridge Scholars Publishing), pp. 120–37

DELEUZE, GILLES and FÉLIX GUATTARI. 1972. *L'anti-Oedipe* (Paris: Les Éditions de minuit)

DELLA COLETTA, CRISTINA. 1996. *Plotting the Past: Metamorphoses of Historical Narrative in Modern Italian Fiction* (West Lafayette, IN: Purdue University Press)

DERRIDA, JACQUES. 1980. 'The Law of Genre', *Critical Inquiry*, 7.1: 55–81

——1995. 'Archive Fever: A Freudian Impression', *Diacritics*, 25.2: 9–63

DESERIIS, MARCO. 2011. '"Lots of Money Because I am Many": The Luther Blissett Project and the Multiple-Use Name Strategy', *Cultural Activism: Practices, Dilemmas and Possibilities*, 21: 65–93

DI MARTINO, LOREDANA. 2011. 'From Pirandello's Humor to Eco's Double Coding: Ethics and Irony in Modernist and Postmodernist Italian Fiction', *MLN*, 126.1: 137–56

——2016. 'Rebuilding Ethical Desire in the Era of Narcissistic *Jouissance*: The Reinvention of Fatherhood in Antonio Scurati's *Il padre infedele*', *Italian Studies*, 71.1: 128–47

DIMOCK, WAI CHEE. 2006. 'Genre as World System: Epic and Novel on Four Continents', *Narrative*, 14.1: 85–101

DI STEFANO, PAOLO. 2008. 'Ecco il manifesto della "Nuova Epic"', *Corriere della sera* (13 May), <http://archiviostorico.corriere.it/2008/maggio/13/Ecco_manifesto_della_Nuova_epica_co_9_080513020.shtml> [accessed 30 June 2018]

DOCX, EDWARD. 2011. 'Postmodernism is dead', *Prospect* (20 July)

DONNARUMMA, RAFFAELE. 2003. 'Postmoderno italiano: Qualche ipotesi', *Allegoria*, 64: 15–50

——2008A. *Da lontano. Calvino, la semiologia, lo strutturalismo* (Palermo: Palumbo)

——2008B. 'Introduzione', *Allegoria*, 57: 7–8

——2008C. 'Nuovi realismi e persistenze postmoderne: narratori italiani di oggi', *Allegoria*, 57: 26–54

DONNARUMMA, RAFFAELE and POLICASTRO, GILDA. 2008. 'Ritorno all realtà? Otto interviste a narratori italiani', *Allegoria*, 57: 9–25

DORAN, STEVEN EDWARD. 2014. 'Identity', *The John Hopkins Guide to Digital Media*, ed. by Marie-Laure Ryan, Lori Emerson and Benjamin J. Robertson (Baltimore: John Hopkins University Press), pp. 266–69

DOUBROVSKY, SERGE. 1999. *Laissé pour conte* (Paris: Grasset)

DUKA and PHILOPAT, MARCO. 2008. *Roma k. o.* (Milan: Agenzia X)

ECO, UMBERTO. 1988. *Apocalittici e integrati* (Milan: Bompiani)

——1995. *Apocalypse Postponed* (London: Flamingo)

——2005. *Il nome della rosa* (Milan: Bompiani)

EGGERS, DAVE. 2009. *Zeitoun* (San Francisco: McSweeney's Books)

ELIAS, AMY. 2001. *Sublime Desire: History and Post 1960s Fiction* (Baltimore and London: John Hopkins University Press)

ELIOT, T. S. 1969. *The Complete Poems and Plays of T. S. Eliot* (London: Faber)

ERLL, ASTRID. 2009. 'Remembering across Time, Space, and Cultures: Premediation, Remediation and the "Indian Mutiny"', in *Mediation, Remediation and the Dynamics of Cultural Memory*, ed. by Astrid Erll and Ann Rigney (Berlin and New York: Walter de Gruyter), pp. 109–38

——2010. 'Cultural Memory Studies: An Introduction', in *A Companion to Cultural Memory Studies*, ed. by Astrid Erll and Ansgar Nünning (Berlin and New York: De Gruyter), pp. 1–18

ERLL, ASTRID and ANN RIGNEY. 2009. 'Introduction: Cultural Memory and its Dynamics', *Mediation, Remediation and the Dynamics of Cultural Memory*, ed. by Astrid Erll and Ann Rigney (Berlin and New York: Walter de Gruyter), pp. 1–11

EVANGELISTI, VALERIO and ANTONIO MORESCO. 2008. *Controinsurrezioni* (Milan: Mondadori)

EVANGELISTI, VALERIO, GIUSEPPE GENNA, WU MING and OTHERS. 2004. *Il caso Battisti. L'emergenza infinita e i fantasmi del passato* (Rimini: NdA Press)

FARRELL, JOSEPH. 1999. 'Walcott's *Omeros*: The Classical Epic in a Postmodern World', in *Epic Traditions in the Contemporary World: The Poetics of Community*, ed. by Margaret Beissinger, Jane Tyler and Susanne Wofford (Berkeley: University of California Press), pp. 270–96

FERRANTE, ELENA. 2011. *L'amica geniale* (Rome: E/O)

——2012. *Storia del nuovo cognome* (Rome: E/O)

——2013. *Storia di chi fugge e di chi resta* (Rome: E/O)

——2014. *Storia della bambina perduta* (Rome: E/O)

FERRARIS, MAURIZIO. 2012. *Manifesto del nuovo realismo* (Rome and Bari: Laterza)

FERRETTI, GIAN CARLO and GIULIA IANNUZZI. 2014. *Storie di uomini e libri. L'editoria letteraria italiana attraverso le sue collane* (Rome: Minimum Fax)

FERRONI, GIULIO. 2010. *Scritture a perdere. La letteratura negli anni zero* (Rome and Bari: Laterza)

FOOT, JOHN. 2009. *Italy's Divided Memory* (Basingstoke: Palgrave Macmillan)

FOREST, PHILLIPPE. 2007. *Le roman, le réel et autres essais* (Nantes: Editions Cécile Defaut)

FRANCHINI, ANTONIO. 2001. *L'abusivo* (Venice: Marsilio)

FRANCHINI, ANTONIO and PARAZZOLI, FERRUCCIO. 1996. *Italiana. Antologia dei nuovi narratori* (Milan: Mondadori)

FULGINITI, VALENTINA, 2009. 'Aedi, rapsodi, contastorie. Intorno all'oralità del New Italian Epic', *Carmilla*, <http://www.carmillaonline.com/2009/05/11/aedi-rapsodi-contastorie/> [accessed 30 June 2018]

——2014. 'The Postapocalyptic Cookbook: Animality, Posthumanism, and Meat in Laura Pugno and Wu Ming', *Thinking Italian Animals: Human and Posthuman in Modern Italian Literature and Film*, ed. by Deborah Amberson and Elena Past (New York: Palgrave Macmillan, 2014), pp. 159–76

GALIMBERTI, JACOPO. 2013. 'Distillare una nuovo Resistenza: Immaginario e storia in *In territorio nemico*', *Carmilla*, <http://www.carmillaonline.com/2013/06/06/distillare-una-nuova-resistenza/> [accessed 30 June 2018]

GALLIPPI, FRANCO. 2013. 'Roberto Saviano e "la sfida al labirinto"', *Negli archivi e per le strade. Il ritorno alla realtà nella narrativa di inizio millennio*, ed. by Luca Somigli (Rome: Aracne), pp. 501–19

GANERI, MARGHERITA. 1999. *Il romanzo storico in Italia* (Lecce: Piero Manni)

——2011. 'Reazioni allergiche al concetto di realtà. Il dibattito intorno al numero 57 di *Allegoria*', *Finzione cronaca realtà: scambi, intrecci e prospettive nella narrativa italian contemporanea*, ed. by Hanna Serkowska (Massa: Transeuropa), pp. 51–68

GARGANI, ALDO. 1984. 'La voce femminile', *Alfabeta*, 64, p. 16

GENNA, GIUSEPPE. 2005. 'Bret Easton Ellis: Lunar Park', *Carmilla*, <http://www.carmillaonline.com/2005/11/23/bret-easton-ellis-lunar-park/> [accessed 30 June 2018]

GENNA, GIUSEPPE. 2007A. 'Babsi Jones su *Vanity Fair*: "Ho scritto il sangue"', *Carmilla*, <http://www.carmillaonline.com/2007/10/03/babsi-jones-su-vanity-fair-ho-scritto-il-sangue/>

——2007B. 'Considerazioni sul romanzo storico italiano oggi: *Una storia romantica* di Antonio Scurati', *Carmilla*, <http://www.carmillaonline.com/2007/10/10/considerazioni-sul-romanzo-sto/> [accessed 30 June 2018]

——2007C. 'De Cataldo: *Nelle mani giuste*', *Carmilla*, <http://www.carmillaonline.com/2007/06/25/de-cataldo-nelle-mani-giuste/> [accessed 30 June 2018]

——2007D. *Medium* (Lulu)

——2008A. *Hitler* (Milan: Mondadori)

——2008B. *Italia De Profundis* (Rome: Minimum Fax)

——2013. *Fine impero* (Rome: Minimum Fax)

——2014. *Dies irae* (Milan: Mondadori)

GHERMANDI, GABRIELLA. 2007. *Regina di fiori e di perle* (Rome: Donzelli)

GIGLIOLI, DANIELE. 2011. *Senza trauma. Scrittura dell'estremo e narrativa del nuovo millennio*, (Macerata: Quodlibet)

GINSBORG, PAUL. 2001. *Italy and its Discontents, 1980–2001* (London: Penguin Books)

——2005. *Silvio Berlusconi: Television, Power and Patrimony* (London and New York: Verso)

GINZBURG, CARLO. 1976. *Il formaggio e i vermi. Il cosmo di un mugnaio del '500* (Turin: Einaudi)

——2006. *Il filo e le tracce. Vero falso finto* (Milan: Feltrinelli)

GIORGIO, ADALGISA (ed.). 2002. *Writing Mothers and Daughters: Renegotiating the Mother in Western European Narratives by Women* (New York and Oxford: Berghahn)

GLYNN, RUTH. 2005. *Contesting the Monument: The Anti-Illusionist Italian Historical Novel* (Leeds: Northern Universities Press)

GLYNN, RUTH, GIANCARLO LOMBARDI and ALAN O'LEARY. 2012. *Terrorism, Italian Style: Representations of Political Violence in Contemporary Italian Cinema* (London: IGRS Books)

GODANI, PAOLO. 2014. *Senza padri. Economia del desiderio e condizioni di libertà nel capitalismo contemporaneo* (Rome: DeriveApprodi)

GORDON, ROBERT. 2006. 'Which Holocaust? Primo Levi and the Field of Holocaust Memory in Post-War Italy', *Italian Studies*, 61.1: 167–88

GORIUNOVA, OLGA and CHIARA BERNARDI. 2014. 'Social Network Sites (SNSs)', in *The John Hopkins Guide to Digital Media*, ed. by Marie-Laure Ryan, Lori Emerson and Benjamin J. Robertson (Baltimore: John Hopkins University Press), pp. 455–62

GREADY, PAUL. 2009. 'Novel Truths: Literature and Truth Commissions', *Comparative Literature Studies*, 46.1: 156–76

HAJEK, ANDREA. 2013. *Negotiating Memories of Protest in Western Europe: The Case of Italy* (Houndmills, Basingstoke and New York: Palgrave Macmillan)

——2014. 'Dalla piazza reale alla piazza virtuale: La Storia del '77 in Rete', *Transmedia: Storia, memoria e narrazioni attraverso i media,* ed. by Emanuela Patti and Clodagh Brook (Milan and Udine: Mimesis). Kindle ebook

HARRIS, KATHERINE. 2014. 'Archive', in *The John Hopkins Guide to Digital Media*, ed. by Marie-Laure Ryan, Lori Emerson and Benjamin J. Robertson (Baltimore: John Hopkins University Press), pp. 16–18

HAY, JAMES and NICK COULDRY. 2011. 'Rethinking Convergence/Culture', *Cultural Studies*, 25.4–5: 473–86

HEGEL, G. W. F. 1975. *Aesthetics: Lectures on Fine Art*, 2 vols, trans. by T. M. Knox (Oxford: Clarendon Press)

HERR, MICHAEL. 1978. *Dispatches* (London: Picador)

HIGHT, ELEANOR, and GARY SAMPSON. 2004. 'Introduction: Photography, "Race", and Post-colonial Theory', in *Colonialist Photography: Imag(in)ing Race and Place* (London: Routledge), pp. 1–19

HIRSCH, MARIANNE. 1989. *The Mother/Daughter Plot: Narrative, Psychoanalysis, Feminism* (Bloomington and Indiana: Indiana University Press)

——2012. *The Generation of Postmemory: Writing and Visual Culture after the Holocaust* (New York: Columbia University Press)

HOLLOWELL, JOHN. 1977. *Fact and Fiction: The New Journalism and the Nonfiction Novel* (Chapel Hill: The University of North Carolina Press)

HOSKINS, ANDREW. 2009. 'Digital Network Memory', in *Mediation, Remediation and the Dynamics of Cultural Memory*, ed. by Astrid Erll and Ann Rigney (Berlin and New York: Walter de Gruyter), pp. 91–106

HUTCHEON, LINDA. 1988. *A Poetics of Postmodernism: History, Theory, Fiction* (London and New York: Routledge)

JACOMELLA, GABRIELA. 2015. 'The Silence of Migrants: The Underrepresentation of Migrant Voices in the Italian Mainstream Media', in *Destination Italy: Representing Migration in Contemporary Media and Narrative*, ed. by Emma Bond, Guido Bonsaver and Federico Faloppa (Bern: Peter Lang), pp. 149–64

JAMESON, FREDERIC. 1991. *Postmodernism, or, The Cultural Logic of Late Capitalism* (London: Verso)

——2009. *Valences of the Dialectic* (London and New York: Verso)

IANNUZZI, GIULIA. 2014. *Fantascienza italiana. Riviste, autori, dibattiti dagli anni cinquanta agli anni settanta* (Milan: Mimesis)

JANECZEK, HELENA. 2002. *Cibo* (Milan: Mondadori)

——2010. *Le rondini di Montecassino* (Parma: Guanda)

——2011. *Lezioni di tenebra* (Parma: Guanda)

——2017. *La ragazza con la Leica* (Parma: Guanda)

JANSEN, MONICA. 2002. *Il dibattito sul postmoderno in Italia: In bilico tra dialettica e ambiguità* (Florence: Franco Cesati Editore)

——2010. 'Laboratory NIE: Mutations in Progress', *Journal of Romance Studies*, 10.1: 97–109

——2012. 'Scritture dell'estremo, postmoderno e narrativa del nuovo millennio', *Bollettino '900*, <http://www.boll900.it/numeri/2012-i/W-bol2/Jansen/Jansen_frame.html> [accessed 30 June 2018]

——2014. 'Narrazioni della precarietà: il coraggio dell'immaginazione', in *Scritture di resistenza*, ed. by Claudia Boscolo and Stefano Jossa (Rome: Carocci), pp. 69–128

JANSEN, MONICA and YASMINA KHAMAL (eds). 2014. *Memoria in Noir. Un'indagine pluridisciplinare*, (Brussels: Peter Lang)

JENKINS, HENRY. 2006A. *Convergence Culture: Where Old and New Media Collide* (New York and London: New York University Press)

——2006B. 'How Slapshot Inspired a Cultural Revolution (Part One): An Interview with the Wu Ming Foundation', <http://henryjenkins.org/2006/10/how_slapshot_inspired_a_cultur.html> [accessed 30 June 2018]

——2006C. 'How Slapshot Inspired a Cultural Revolution (Part Two): An Interview with the Wu Ming Foundation', <http://henryjenkins.org/2006/10/how_slapshot_inspired_a_cultur_1.html> [accessed 30 June 2018]

JONES, BABSI. 2007. *Sappiano le mie parole di sangue* (Milan: Rizzoli)

KERMODE, FRANK. 2000. *The Sense of an Ending: Studies in the Theory of Fiction with a New Epilogue* (New York: Oxford University Press)

LAMPEDUSA, GIUSEPPE TOMASI DI. 1969. *Il gattopardo* (Milan: Feltrinelli)

LOMBARDI-DIOP, CRISTINA and CATERINA ROMEO. 2012. 'Introduction', *Postcolonial Italy: Challenging National Homogeneity* (New York: Palgrave Macmillan), pp. 1–29

LUCAMANTE, STEFANIA. 2001. 'Introduction: "Pulp", Splatter, and More: The New Italian Narrative of the *Giovani Cannibali* Writers', in *Italian Pulp Fiction: The New Narrative of the Giovani Cannibali Writers*, ed. by Stefania Lucamante (Madison and Teaneck: Fairleigh Dickinson University Press and London: Associated University Presses), pp. 13–37

——2008. *A Multitude of Women: The Challenges of the Contemporary Italian Novel* (Toronto, Buffalo and London: University of Toronto Press)

LUCARELLI, CARLO. 2008. *L'ottava vibrazione* (Turin: Einaudi)

——2009. *G8: Cronaca di una battaglia* (Turin: Einaudi)

LUKÁCS, GEORG. 1978. *The Theory of the Novel: A Historico-Literary Essay on the Forms of Great Epic Literature*, trans. by Anna Bostock (London: Merlin Press)

LUPERINI, ROMANO. 2005. *La fine del postmoderno* (Naples: Guida)

MAGINI, GREGORIO and SANTONI, VANNI. 2008. 'Verso il realismo liquido', *Carmilla*, <http://www.carmillaonline.com/archives/2008/06/002663.html#002663> [accessed 30 June 2018]

MAGNÚSSON, SIGURDUR and SZIJÁRTÓ, ISTVÁN. 2013. *What is Microhistory? Theory and Practice* (London and New York: Routledge)

MANTEL, HILARY. 2014. *The Assassination of Margaret Thatcher and Other Stories* (London: Fourth Estate)

MANZONI, ALESSANDRO. 1972. *The Betrothed*, trans. by Bruce Penman (London: Penguin Books)

——1973. 'Del romanzo storico e, in genere, de' componimenti misti di storia e d'invenzione', in *Tutte le opere*, ed. by Mario Martelli, II (Florence: Sansoni Editore), pp. 1727–64

——1984. *On the Historical Novel*, trans. by Sandra Bermann (Lincoln, NB and London: University of Nebraska Press)

——1987. 'Storia della colonna infame', in *I promessi sposi e storia della colonna infame*, ed. by Tommaso Di Salvo (Bologna: Zanichelli)

——2010. *I promessi sposi* (Milan: Mondadori)

MARI, LORENZO. 2008. 'Una carezza in un Pugno', *Tabard* (28 May), <http://rivistatabard.blogspot.co.uk/2008/05/una-carezza-in-un-pugno.html> [accessed 30 June 2018]

McCaffery, Larry. 1993. 'An Interview with David Foster Wallace', *The Review of Contemporary Fiction*, 13.2: 127–50

Mecchia, Giuseppina. 2009. 'Wu Ming: Anonymous Hatchet Throwers at the Dawn of the 21st Century', in *Creative Interventions: The Role of Intellectuals in Contemporary Italy*, ed. by Eugenio Bolongaro, Mark Epstein and Rita Gagliano (Newcastle: Cambridge Scholars Publishing), pp. 195–214

Melandri, Erica, Marialuisa Menegatto, Valentina Moroni and Adriano Zamperini. 2011. 'Il lavoro della memoria come azione sociale', *Cittadinanza ferita e trauma psicopolitico. Dopo il G8 di Genova: il lavoro della memoria e la ricostruzione di relazioni sociali*, ed. by Marialuisa Menegatto and Adriano Zamperini (Naples: Liguori Editore), pp. 129–55

Mohamed, Antar and Wu Ming 2. 2012. *Timira. Romanzo meticcio* (Turin: Einaudi)

Mondello, Elisabetta. 2007. *In principio fu Tondelli. Letteratura, merci, televisione nella narrativa degli anni novanta* (Milan: il Saggiatore)

——2010. *Crimini e misfatti: La narrativa noir italiana degli anni Duemila* (Rome: Giulio Perrone Editore)

Morgan, Ted. 1988. *Literary Outlaw: The Life and Times of William S. Burroughs* (New York: Henry Holt and Company)

Mosca, Raffaello Palumbo. 2009. 'Prima e dopo Gomorra: *non-fiction novel* e impegno', in *Postmodern Impegno: Ethics and Commitment in Contemporary Italian Culture*, ed. by Pierpaolo Antonello and Florian Mussgnug (Bern: Peter Lang), pp.304–26

——2013. 'Sono arrivati gli unni: ibridismo e tensione civile nella narrativa italiana contemporanea', in *Negli archivi e per le strade. Il ritorno alla realtà nella narrativa di inizio millennio*, ed. by Luca Somigli (Rome: Aracne), pp. 157–71

——2014. *L'invenzione del vero. Romanzi ibridi e discorso etico nell'Italia contemporanea* (Rome: Gaffi)

Moynihan, Michael. 2015. 'Mafia Author Roberto Saviano's Plagiarism Problem', *Daily Beast* (24 September), available at <https://www.thedailybeast.com/mafia-author-roberto-savianos-plagiarism-problem> [accessed 30 June 2018]

Muraro, Luisa. 2006. 'Il pensiero dell'esperienza', *diotima*, numero 5, available at <http://www.diotimafilosofe.it/larivista/il-pensiero-dellesperienza/> [accessed 30 June 2018]

Muratori, Letizia. 2007. *La vita in comune* (Turin: Einaudi)

Murgia, Michela. 2017. *Il mondo deve sapere. Romanzo tragicomico di una telefonista precaria* (Turin: Einaudi)

Mussgnug, Florian. 2012. 'Naturalizing Apocalypse: Last Men and Other Animals', *Comparative Critical Studies*, 9.3: 333–47

Neumann, Birgit. 2010. 'The Literary Representation of Memory', in *A Companion to Cultural Memory Studies*, ed. by Astrid Erll and Ansgar Nünning (Berlin and New York: De Gruyter), pp. 333–44

Niwot, Melody. 2011. 'Narrating Genoa: Documentaries of the Italian G8 Protests of 2001 and the Persistence and Politics of Memory', *History & Memory*, 23.2: 66–89

Nove, Aldo. 2006. *Mi chiamo Roberta, ho 40 anni, guadagno 250 euro al mese. . .* (Turin: Einaudi)

——2011. *Mi chiamo Roberta, ho quarant'anni, guadagno 250 euro al mese. . . Versione 2.0* (Massa: Transeuropa)

O'Leary, Alan and O'Rawe, Catherine. 2011. 'Against Realism: On a "Certain Tendency" in Italian Film Criticism', *Journal of Modern Italian Studies*, 16.1: 107–28

Pardi, Alessandro. 2008. 'Alzare il culo, adesso! Riflessioni su *New Italian Epic 2.0*', *Carmilla*, <http://www.carmillaonline.com/archives/2008/12/002861.html> [accessed 30 June 2018]

Pasolini, Pier Paolo. 1974. 'Cos'è questo golpe? Io so', *Corriere della Sera* (14 November), <http://www.corriere.it/speciali/pasolini/ioso.html> [accessed 30 June 2018]

——1992. *Petrolio* (Turin: Einaudi)

PATTI, EMANUELA. 2010. '*Petrolio*, a Model of UNO in Giuseppe Genna's *Italia De Profundis*', *Journal of Romance Studies*, 10.1: 83–96

——2014. 'Il romanzo nella "galassia internet": sperimentazioni transmediali nella narrativa italiana del XXI secolo', in *Transmedia: Storia, memoria e narrazioni attraverso i media*, ed. by Emanuela Patti and Clodagh Brook (Milan and Udine: Mimesis). Kindle ebook

——2016. 'From Page to Screen/From Screen to Page: Collaborative Narratives in Twenty-First-Century Italian Fiction — The Wu Ming Case', *Journal of Romance Studies*, 16.1: 39–61

PELLINI, PIERLUIGI. 2011. 'Lo scrittore come intellettuale. Dall'*affaire* Dreyfus all'*affaire* Saivano: modelli e stereotipi', *Allegoria* 63: 135–63

PETRELLA, ANGELA. 2006. 'Dal postmoderno al romanzo epico: linee per la letteratura italiana dell'ultimo Novecento', *Allegoria*, 52–53: 134–48

PIGA, EMMANUELA. 2010. 'Metahistories, Microhistories and Mythopoeia in Wu Ming', *Journal of Romance Studies*, 10.1: 51–68

——2012. 'Epica, storia e memoria. *Le rondini di Montecassino* di Helena Janeczek', *Bollettino '900*, 1–2, <https://boll900.it/2012-i/Piga.html>

——2014. 'Comunità, intelligenza connettiva e letteratura: dall'open source all'opera aperta in Wu Ming', in *Transmedia: Storia, memoria e narrazioni attraverso i media*, ed. by Emanuela Patti and Clodagh Brook (Milan and Udine: Mimesis). Kindle ebookPincio, Tommaso. 2008. *Cinacittà* (Turin: Einaudi)

PISANI, DANIELE. 2007. 'Carlo Ginzburg e Hayden White. Riflessioni su due modi di intendere la storia', *Engramma*, 55 (marzo), <http://www.engramma.it/eOS/index.php?id_articolo=2296>

POCCI, LUCA. 2011. '"Io so": A Reading of Roberto Saviano's *Gomorra*', *MLN*, 126.1: 224–44

——2012. 'Ginzburg e Manzoni: Tra la storia e il romanzo', *Italica*, 89.2: 219–35

POLICASTRO, GILDA. 2008. 'Roberto Saviano, *Gomorra*', *Allegoria*, 57: 185–90

PONZANESI, SANDRA. 2005. 'Beyond the Black Venus: Colonial Sexual Politics and Contemporary Visual Practices' in *Italian Colonialism: Legacies and Memories*, ed. by Jacqueline Andall and Derek Duncan (Oxford: Peter Lang), pp. 165–89

PRUDENZANO, ANTONIO. 2013. 'Chiude ("per inerzia") il blog di Generazione TQ', *Affari italiani* (21 August), <http://www.affaritaliani.it/culturaspettacoli/chiude-per-inerzia-il-blog-di-generazione-tq210813.html> [accessed 30 June 2018]

PUGNO, LAURA. 2007. *Sirene* (Turin: Einaudi)

PURINI, PIERO. 2014. 'Come si manipola la storia attraverso le immagini: il #GiornodelRicordo e i falsi fotografici sulle #foibe', *Giap*, <http://www.wumingfoundation.com/giap/?p=20649> [accessed 30 June 2018]

QUINT, DAVID. 1989. 'Epic and Empire', *Comparative Literature*, 41.1: 1–32

RANCIÈRE, JACQUES. 2004. *The Flesh of Words: The Politics of Writing*, trans. by Charlotte Mandell (Stanford, California: Stanford University Press)

RAVAGLI, VITALIANO and WU MING. 2005. *Asce di guerra* (Turin: Einaudi)

RE, LUCIA. 1993. 'Utopian Longing and the Constraints of Racial and Sexual Difference in Elsa Morante's *La storia*', *Italica*, 70.3: 361–75

——2014. 'Pasolini vs. Calvino, One More Time: The Debate on the Role of Intellectuals and Postmodernism in Italy Today', *MLN*, 129.1: 99–117

RECALCATI, MASSIMO. 2011. *Cosa resta del padre? La paternità nell'epoca ipermoderna*, (Milan: Rafaello Cortina Editore)

——2013. *Il complesso di Telemaco. Genitori e figli dopo il tramonto del padre* (Milan: Feltrinelli)

——2015. *Le mani della madre. Desiderio, fantasmi ed eredità del materno* (Milan: Feltrinelli)

RICOEUR, PAUL. 2006. *Memory, History, Forgetting*, trans. by Kathleen Blamey and David Pellauer (Chicago: University of Chicago Press)

RONCHETTI, ALESSIA. 2009. 'Postmodernismo e pensiero italiano della differenza sessuale: una questione politica', in *Postmodern Impegno: Ethics and Commitment in Contemporary Italian Culture*, ed. by Pierpaolo Antonello and Florian Mussgnug (Bern: Peter Lang), pp. 99–120

RONDOLINO, FABRIZIO. 2009. 'Wu Ming se questa è letteratura. Una parodia dell'antipolitica applicata alla narrativa', *La Stampa* (15 February)

ROTH, PHILIP. 1999. *Patrimony: A True Story* (London: Vintage)

ROTHBERG, MICHAEL. 2009. *Multidirectional Memory: Remembering the Holocaust in the Age of Decolonization* (Stanford, CA: Stanford University Press)

RUSHING, ROBERT A. 2011. 'Sirens without Us: The Future after Humanity', *California Italian Studies*, 2.1, <https://escholarship.org/uc/item/0cc3b56b> [accessed 30 June 2018]

SABA, UMBERTO. 1993. *Scorciatoie e raccontini* (Milan: Mondadori)

SABELLI, SONIA. 2013. 'Quale razza? Genere, classe e colore in *Timira* e *L'ottava vibrazione*', *Giap*, <http://www.wumingfoundation.com/giap/?p=13861> [accessed 30 June 2018]

SAMBUCO, PATRIZIA. 2012. *Corporeal Bonds: The Daughter–Mother Relationship in Twentieth Century Italian Women's Writing* (Toronto: University of Toronto Press)

SANTONI, VANNI. 2017. *Personaggi precari* (Rome: Voland)

SANTORO, VITO. 2010. 'Privato è pubblico. (Dis)avventure dell'Io nella narrativa italiana degli anni Zero', *Notizie dalla post-realtà. Caratteri e figure della narrativa italiana degli anni Zero*, ed. by Vito Santoro (Macerata: Quodlibet), pp. 13–60

SAVIANO, ROBERTO. 2006. *Gomorra. Viaggio nell'impero economico e nel sogno di dominio della camorra* (Milan: Mondadori)

——2008. *Gomorrah: Italy's Other Mafia*, trans. by Virginia Jewiss (Basingstoke and Oxford: Pan Macmillan)

——2009. *La bellezza e l'inferno: Scritti 2004–2009* (Milan: Mondadori)

——2013. *Zero Zero Zero* (Milan: Feltrinelli)

——2016. *ZeroZeroZero*, trans. by Virginia Jewiss (London: Penguin Books)

SBANCOR. 2007. 'Sbancor: su Babsi Jones', *Carmilla*, <http://www.carmillaonline.com/2007/09/26/sbancor-su-babsi-jones/>

SCEGO, IGIABA. 2005. 'Dismatria', in Gabriella Kuruvilla, Ingy Mubiayi, Igiaba Scego, and Laila Wadia, *Pecore nere* (Rome and Bari: Laterza), pp. 5–21

——2008. *Oltre Babilonia* (Rome: Donzelli)

——2012. *La mia casa è dove sono* (Turin: Loescher)

SCEGO, IGIABA and RINO BIANCHI. 2014. *Roma negata: Percorsi postcoloniali nella città* (Rome: Ediesse)

SCIASCIA, LEONARDO. 1978. *La Sicilia come metafora* (Milan: Mondadori)

——1994. *L'affaire Moro* (Milan: Adelphi)

SCRITTURA INDUSTRIALE COLLETTIVA, 2013. *In territorio nemico* (Rome: Minimum Fax)

SCURATI, ANTONIO. 2003. *Televisioni di guerra. Il conflitto del Golfo come evento mediatico e il paradosso dello spettatore totale* (Verona: ombre corte)

——2006A. *La letteratura dell'inesperienza* (Milan: Bompiani)

——2006B. *Il rumore sordo della battaglia* (Milan: Bompiani)

——2007A. *Il sopravvissuto* (Milan: Bompiani)

——2007B. *Una storia romantica* (Milan: Bompiani)

——2009. 'L'epica è rediviva e lotta insieme a noi', *La Stampa* (Tuttolibri, 7 February)

——2010. *Il bambino che sognava la fine del mondo* (Milan: Bompiani)

——2013. *Il padre infedele* (Milan: Bompiani)

——2016. *Il tempo migliore della nostra vita* (Milan: Bompiani)

——2018. *M. Il figlio del secolo* (Milan: Bompiani)

SEBASTE, BEPPE. 2007. *H. P. L'ultimo autista di Lady Diana* (Turin: Einaudi)

SELF, WILL. 2014. 'The Novel is Dead (This Time it's for Real)', *The Guardian* (2 May), <http://www.theguardian.com/books/2014/may/02/will-self-novel-dead-literary-fiction> [accessed 30 June 2018]

SERKOWSKA, HANNA. 2011. 'Introduzione: Scambi e intrecci tra *fiction* e reale', in Serkowska, *Finzione cronaca realtà: scambi, intrecci e prospettive nella narrativa italian contemporanea* (Massa: Transeuropa), pp. ix–xlv

——2012. *Dopo il romanzo storico. La storia nella letteratura italiana del '900* (Pesaro: Metauro)

SHIELDS, DAVID. 2010. *Reality Hunger: A Manifesto* (London and New York: Penguin)

SIEGEL, LEE. 2010. 'Where Have All the Mailers Gone?', *New York Observer* (22 June), <http://observer.com/2010/06/where-have-all-the-mailers-gone/> [accessed 30 June 2018]

SIMONARI, ROSELLA. 2008. '*Sappiano le mie parole di sangue* e New Italian Epic', *Carmilla*, <http://www.carmillaonline.com/2008/09/28/sappiano-le-mie-parole-di-sang/> [accessed 30 June 2018]

SITI, WALTER. 2006. *Troppi paradisi* (Turin: Einaudi)

——2008. *Il contagio* (Milan: Mondadori)

SOMIGLI, LUCA. 2013. 'Negli archivi e per le strade: considerazioni meta-critiche sul "ritorno alla realtà" nella narrativa contemporanea', *Negli archivi e per le strade. Il ritorno alla realtà nella narrativa di inizio millennio* (Rome: Aracne), pp. i–xxii

SPINAZZOLA, VITTORIO (ed.). 2010. *Tirature '10. Il new Italian realism* (Milan: Il Saggiatore)

STANDEN, ALEX. 2015. 'Introduction', in *Gendering Commitment: Re-Thinking Social and Ethical Engagement in Modern Italian Culture*, ed. by Alex Standen (Newcastle: Cambridge Scholars Publishing), pp. 1–8

STEFANI, GIULIETTA. 2010. 'Coloniali. Uomini italiani in Africa da Flaiano a Lucarelli', *Storie in movimento*, <http://www.storieinmovimento.org/articoli/zapruder_n23_p040–056.pdf> [accessed 30 June 2018]

STORINI, MONICA CRISTINA. 2010. 'Nella valle perturbante: moderno, postmoderno e *noir* secondo Wu Ming', *Roma noir 2010. Scritture nere: narrativa di genere, New Italian Epic o post-noir?*, ed. by Elisabetta Mondello (Rome: Robin Edizioni), pp. 73–98

TABUCCHI, ANTONIO. 2004. *Tristano muore* (Milan: Feltrinelli)

——2006. *L'oca al passo. Notizie dal buio che stiamo attraversando* (Milan: Feltrinelli)

TAVIANI, GIOVANNA. 2008. 'Inventare il vero. Il rischio del reale nel nuovo cinema italiano', *Allegoria*, 57: 82–93

TONDELLI, PIER VITTORIO. 1998. *Un weekend postmoderno: Cronache dagli anni ottanta* (Milan: Bompiani)

TRICOMI, ANTONIO. 2008. 'Roberto Saviano, Gomorra', *Allegoria*, 57: 190–95

TRIULZI, ALESSANDRO. 2012. 'Hidden Faces, Hidden Histories: Contrasting Voices of Postcolonial Italy', in *Postcolonial Italy: Challenging National Homogeneity*, ed. by Cristina Lombardi-Diop and Caterina Romeo (New York: Palgrave Macmillan), pp. 103–13

VAN DIJCK, JOSÉ. 2007. *Mediated Memories in the Digital Age* (Stanford, CA: Stanford University Press)

VARESE, FEDERICO. 2013. '*Zero Zero Zero*. Più romanzo che documento', *La Stampa* (6 April), <http://www.lastampa.it/2013/04/06/cultura/tuttolibri/piu-romanzo-che-documento-cHvxBul2hQWeUBjUmEREYK/pagina.html> [accessed 30 June 2018]

VESPA, MARY. 1979. 'Sued by Gore Vidal and Stung by Lee Radziwill, a Wounded Truman Capote Lashes Back at the Dastardly Duo', *People* (25 June), <http://www.people.com/people/archive/article/0,,20073969,00.html> [accessed 30 June 2018]

VICARI, DANIELE. 2008. 'Il reale è razionale, ma non sempre', *Allegoria*, 57: 74–81

VITO, MAURIZIO. 2009. 'Epica moderna e New Italian Epic', *Carmilla*, <http://www.carmilla online.com/2009/05/06/epica-moderna-e-new-italian-ep/> [accessed 30 June 2018]

WALLACE, DAVID FOSTER. 1998. *A Supposedly Fun Thing I'll Never Do Again* (London: Abacus)

WHITE, HAYDEN. 1987. *The Content of the Form: Narrative Discourse and Historical Representation* (Baltimore: John Hopkins University Press)

WILLMAN, KATE. 2016. 'Qualsiasi narrazione è un'opera collettiva: Wu Ming's Collective Writing', *Reading Italy*, <https://readingitaly.wordpress.com/2016/10/03/collective-writing-academia/> [accessed 30 June 2018]

——2017. 'Unidentified Narrative Objects: Approaching Instant History through Experiments with Literary Journalism in Beppe Sebaste's *H. P. Lady Diana's Last Driver* and Frédéric Beigbeder's *Windows on the World*', *Journalism* (2017), <http://journals. sagepub.com/eprint/FznuFSbKAkgxxuvaUNYi/full> [accessed 30 June 2018]

WOLFE, TOM. 1975. 'Part One: The New Journalism', in *The New Journalism*, ed. by Tom Wolfe and E. W. Johnson (London: Pan Books), pp. 15–68

WU MING. 2002. *54* (Einaudi: Turin)

——2005. 'Prefazione', *La prima volta che ho visto i fascisti*, <http://www.wumingfoundation. com/italiano/outtakes/antifa/primavolta.pdf>, pp. 8–10 [accessed 30 June 2018]

——2007A. *Manituana* (Einaudi: Turin)

——2007B. 'Prefazione a Cultura convergente di Henry Jenkins', *Giap*, <http://www. wumingfoundation.com/italiano/outtakes/culturaconvergente.htm> [accessed 30 June 2018]

——2009A. *Altai* (Turin: Einaudi)

——2009B. *New Italian Epic. Letteratura, sguardo obliquo, ritorno al futuro* (Turin: Einaudi), pp. 3–100

——2009C. 'Premessa', in Wu Ming, *New Italian Epic. Letteratura, sguardo obliquo, ritorno al futuro* (Turin: Einaudi), pp. vii–xiii

——2011. *Anatra all'arancia meccanica. Racconti 2000–2010* (Turin: Einaudi)

——2013. 'Speciale #Timira e #PointLenana: quattro autori, due libri, molte voci, la storia', *Giap*, <http://www.wumingfoundation.com/giap/?p=14745> [accessed 30 June 2018]

——2014A. *L'Armata dei Sonnambuli* (Turin: Einaudi)

——2014B. 'Peter Kolosimo, 30 anni "across the universe" (1984–2014)', *Giap*, <http:// www.wumingfoundation.com/giap/?p=16648>

WU MING 1. 2008A. 'New Italian Epic 2.0: Memorandum 1993–2008', *Giap*, <http://www. wumingfoundation.com/italiano/WM1_saggio_sul_new_italian_epic.pdf> [accessed 30 June 2018]

——2008B. 'L'uomo che volle essere Perón, Giovanni Maria Bellu', *Giap* <http://www. wumingfoundation.com/italiano/Giap/nandropausa14.htm#bellu> [accessed 30 June 2018]

——2009A. 'New Italian Epic 3.0. Memorandum 1993–2008', in Wu Ming, *New Italian Epic. Letteratura, sguardo obliquo, ritorno al futuro* (Turin: Einaudi), pp. 3–100

——2009B. 'Noi dobbiamo essere i genitori', in Wu Ming, *New Italian Epic. Letteratura, sguardo obliquo, ritorno al futuro* (Turin: Einaudi), pp. 101–26

——2009C. 'Reazioni *de panza* — 1° parte', *Carmilla*, <http://www.carmillaonline.com/ archives/2009/02/002945.html> [accessed 30 June 2018]

——2009D. 'Wu Ming / Tiziano Scarpa: face off. Due modi di gettare il proprio corpo nella lotta. Note su affinità e divergenze, a partire dal dibattito sul NIE', *Giap*, <http:// www.wumingfoundation.com/italiano/outtakes/Wu_Ming_Tiziano_Scarpa_Face_ Off.pdf> [accessed 30 June 2018]

——2010A, '2008–2010: Lo "sfondamento"', *Carmilla*, <http://www.carmillaonline. com/2010/01/06/speciale-new-italian-epic-te/> [accessed 30 June 2018]

——2010B. 'Da lontano /da dentro: Note su nebulose, sguardi sovraccarichi e oggetti narrativi non-identificati in letteratura e negli audiovisivi', <http://dl.dropbox.com/ u/8820520/Da_lontano_Da_dentro.pdf> [accessed 30 June 2018]

——2010C. 'Note sul "Potere Pappone" in Italia, 1a parte: Berlusconi non è il padre', *Giap*, <http://www.wumingfoundation.com/giap/?p=1675> [accessed 30 June 2018]

——2010D. 'Wu Ming Foundation: Chi siamo, cosa facciamo', *Giap*, <http://www. wumingfoundation.com/italiano/biografia.htm> [accessed 30 June 2018]

——2016. 'Zeppo's Gone. Riccardo/Wu Ming 5 è uscito dal collettivo', *Giap*, <http:// www.wumingfoundation.com/giap/2016/02/comunicato-di-wu-ming-riccardo-gia- wu-ming-5-e-uscito-dal-collettivo/> [accessed 30 June 2018]

Wu Ming 1 and Roberto Santachiara. 2013. *Point Lenana* (Turin: Einaudi)

Wu Ming 1 and Wu Ming 2. 2007. 'Mitologia, epica e creazione pop al tempo della Rete', *Carmilla*, <http://www.carmillaonline.com/archives/2007/01/002124.html> [accessed 30 June 2018]

Wu Ming 2. 2009. 'La salvezza di Euridice', *New Italian Epic. Letteratura, sguardo obliquo, ritorno al futuro* (Turin: Einaudi), pp. 127–203

——2012. 'Orizzonti d'Impero e paesaggi coloniali — Una riflessione di Wu Ming 2', *Giap*, <https://www.wumingfoundation.com/giap/2012/06/orizzonti-dimpero-e-pae saggi-coloniali/> [accessed 30 June 2018]

Wu Ming 4. 2008. *Stella del mattino* (Turin: Einaudi)

Wu Ming 5. 2006. Free Karma Food (Milan: Rizzoli)

INDEX